Roy Medvedev

Verso

Leninism and Western Socialism

Translated by A.D.P. Briggs

British Library
Cataloguing in Publication Data

Medvedev, Roy A.
   Leninism and western socialism.
   1. Socialism   2. Communism—Soviet Union
   I. Title
   335 .00171˙3   HX44

ISBN 0-86091-042-3 (Cloth)
     0-86091-739-8 (Paper)

First published, 1981
©   Roy A. Medvedev, 1981

Verso Editions and NLB,
15 Greek Street, London W1

Typeset in Times by
Review Design Services,
182 Oxford Road, Manchester 13

Printed and bound in Great Britain by
Blackwell Press Ltd
Worcester

Contents

	Introduction	1
1	Marxism, Leninism, and Marxism-Leninism	11

I

2	The Dictatorship of the Proletariat	29
3	Soviets as a Form of Revolutionary Power	94
4	Majority and Minority in Revolution	139
5	Socialism in One Country	167

II

6	Communists and Social Democrats in the West	203
	References	297
	Index	308

Introduction

The profound crisis afflicting the world Communist movement today is no secret. Its numbers throughout the world have continued to increase, and about a hundred parties are affiliated to the movement. Since the Second World War, the countries ruled by Communist parties have become ever more numerous. However, this quantitative growth has been matched by the loss of the movement's former solidity and unity. Perfectly natural differences of opinion and healthy controversy have escalated into bitter exchanges. Apart from the one great and obvious split, the monolith of Communism today is cracked in every direction. Political differences between some Communist countries have spilled over into military confrontation, culminating on more than one occasion in warfare and bloodshed. Paradoxically, the capitalist countries often display greater unity, mutual understanding and ability to compromise than those countries professing allegiance to socialism.

There are many reasons for this crisis. In some cases, dissent has been caused by the triumph of nationalism, albeit in the guise of Communism, over internationalism. No small part of the blame for the occurrence and development of much of the conflict must be placed also at the door of individual leaders of the movement and their personal ambitions. Nevertheless, there are objective reasons for disagreement or mutual misunderstanding between Communist parties, and these arise from their quite distinct social, economic and political circumstances. The problems and the historical experience determining the activity of Communist parties that came to power sixty, thirty, or perhaps as recently as ten years ago, are by no means identical. Neither are the problems and historical experience determining the activity of those parties that have come to power in countries of medium capitalist development and in underdeveloped colonial or semi-colonial countries—or, indeed, those parties still struggling for power in mature capitalist and democratic countries. The problems confronting the numerically substantial Communist parties of Southern Europe are not those of the relatively small ones of Northern Europe. Similar differences divide the French Communists from those in East Germany, and Western European Communists from those in the USA, where so far it has proved impossible to establish even a mass socialist party, let alone a Communist one. Markedly different strategies and tactics are employed by parties working legally in the West and those operating illegally in South America.

The technological revolution is one new factor that has not only brought about vast changes in the social structure and the very scientific and economic basis of capitalist society but has also aggravated inequalities in development between individual countries and even whole continents. Not that the question is simply one of economic or social development. Quite separate ideological problems arise for the Communists in the Indian State of Kerala, which has a substantial Hindu majority and where there are two parallel Communist parties which frequently come together in a united front to form the government there, and for the Communists in Afghanistan with its Muslim majority. Catholic Italy, Lutheran Switzerland, Social-Democratic Austria, Zionist Israel are all countries in which Communists are faced with distinctive ideological problems.

It is, of course, still true, even given these extremely diverse circumstances, that Communists retain a good deal in common—their general outlook, strategy and tactics, structure and traditional party methods. Without all this one could scarcely speak of a world Communist movement. But the occasional attempts to bring together Communist parties by tightening the bands of a single doctrine around them or imposing a single leadership upon them are quite unrealistic and are invariably met with a firm and justified rebuff. It is unfortunate, at the same time, that the fear of a return to old-fashioned Comintern centralism has also precluded the creation of any machinery for co-ordinating and exchanging information like that which has survived in the Socialist and Social-Democratic parties without in any way undermining their independence and authority, even though the differences between them are at least as great as those dividing the Communist parties.

Every success of the Communist movement, from massive triumph to partly achieved revolution, seems to create the illusion that at long last it has discovered the key to further success, which can be re-used in other countries. This happened after the October Revolution; it also followed the revolutionary triumphs in China and Cuba. Sometimes the illusion persists for years on end, though nowadays we tend to hear more to the effect that 'no two revolutions are alike' than that 'Bolshevism should be considered a suitable model for everyone else'. The experience amassed by world Communism is, of course, very substantial and may be disregarded only at the risk of many costly mistakes, but it is equally true that blind repetition of that experience, even including the experience of Lenin's party, may also lead to serious errors. For this reason we should welcome the search for an individual road to socialism that preoccupies many Communist parties today. Such searches are both normal and essential, despite the fact that they are not always successful. Perhaps it is even true to say that, so far, Communists have experienced more failures than successes, and that this is why many of these parties, while maintaining basic common loyalties, are doing their utmost to discover not only their own road to socialism but their own understanding of socialism, distinct from that enshrined in the present social and economic reality of the Soviet Union—to say nothing of the People's Republic of China.

The absence of any single centre of control, the independence and equal rights enjoyed by the various parties and countries should not be taken to indicate a refusal to undertake joint action or the absence of any kind of *leadership* arising either from a given country's status within its region or the qualities of a particular party or even an individual politician. Thus, for example, for most of the post-war period, the USA has been the undisputed leader of the capitalist world not only because of its pre-eminently large population but also by virtue of its economic, financial and technological potential together with its military might. Yugoslavia, on the other hand, although by no means the largest or most powerful country among the non-aligned nations, was for many years their unquestioned leader, because of the massive authority of President Tito.

The USSR is the leader of two groups of countries, those of the

Warsaw Pact and of Comecon (including its full members and associates). The Communist Party of the Soviet Union now claims leadership of world Communism not only as the ruling party in the strongest of the socialist states, in economic and in military terms, but also as the party that led the world's first socialist revolution, going on then to acquire enormous political experience including many outstanding achievements and many tragic but exemplary failures. It is unfortunate that our party has proved so often incapable of profiting from the lessons taught by its own rich experience. In consequence, the CPSU leadership in recent decades has been unable to advance anything in the way of new ideas for consideration by the international Communist movement. Is it any wonder that this leadership has lost some of its lustre abroad? The same applies to the leaders of the Cuban Revolution, which stood until recently at the head of the Communist movement in Latin America, and even more to the leaders of the People's Republic of China, which also until recently could claim leadership of the national liberation and revolutionary movements in Asia and Africa but which has spent the last thirty years trying unsuccessfully to solve the most elementary problems arising in its own economic and cultural life.

A year or two ago, in an address to the US Senate, Alexander Sozhenitsyn exclaimed: 'Very soon, all too soon, your state will have need of men who are not merely outstanding but who are great. Find them in your souls. Find them in your hearts. Find them—in the very depths of your country!'[1] It might have been possible to associate oneself with this appeal, safe in the knowledge that if great men did come to power in the USA they would certainly not adopt the policies recommended by Solzhenitsyn. Unhappily, the 1980 Presidential election has once more shown the American political establishment to be incapable of presenting the electorate with anything better than a set of relatively mediocre politicians as candidates for the leadership of the capitalist world. If this deficiency is important for the capitalist world, itself plunged into a period of deep crisis, it is no less so for the socialist countries and Communist parties. Here too, as things stand today, there is a marked shortage of outstanding political leaders.

One particularly important reason for the present crisis in world Communism is the large gap that has opened up between the practice of the movement and the development of scientific socialist theory. It is not the first such gap. A similar one occurred at the beginning of the twentieth century, prompting the emergence and development of Leninism. At that time, Lenin produced a stream of new ideas on the theory and practice of socialism. He loved to repeat the assertion that 'Marxism is not dogma, it is leadership towards action'. In 1917. he wrote: 'We do not claim that Marx or Marxists know the road to socialism in its last concrete detail'.[2] Nowadays, these very words are being repeated by some of the leaders of the Communist parties of Western Europe and Japan in relation to the theoretical and practical inheritance that has come down to them from Lenin himself and from Leninism. These leaders consider, not without good reason, that the new circumstances of the modern world, especially in developed capitalist countries, call for a new approach and a complete overhaul of everything—not only Lenin's tactical and theoretical directives, but some of the basic underlying principles of Leninism, including for example, possible attitudes to 'bourgeois' democracy and parliamentarism, the role and significance of general elections, the problems of the majority and the minority in revolutionary situations, the whole question of the dictatorship of the proletariat, and issues such as the possibility of Communists and social democrats joining forces in the run-up to socialist revolution. A whole series of ideas, on revolution and the revolutionary situation, the allies of the proletariat, the relationships between party and state and also between the party and other mass working-class organizations, are being subjected to fresh scrutiny. Old questions are being asked again. What kind of oppositional activity is possible within Communist parties? What are the functions of the various parties and political groups once the working class has assumed power? Careful consideration is being given to problems arising from the economic and social consequences of the technological revolution and the positions and political attitudes of every section of the working class.

Left-wing theoreticians in the West now query—with clear justification—the relevance and usefulness today of the slogans and formulae that proved effective sixty or 120 years ago. This does not mean that they are now having doubts about the authority and merits of Karl Marx and Friedrich Engels as founders of the working-class socialist movement in the nineteenth century. It does not mean that they are beginning to doubt the authority and the merits of Lenin as the initiator of the Communist movement in the twentieth century. This new attitude indicates that they have come to consider Marxism and Leninism as a *principle* worthy of development rather than the culmination of a new tendency in scientific research into the means by which human society functions and develops, its material foundations, its political institutions, its class structures and class struggles. The last decade has seen a renewal of interest in the works of contemporary opponents of Lenin such as Luxemburg, Plekhanov, Kautsky, Bauer and James Connolly. This has extended also to writers who considered themselves Lenin's disciples—Gramsci, Bukharin, Dimitrov and Lukács. Political figures as disparate as Mao Tse Tung and Stalin, Trotsky and Castro, Tito and Ho Chi Minh have attracted attention; and considerable interest has been aroused in the works of contemporary writers such as Marcuse, Debray, Fanon and Althusser.

In recent years, the not always successful efforts towards a new political direction and new theoretical principles have been given the extremely imprecise title of 'Eurocommunism', a term to which we shall have to resort on occasion for want of a more exact political formulation. The appearance of Eurocommunism has provoked much discussion and various comment for and against. Without going into detail, we may safely say that in the Soviet press and in that of a number of other Communist parties, Eurocommunism is usually taken to be a form of revisionism or opportunism within the Communist movement, or even a bourgeois diversionary manoeuvre. This view is examplified in the following statement by Papaioannu, General Secretary of the Progressive Party of the Working People of Cyprus (AKEL): 'Having invented the term "Eurocommunism", bourgeois propaganda uses it as anything but an inoffensive euphemism or, to put it more simply, they use it as more than just a roundabout phrase denoting similar positions adopted by a series of parties in our region with regard to certain issues... The bourgeoisie invests the term with its own tendentious anti-Communist connotations and employs it to put pressure on our movement as a method fighting the Communist parties..., in order to insinuate mistrust and alienation into relations between Communist parties, to incite them to confrontation and the severing of contacts.'[3] The Hungarian Communist Ferenc Barnai has said: 'The introduction of the concept of "Eurocommunism" into the political arena is an obvious manoeuvre. The aim is to distract attention from the struggle being waged against monopolies, to depict a section of the Western European Communist parties, labelled "Eurocommunist", as anti-Soviet, and to create dissension between fraternal parties, especially those in power and those fighting for it.'[4]

In this instance both Barnai and Papaïoannu are clearly exaggerating the part played by bourgeois propaganda in the emergence of the term 'Eurocommunism' and undervaluing the ideological processes, in some of the western Communist parties, which have given rise to the concept. Although the term itself first appeared in the non-Communist press, it has nevertheless been widely used in the western Communist and left-wing press with reference to those essential changes which have been introduced into political programmes and their theoretical bases in the Communist parties of such countries as Italy, France, Spain, Japan, Sweden, Australia and elsewhere. It is no exaggeration to say that, with a few small exceptions, Socialist and Social Democratic parties have shown a close interest in the policy changes occurring in several influential Communist parties, though this has often been tinged with deep scepticism. Bourgeois political parties, bourgeois politicians and bourgeois propaganda have all proved overtly hostile to these changes. Henry Kissinger, as US Secretary of State, spoke out several times in 1976 on the dangers of Eurocommunism. Ex-President Ford also claimed in 1977 that it was not 'Communism with a human face or democratic tendencies but Stalinism in disguise, hidden tyranny.'[5] Prominent Western politicians have described Eurocommunism as 'the Trojan Horse of Communism by means of which the Communists would like to destroy the free world.'[6] The bourgeois ideologist Klaus Menert, speaking to an invited audience in the offices of the West German periodical *Osteuropa*, claimed that Eurocommunism was nothing more than 'tactical camouflage' adopted by Communists with the aim of seizing power in the West.[7] Bourgeois propagandists have vied with each other in assuring their readers that Communism is incapable of changing its aims, its image or any of the methods it has employed ever since the October Revolution. It came as no surprise when Solzhenitsyn, in his speech to the Second Sakharov Hearing (Rome 1977), spoke of a 'healthy awareness in Europe' of the dangers posed by the 'insidious songs of Eurocommunism.'

This is not the time to go deeply into the controversy surrounding the success or failure of recent ideas. Suffice it to say that the search for new theories, new political approaches and new initiatives undertaken during the 1970s deserves every kind of support and continuation. No one can predict the exact outcome of the present differences of opinion within the Communist movement. It is perfectly possible that the split between individual socialist countries will go on widening and that the cracks appearing today in relations between some Communist parties will be even more noticeable tomorrow. It is equally possible that things will go the other way, towards a strengthening of the outward unity and inner solidarity of world Communism. Even in the latter case the road to unity is bound to lead through argument and discussion. It is unrealistic even to think of re-establishing the former 'indivisible' unity based upon principles of ultimate authority that would, in any case, ruin the health and development of Communist parties. Differences of opinion and discussion are not only normal, they are actually beneficial to any political movement and to Communists in particular since they claim to possess an ideology with a scientific basis. The very freedom of criticism and opposition that is excluded from the framework of most individual Communist parties, and whose lack impoverishes their inner political life, does exist today within world Communism taken as a whole. Communist leaders, not least those in the USSR, can no longer count on virtually automatic approval of their activities by Communist parties abroad. This fact is helping gradually to overcome the intolerance and *active dogmatism* that have characterized many Communist leaders in days gone by and inseminated fellow Communists with theoretical inertia and *passive dogmatism*.

Discussions concerning the theory of scientific socialism have taken place in recent years mainly in Communist parties and other left-wing movements in the West. Their true significance extends, however, to other countries including those of 'real socialism'. Communists cannot and must not lightly undertake a revision of the basic tenets of their inherited ideology. A measure of doctrinal tenacity, a *moderate dogmatism,* so to speak, is often necessary and useful both in science and in politics. Excessive dogmatism, on the other hand, would be fatal for the Communist movement in capitalist countries and it has a perceptible braking effect on the economies and the political development of the socialist countries. This is the standpoint from which the present book proposes to examine a number of vitally important problems arising from Leninism and which in recent years have come to the very centre of the discussions taking place within the world Communist movement.

April 1980

1
Marxism, Leninism, and Marxism-Leninism

'Marxism'

The concept of 'Marxism' came into use in Karl Marx's own lifetime as a means of defining the new revolutionary doctrine propounded by him which aimed at a transformation of the surrounding world and the creation of a new, just society, that is, socialism and communism. This doctrine was a bringing together of ideas taken from different disciplines, philosophy, history, economic theory and politics, which had been advanced and substantiated in the writings of Marx and further developed, first of all in the work of his close friend and comrade-in-arms, Friedrich Engels and then by a group of like-minded disciples and followers.

Unlike his socialist predecessors, Marx made an extremely fruitful attempt to create a scientific basis for socialist and communist ideology. This is why, despite some obvious relics of utopian thinking in his outlook, he came to be considered the founder of scientific socialism. Taking the legacy of classical German philosophy as his starting point, Marx developed a new philosophical doctrine, dialectical materialism and the materialist interpretation of history. Starting also with contemporary political economy and a deep study of mid-nineteenth-century capitalist society, Marx developed a new line of economic thought. This envisaged the inevitable construction of socialism and portrayed the proletariat as a class whose historic mission was to overturn capitalism by means of revolution and to create the socialist order. Thus it was Marx himself who worked out the tactics of the proletarian class struggle and laid the foundation stone of unity between scientific socialism and the working-class movement. It was under his guidance or with his participation that many of the first working-class political organizations were formed.

Marxism was by no means the only political or socio-philosophical movement of the time aiming at the transformation of capitalist society. In the battle to win over the working-class movement, Marx and Engels had to take issue continually with all manner of theories pertaining to socialism that are now commonly described as 'petty bourgeois'—Proudhonism and the closely related anarchism, the schools of Lassalle and Blanqui, French Possibilism and English Fabianism. Marxism came out on top and by the end of the nineteenth century it had become the basic ideology of the working-class movement. The Russian Social Democratic Workers' Party, founded in 1903, proclaimed Marxism as the fundamental theory underlying its practical activities.

'Leninism'

No one nowadays has any reason to doubt the enormous significance of the events connected with the name of Vladimir Ilyich Lenin, though for some people these amounted to a catastrophe, or the beginnings of one, whereas for others they created the hope that a new and just society might one day be created. The concept of 'Leninism' is something different. During Lenin's lifetime, the expressions 'Leninist' and 'Leninism' were generally used by enemies of the Bolsheviks, more often than not in a pejorative sense. Lenin described himself as a Marxist and even his closest comrades took the view that he was not the creator of any new doctrine or independent line of thought: he had merely put into practice the doctrines propounded by Marx and Engels. 'Marx is theory, Lenin is practice' was a saying often heard in Lenin's own company.

This underestimation of Lenin's theoretical bequest is explicable in several different ways. For some time after the appearance of Lenin in the political arena of Russia, and the creation of the Bolshevik faction of the Social Democratic Party, Leninism failed to emerge as a relatively independent and original body of thought or as a new stage in the development of scientific socialism. In the majority of his works, especially in the first decade of his activity, Lenin spoke largely as a popularizer and interpreter of Marxism, which he defended against Populism, 'Economism' and 'Legal

Marxism'. He was at pains to indicate the applicability of the basic tenets of Marxism to Russia, in which respect he was essentially continuing the work carried out much earlier, and with greater literary merit, by Plekhanov. Similar work had been conducted in other countries by Bebel, Kautsky, Lafargue, Liebknecht, Mehring, Labriola and other followers of Marx and Engels. It goes without saying that neither Lenin nor the other Marxist theoreticians simply reiterated what their teachers had said. They were all developing the theory of Marxism, though essentially within its classical framework. In their consideration of Russia's economy, the agrarian problems of Europe and Russia, the origins of private property, the question of women, the role of the individual in history, the strategy and tactics of the political struggle of the proletariat, the disciples and followers of Marx were concerned to stay within the limits of the fundamental ideas laid down by Marxism and to multiply arguments confirming them. This was an inevitable stage in the development of Marxism in breadth and depth. As Lenin himself wrote: 'Seventy Karl Marxes could never embrace all the variations, in all their ramifications, of a capitalist economy. All that matters is that the rules governing these variations have been exposed and that the logic which lies behind their historical evolution has been demonstrated.'[1]

At the time of the first Russian Revolution and in the period of reaction that followed, Lenin did put forward and develop a number of original conceptions, particularly in regard to political tactics and organizational structure as they affected his party. These were quite distinct from the traditional ideas that had been adopted by the Social Democratic movement world-wide. They were truly *Leninist* ideas; they were to form the theoretical basis of Bolshevism at that time, and eventually they would lead to the division of the Social Democratic Party into two independent factions.

The beginning of the twentieth century was marked by the emergence of new problems and new variations in the nature of capitalism sufficient to transform its character. When these problems came to be analysed, some western Social Democrats (Bernstein, Millerand and others) began to diverge from Marxism and scientific socialism and, particularly, to dissociate themselves from revolutionary methods. Others showed themselves to be prisoners of dogmatism, attempting to find the answers only with reference to earlier ideas. Lenin turned out to be the only person capable of formulating a new and revolutionary approach to the solution of such problems as the development of imperialism, workers' opposition to the First World War, the appearance of national liberation movements in the colonial world, and the possibility of the socialist revolution achieving victory at first in a single capitalist country. However, the most important period in the formation of Leninism as a doctrine coincided with the start of the new Russian Revolution and embraced the last five or six years of Lenin's life. At this time not only was Lenin the leader of the world's first socialist revolution, he was head of the world's first socialist state.

There are historians who (quite without foundation) consider that Marxism as a doctrine depends first and foremost on the works of the young Marx. With Lenin the reverse is true. It was during the stormy events of the October Revolution and the first years of Soviet power that Lenin's real quality as a strategist and tactician in the revolutionary struggle emerged. Lenin alone had to come up with the first solutions to all the problems of proletarian revolution, theoretical and practical—the Soviets as a new form of power, the union between the proletariat and the peasantry, the building of a new society in post-revolutionary Russia, the new economy, the new state itself. In all of this Lenin was beating an entirely new path and not infrequently he was compelled to take up and defend positions quite different from those indicated by orthodox Marxism. It was this original contribution to the theory of scientific socialism, based on experience gained during the creation of the world's first Socialist state, that came rapidly to be known as *Leninism*.

Lenin wrote a fair number of books and many more articles. He made speeches and statements without number. Many of his letters have been preserved, as have his personal directives and decrees in the name of the Soviet government. His collected works outnumber those of Karl Marx; in fact they are approximately equal to all the works written by Marx and Engels together. However, he lacked the time and the opportunity to systematize his writings, to reconcile the numerous contradictions within them, to distinguish between what was vital and what was of secondary importance, between works of popularization in which he spoke merely as a 'practitioner' of Marxism and pieces in which he wrote as an original and penetrating theoretician. It is also true that Lenin made many mistakes and usually did not attempt to deny them. His writings and speeches are peppered with such comments as 'I have made a mistake', 'We have made a serious mistake', 'I seem to have been quite wrong and I owe an apology to the working-class movement', 'We have committed, and we shall continue to commit, a lot of stupid errors', 'I was wrong', 'I have failed', and so on. To take one specific example, Lenin never managed to square the practicalities of the first years of the Soviet state with the views he had expressed in his *The State and Revolution* and in a number of policy articles written before October 1917, although the disparities between pre-revolutionary theory and post-revolutionary practice were considerable.

It should also be borne in mind that, even in the most original of his works, Lenin was not a man who introduced new concepts, or a new kind of logic into the theory of scientific socialism. He tended to make use of the basic concepts advanced by Marx: 'productive forces', 'industrial relations', 'socio-economic stage of development', 'surplus value', 'the dictatorship of the proletariat', 'base and superstructure', etc. He also employed many concepts that had come into scientific use before the time of Marx and Engels and retained the same implications that the founders of Marxism had intended—expressions such as 'class', 'the class struggle', 'the bourgeoisie', 'the petty bourgeoisie', 'exploitation', 'capitalism, 'feudalism', 'socialism', 'revolution' and so on. Any new concepts which may be said to arise exclusively in Lenin's works—'NEP', 'revolutionary situation', 'state capitalism,' 'monopoly of foreign trade', and so on—have a basis in previously established formulations. Thus Lenin was neither the creator of a new philosophy nor the initiator of a new research method. Not that this relegates him to the role of a mere 'practitioner' of revolution. Speaking at a solemn assembly of the Communist Academy on February 17, 1924, less than a month after Lenin's death, Nicolai Bukharin said: 'There is a widespread impression within our Party, and outside it too, that Vladimir Ilyich must disputably be considered an incomparable practitioner of the working-class movement, a genius in that field. When it comes to his position as a theorist the estimation is generally much lower... I believe this estimation to be an undervaluation...conditioned by a particular psychological aberration which affects everyone of us. The theory propounded by Lenin is not to be found in a condensed or compressed form, it is not nearly packaged in one or two well-finished volumes. The theoretical principles, statements and generalizations which Comrade Lenin formulated were mostly—ninety per cent—occasional ones. You will find them scattered throughout the many volumes of his works simply because they *are* scattered observations, they are not offered to our reading public in compact, nicely wrought, finished form. For this reason there are many people who consider that Lenin the theoretician falls well short of Lenin the practitioner. I think it will not be long before this idea is demolished and in the course of time Comrade Lenin will rise before us to his full height, not only as a genius in the practical affairs of the working-class movement but also as a genius in the realm of theory.'[2]

The need for a systematized arrangement of Lenin's views and a relatively condensed exposition of 'Leninist principles' was felt immediately following his death. This arose to a great extent from an acrimonious internecine struggle that had started in the party in 1923, between factions eager to present their own views as 'authentic' Leninism. Many Party leaders and theoreticians made individual attempts to settle this issue. Stalin, for instance, went to Sverdlov University in early April 1924 and read a series of lectures which were then published in *Pravda* under the general heading 'Concerning the Basic Principles of Leninism'. (He was, in fact, drawing on the manuscript of his assistant F. Ksenofont—'Lenin's Doctrine of Revolution', which the author did not publish until 1925.) For the same reason, Bukharin's speech, referred to above, was published, under the heading 'Lenin as a Marxist'; another such work of his was 'The Road to Socialism and the Worker-Peasant Union' (1925). Leon Trotsky also published works on Lenin and Leninism. One of these, in which he drew a comparison between Marx and Lenin, was written in the latter's lifetime. Trotsky sent it to Lenin in Gorki, where it was read to him a month before his death by Nadezhda Krupskaya. At the same time, Zinoviev published his *Leninism* and an article entitled 'Philosophy of the Age'; Kamenev issued a pamphlet called 'Lenin and His Party'. In Leningrad, Safarov's big book, *Fundamentals of Leninism,* went through three editions in 1924 alone. Stalin wrote two further articles on Leninism, 'The October Revolution and the Tactics of the Russian Communists' and 'Towards Questions of Leninism'. There were also a number of Leninist anthologies, short biographies and collections of articles, *About Ilyich,* and so on.

The content of all these articles, pamphlets and books was bound to be reflected in the intensifying Party struggle of 1924-26. Many of the authors singled out those aspects of Leninism which seemed particularly significant for their own arguments. Stalin and Bukharin were sharply critical of works written by Trotsky and Zinoviev but the latter were not to be outdone; Trotsky, for instance, described Stalin's articles and pamphlets as 'primitive and abounding in schoolboy errors'. This is not the time to go deeply into that series of attacks, accusations and counter-claims. One may assert with justification that all the works outlined above were of value in defining Lenin's contribution to the theory of scientific socialism and that from then on the concept of 'Leninism' was firmly established in the literature of socialism and communism.

'Marxism-Leninism'

We have seen that Lenin leaned heavily on Marx and Engels in developing his own ideas. He also attempted, however, to solve many theoretical and practical problems that had not presented themselves to the workers' movement in the nineteenth century. Moreover, in many instances, he reconsidered certain premises that Marx and Engels had believed to be vital for their doctrine. They considered, for example, that under socialism commodity production would be eliminated and that, along with it, trade and barter would die out. Lenin in 1920 did not doubt that this was true, and this false premise of Marxism cost the Bolsheviks dearly. Learning from the experience gained by the young Soviet state, Lenin was quick to abandon the dogma. In 1921, he wrote: 'Trade—this is the "link" in the historical chain of events which we must grasp with all our strength, we leaders of proletarian state power and the Communist Party. If we can "grasp" that link firmly enough now we shall probably control the whole chain in the near future. There is no other way for us to lay the foundation of socio-economic relations'.[3]

Whole pages could be filled with examples of this sort of thing. What is obvious is that 'Marxism' and 'Leninism' are not synonymous. Thus, it became necessary to create a new general formula, since references in the policy documents of the Russian Communist

Party and the Comintern had been limited to the 'revolutionary teachings of Marx'. Proposals came thick and fast. 'Leninism is living Marxism', 'Leninism is Marxism in action', 'Leninism is Marxism adapted to Russian conditions', 'Marxism for theory—Leninism for tactics', and so on. All of these were rejected because they laid a greater emphasis on the practical significance of Leninism than on its theory. In one of his lectures Stalin refined a formula proposed by Ksenofont as follows: 'Leninism is Marxism in the age of imperialism and of the proletarian revolution. Or, to be more exact, Leninism is the theory and tactics of proletarian revolution in general, the theory and tactics of the dictatorship of the proletariat in particular.'[4]

Here was a more precise formula, and it became entrenched in our theory as an indisputable dogma. Even this proved unsatisfactory, however. Lenin had developed Marxism only in certain directions. Many important aspects of the teaching of Marx and Engels, vital though they were in nineteenth-century conditions (and in the circumstances of the better developed countries of Western Europe), were of little interest to Lenin, whose views, although not spelt out in their last detail, clearly derived from circumstances and conditions specific to Russia. Lenin was also much influenced in the formulation of his principles by the ideological legacy inherited from the revolutionary and democratic movement that had been active in Russia in the second half of the nineteenth century, particularly the writings of Herzen, Chernyshevsky and Tchakev. Thus, a growing need was felt for yet another formula which would not only define the theoretical content of Leninism, but would actually embrace the theory laid down collectively by Marx, Engels and Lenin. Zinoviev was the first person to offer one, though his concept of 'Marxo-Leninism' seemed a very awkward one at the time.[5] It was accepted however, as a useful theoretical discovery and was used in subsequent propagandist works. Nevertheless, the Russian Communist Party and the Comintern continued to speak of Marxism and Leninism (unhyphenated) in their fundamental policy documents. The Comintern Programme adopted by the Sixth Congress in 1928, for instance, included the following statement: 'Drawing on the historical experience of the revolutionary working-class movement on all continents and in all peoples, the Communist International in its theoretical and practical work stands wholly and without qualification behind the viewpoint of *Revolutionary Marxism* and its further development in *Leninism* which is nothing other than Marxism in the age of imperialism and proletarian revolution.'[6] There was no mention of 'Marxism-Leninism' in the text of the Rules of the All-Union Communist Party (Bolsheviks) adopted at the Fourteenth Party Congress at the end of 1925, though the term was used in the revised Rules adopted at the Seventeenth Congress early in 1934. For example, a party member is enjoined 'to work indefatigably at improving his ideological battle-readiness, at mastering *Marxism-Leninism* and the vital political and organizational decisions taken by the Party and to explain these in detail to the masses outside the Party.'[7]

In the 1930s the concept of 'Marxism-Leninism' came into general currency as the main term used in defining the theoretical basis of the Communist movement. It came to be used in the policy documents of all Communist parties. Sometimes propaganda literature continued to refer separately to 'Marxism' and 'Leninism' but usually the intention was to denote 'Marxism-Leninism'. Significantly, the latest edition of the *Great Soviet Encyclopaedia (3rd Edition)* does not contain separate articles on Marxism and Leninism but has only a single article on 'Marxism-Leninism'. The secretary of the CPSU Central Committee, Boris Ponamaryov wrote recently: 'The continuity in Marxist-Leninist theory and politics reflects the objective international unity of a world-wide historical process and the profound interrelationship between its various stages... It is impossible to divide the indivisible, to sunder the unified, organic wholeness of this doctrine to set Marx against Lenin or Marxism against Leninism. Nowadays the question of the historical place of Leninism, of the unity of Marxist-Leninist theory is of vital significance. It has become one of the main ideological weapons in the confrontation between imperialism and reaction on the one hand and the forces of democracy, socialism and progress on the other. It keeps appearing on the agenda of debates taking place in the Communist world.'[8]

Let us refrain from commenting on the adherents of imperialism and reaction. We are still left with the awkward question, 'Why does the question of Marxism-Leninism keep appearing on the agenda of debates taking place in the Communist world'?

Leninism and Marxism-Leninism after Lenin's death

After Lenin's death, Leninism met with virtually the same fate as did Marxism after the death of Marx. The authority of Lenin and Leninism, based on victory in the October Revolution and the creation of the Soviet state, was remarkably well established in the minds of revolution-inclined young people and intellectuals. All over the world, many new followers of Leninism and Bolshevism began to emerge. In the Communist world, no one had a word to say against Leninism or Marxism-Leninism. However, there was no shortage of politicians claiming that they, or their faction, represented the only 'authentic Leninism', everyone else being 'revisionist' or 'opportunist'. All the debates occurring within the Communist movement in the 1920s were part of a struggle to establish 'authentic Leninism'. Stalin and his entourage emerged as winners, though by no means because they followed Lenin's precepts more closely than anyone else. On the contrary, almost all Stalin's actions from the late 1920s to the early 1950s represented a departure from Leninism, though they disguised themselves in various words and formulas belonging to Marxism-Leninism. Stalin, in fact, was unscrupulous enough to distort many of Lenin's premises and still retain the description 'Leninist' for his new excursions. For instance, Lenin had spoken of strengthening opposition to the overthrown classes *after the triumph of socialist revolution,* that is, after the formation of the Socialist state. This was his explanation of Civil War and all its atrocities. But Stalin imposed on the Party his own conception of intensifying the class struggle according to the success-rate in the building of socialism *even after the triumph of socialism in the USSR,* even after antagonistic classes had disappeared throughout the country. This conception was needed by Stalin to justify mass repression in the late 1930s. A number of Lenin's works either ceased to be published or were abbreviated or even subjected to arbitrary editing in a spirit conforming to Stalin's policies. Briefly speaking, it was Stalinism that became institutionalized in our country in the 1930s even though Soviet propaganda continued to speak only of carrying through or developing 'Marxism-Leninism'. Naturally, this does not mean that Lenin and Leninism were wholly forgotten or entirely betrayed by

Stalinism; they were merely pushed into the background. It is typical that even pamphlets devoted to Lenin's works were half filled with quotations from Stalin.

The removal of the incrustation of Stalinism was delayed for us, in our theoretical work and practical experience, until the 20th Party Congress. This process is still incomplete, but that is not the point. The world Communist movement and the CPSU now not only face the problem of returning to certain Leninist precepts, 'Leninist Party norms' or 'Leninist norms for the building of a state'; they have to consider the more urgent question of adapting Leninism or Marxism-Leninism to suit the conditions of an entirely new age of human development. By 1964, forty years on from Lenin's death, many more changes had occurred throughout the world than in the forty-year period between the deaths of Marx and Lenin. The causes and consequences of the Second World War had still to be scrutinized, as had the historical process by which a whole camp of socialist countries had grown up, and the divisions that had appeared between them. A study had to be made of the collapse of the colonial and semi-colonial world and the formation of a vast new zone called the 'Third World'. Phenomena like Stalinism and Maoism called for analysis and explanation. There was a need to interpret the technological revolution of the 1950s and 1960s, the unprecedented rise in capitalist productivity, the formation of multinational monopolies and the numerous changes that had taken place in the structure of property-owning under capitalism. Social change in capitalist societies and changes in the society and economy of socialist countries also needed to be explored. Global problems that had scarcely worried mankind at the beginning of the twentieth century now took on vast significance: problems of ecology, disarmament, demographic revolution and the like. Despite Lenin's predictions to the contrary, democratic institutions in capitalist societies, far from disappearing, had developed and become firmly established, whereas in socialist countries it was clear that many serious and unjustified breaches of socialist democracy had occurred.

There is no end to this list of problems, vital to all societies, which never even occurred to Lenin, let alone Marx and Engels, but which now need to be solved in order to determine the strategy and tactics of Communist parties. Naturally enough, some steps have been taken towards the analysis, explanation and solution of these and other problems. Much of this work has taken place in theoretical discussions within the CPSU, or has been conducted by many leading politicians and theorists belonging to other Communist parties. But whatever has been done in this respect is patently inadequate, and, in any case, the results of the work so far carried out are anything but generally accepted. It was predictable that, after Lenin's death, the Communist movement would be unlikely to produce still more doughty warriors of the calibre of Marx, Engels and Lenin in their times. The movement has proved unable to form people capable of indicating in a convincing and authoritative manner even the main approaches towards a resolution of problems now arising in the modern world. Indeed it is very doubtful whether any single thinker, however great, could possibly have done so, given the multiform complexity of these new problems.

A problem that proves insoluble by any single individual within a scientific discipline or ideological current usually has to be solved collectively. It is unfortunate that, in the Communist movement, collaboration has been badly obstructed by the dogmatism of many leaders and theoreticians. One of the most striking forms of this dogmatism is the demand that all concepts must be worked out within the framework of Marxism-Leninism or Leninism alone, while we are really faced with entirely new issues that never even occurred to Lenin, let alone Marx, or else with political and socio-economic developments that simply do not conform to the predictions and expectations of the Marxist-Leninist classics, and in fact confound them.

Let us take the example of Lenin's prediction that the colonial system of imperialism would collapse. He could never have envisaged that this collapse would coincide with a renewal of stability and even a rapid growth of the economy in most capitalist countries. Lenin also foresaw the rapid development of science and technology, but he said it would occur in the socialist countries. He also failed to predict that the pioneer work in the new technological revolution would be carried out in the very countries where capitalism was 'in decay'; that these countries would not only still be in existence as such sixty or seventy years after the October Revolution but would still be ahead of the socialist countries in economic and technological achievement. Lenin pointed out often enough that it would be more difficult to begin a socialist revolution in the countries of advanced capitalism than in Russia. He could not have foreseen, however, that even after the devastation of a second world war they would still be showing no signs of a socialist revolution. He failed also to predict that bourgeois-democratic institutions would not only continue to survive in these countries but would go on developing, that the Socialist International would long outlive the Comintern, and that, even sixty years after the formation of the Comintern, majorities of workers in capitalist countries would continue to cast their votes not for Communist, but for Social Democratic parties. Lenin had no means of foretelling the urgency for the whole of humanity of our newly arrived ecological and demographic problems, or the issues facing us now because of our limited raw materials and energy. We are well aware that Lenin saw the danger of a degeneration of the Bolshevik Party; he even indicated where the danger lay, pointing specifically to Stalin and recommending that he be demoted to a more modest role in Party affairs. But even Lenin could never have imagined the monstrous forms to be assumed by the Party during its actual degeneration under Stalinism, or that within twenty years of the glorious October Revolution our country would see the rise of appalling terror and, with it, the liquidation of most of the founder-members of the Bolshevik Party.

If this is the truth of the matter, then why do the Communist parties, or individual theoreticians within the Communist movement, continue to think out their new positions with reference to all that has passed as 'Leninism' or 'Marxism-Leninism'. This approach, demanded by dogmatists like Ponomaryov, inhibits and bedevils the search for new and fertile ideas, stifles discussion and prevents the solution of all sorts of problems—the dictatorship of the proletariat, the emergence of new forms of revolutionary transition towards socialism, new organizational procedures for Communist parties, new attitudes towards the values and institutions of 'bourgeois' democracy, new relations between Communist and Social Democratic parties, new relations between Communism and the churches as well as many other issues of lesser importance.

It seems nothing less than normal and reasonable, then, for Western Communist parties to refuse to be bound by the concepts of 'Leninism' or 'Marxism-Leninism' when drawing up their fundamental documents, but to prefer the broader, yet at times more useful and specific concepts of 'scientific socialism' or 'scientific communism'. In one Soviet publication after another, these parties are criticized for doing so as if their departure from Leninism can lead only to the ideological disarmament of the Communist movement. As it happens, this is not a departure from Leninism, but a reconsideration of many of his premises with a view to forward movement in the ideological realm, in other words not 'disarmament' but a more relevant 'rearming' of the Communist movement. This problem arose long ago not just in Western Communist parties but actually in the CPSU.

The 1978 Congress of the Spanish Communist Party excluded from its documents the concept of 'Marxism-Leninism', characterizing itself as 'Marxist, democratic and revolutionary'.[9] The concepts of 'Leninism' and 'Marxism-Leninism' were avoided also by the Italian Communist Party in the formulation of its basic principles; and its leader, Enrico Berlinguer, made it clear in an interview that the Party was against the institutionalization of Lenin and the conversion of his teaching into a school text-book. Nevertheless, he was at pains to stress the importance of many of Lenin's ideas. 'From the time of our birth, and throughout our analytical processes and all our struggles, Lenin has played a vastly important role, though we stop short of investing him with exclusive preeminence and doctrinaire certainty.'[10] The term 'Marxism-Leninism' was replaced by that of 'scientific socialism' in the policy documents of the Communist parties of Japan, Sweden and Australia. The same thing occurred at the 23rd Congress of the French Communist Party. *Pravda* published a summary of Georges Marchais's speech on this occasion. Readers were informed that, '... touching on proposed changes in the Rules of the French Communist Party the speaker announced that the ideological basis of French Communism was Scientific Socialism as laid down by Marx, Engels and their great successors, with V.I. Lenin foremost among them. It was proposed to introduce into the Rules of the Party the phrase 'Scientific Socialism' rather than 'Marxism-Leninism'.'[11].

At the very outset of his revolutionary career, Lenin wrote; 'We most certainly do not look upon the theory of Marx as something permanent and immutable; on the contrary, we remain convinced that it has merely laid the foundation stone of the science which socialists must advance in all directions if they want to keep abreast of life.'[12] The same could be said today (and could have been said yesterday) of the theories of Lenin himself. We have no intention of repudiating 'Leninism', a concept denoting an entire age in the development of scientific communism, or, for that matter, 'Marxism' itself. The study of Leninism and the practical development of socialist revolution in Russia remains as urgently relevant to all of us as the study of Marxism and the practical development of the working-class movement in the nineteenth century did for Lenin himself. But we live today in an entirely new era, one that Lenin could not have known. If it is true that the revolutionary movement forty to forty-five years after the death of Marx could not be circumscribed by the simple formula 'Marxism' in defining its ideology but had to substitute the term 'Marxism-Leninism', it is no less certain that the same thing is happening again today when the 'Marxism-Leninism' formula begins to seem inadequate. It is a mistake to believe in the formula 'Leninism is the Marxism of today' even when it is expounded in a more complex form such as this: 'Leninism is Marxism in the age of imperialism and proletarian revolution, the age of the collapse of colonialism and the triumph of national liberation movements, the age of transition as mankind moves from capitalism to socialism and of the building of communist society.'[13] This was a relevant statement in the early 1920s; it is not so in the early 1980s. The claim that Leninism is present-day Marxism amounts to a voluntary acceptance of the limitations of *yesterday's Marxism,* which is impermissible.

I have suggested elsewhere that the identification of a given science or scientific tendency with a single person occurs only in the earliest stages of its development, as a token of gratitude for the achievements of its founder. It was Darwin who provided the powerful impulse needed for the development of the biological sciences, and for decades afterwards those biologists who shared his views called themselves Darwinists. Similarly, geneticists called themselves Mendelists, then Mendelist-Morganists or Mendelist-Weismannists. We can also point to Freudians, Copernicans, Newtonians or to the sad memory of the Michurin school. Nowadays, however, men and women who study flora and fauna are simply biologists or geneticists. The teachings of Freud developed into psychoanalysis, those of Copernicus became astronomy, those of Newton are now described as mechanics. And so it goes on. Many religious and ethical doctrines have developed along different lines, retaining the name of their founder even today. This applies for example, to Confucianism, Mohammedanism, Christianity, Buddhism, Ghandism, Lutheranism and Tolstoyism. Neither the teachings of Marx and Engels, however, nor those of Lenin, amount to a religion or an ethical doctrine. Marx and Engels were the founders of scientific socialism. Under Lenin, this science took a further step forward. Today, it has reached an even more exalted stage of development which it is not proper to associate with the name of any one of its scientific or revolutionary founding fathers. We must now concern ourselves first and foremost not with the restoration of old appellations from the past but with the future development of scientific socialism.

I

2
The Dictatorship of the Proletariat

Marx and Engels on the Dictatorship of the Proletariat

In the *Communist Manifesto* (1848) and several articles and speeches of 1847-49, Marx and Engels made numerous references to the necessity for the proletariat to win political power and become organized as the 'ruling class'. Expressions such as 'revolutionary dictatorship' or 'revolutionary violence' were commonly used by Marx and Engels when they outlined the conditions necessary for the victory of socialist revolution and the building of socialist society. The phrase 'the dictatorship of the proletariat' was first used by Marx in *The Class Struggles in France 1848 to 1850*, which was written between January and November 1850 and serialized in the *Neue Rheinische Zeitung*. Marx himself claimed that in the course of the class struggle in France the proletariat had invented a 'bold, revolutionary battle-cry'—*'Overthrow of the bourgeoisie! Dictatorship of the working class!'*.[1]

The leading revolutionary groups of French workers were controlled in 1848 by a political club founded by Louis Auguste Blanqui. Marx wrote that, in the process of their intense class struggle, the French proletariat 'rallies ever more around *revolutionary socialism,* around *communism,* for which the bourgeoisie itself has invented the name of Blanqui. This socialism is the declaration of the permanence of the revolution, the class dictatorship of the proletariat as a necessary intermediate point on the path towards the abolition of class differences...'.[2] The identification between Marx, Engels and Louis Blanqui at this time was so close that, in the first half of 1850, Marx and Engels, on behalf of the

Communist League, personally signed an agreement with the Blanquists Adam and Vidille, according to which English, French and German communists were to form a 'World-wide Society of Communist Revolutionaries'. The first article of this agreement was: 'The purpose of the society shall be the overthrow of the privileged classes, the subjugation of these classes to the dictatorship of the proletariat by the waging of permanent revolution pending the establishment of Communism, which shall be the final form of organization for the human species.'[3]

The intended agreement between the Communist League and the Blanquist organizations, together with other left-wing Chartist groups, in fact never came into effect. A wave of reaction spread over Western Europe. Blanqui was sentenced to a long term in prison, the Communist League suffered a split and was soon dissolved. However, the development of revolutionary thinking that would come to be known as Marxism did continue. In 1852, Marx wrote to a friend, Wedemeyer, who had emigrated to the United States: 'What I did that was new was to prove: (1) that the *existence of classes* is only bound up with *particular, historic phases in the development of production;* (2) that the class struggle necessarily leads to the *dictatorship of the proletariat;* (3) that this dictatorship itself only constitutes the transition to the *abolition of all classes* and to a *classless society.*'[4]

Occupied as he was from now on with his researches into economics, Marx did not use the phrase 'the dictatorship of the proletariat' for some years. It is not used in the policy documents of the First International, the organizers and leaders of which were, to all intents and purposes, Marx and Engels themselves. Marxism had not yet been adopted by the working-class movement as its prime ideology, and therefore the International needed a programme that 'would keep its doors open to British trade unionists, followers of Proudhon in France, Belgium, Italy and Spain, and those of Lassalle in Germany.'[5] The options of Marx and Engels had not changed, however, and in his critical observations directed against the Gotha Programme of the German Social Democratic Party in 1875, Marx was to write: 'Between capitalist and communist society lies the period of revolutionary transformation of the one into the other. Corresponding to this is also a political transition period in which the state can be nothing but *the revolutionary dictatorship of the proletariat.*[6] The authors of the Gotha Programme, however, virtually ignored Marx's numerous criticisms, which were not published until 1891.

The concept of 'the dictatorship of the proletariat' was absent also from the policy documents of the various workers' parties that came together in 1889 to form the Second International. It was not to be found either in the Erfurt programme of the German Social Democratic Party, which Engels had a hand in writing and which did take into consideration many earlier observations made by Marx. This programme, which was considered by Lenin to be in many ways exemplary,[7] contained only a reference to 'the necessity for the proletariat to gain political power and eliminate classes and class rule.'[8] Engels had in mind the timid reluctance of Social Democrats to use the formula 'the dictatorship of the proletariat' when he wrote in 1891: 'of late the Social Democratic philistine has once more been filled with wholesome terror at the words: Dictatorship of the Proletariat...Gentlemen, do you want to know what this dictatorship looks like? Look at the Paris Commune. That was the Dictatorship of the Proletariat.'[9] The wish to avoid this formula, however, remained with Western Social Democrats, especially those on the right. One of the German leaders Eduard Bernstein, wrote in the late 1890s: 'Is there any sense in going on about the "dictatorship of the proletariat"?... This phrase has outlived itself.'[10]

Not only the left-wing Social Democrats, but also those in the moderate centre group took issue with Bernstein, though before long the overwhelming majority of theoreticians and leaders of the Western Social Democratic parties had stopped using the formula. Karl Kautsky went so far as to suggest that it had been an off-the-cuff phrase for Marx himself and had no serious significance for Marxism. His Social Democratic contemporaries went further still in rejecting 'the dictatorship of the proletariat' as a formula, and, in fact, repudiating all formulae to do with revolutionary dictatorship. They held that the expressions 'socialism' and 'dictatorship' were mutually exclusive. If there was a dictatorship, there was no socialism, and vice versa.[11] Only the Russian Social Democrats took a different attitude.

Lenin on the Dictatorship of the Proletariat.

The Russian Social Democratic movement showed from the first that it was unafraid of words describing the dictatorship of the proletariat. The expression itself is found repeatedly in Plekhanov's writings in the 1890s. He saw to it that the phrase was included in the first draft programme of the Social Democratic Party. It was omitted from the second draft, only for Lenin to insist on its inclusion in the final text.[12]

In the revolutionary period of 1905-1907, Lenin spoke much more frequently of the revolutionary-democratic dictatorship of the proletariat and the peasantry, or of revolutionary dictatorship in general, than of the dictatorship of the proletariat in particular. Like Marx before him, Lenin was reluctant to project too detailed a model of the future society. Thus he wrote in 1905: 'A time will come when the battle against the Russian autocracy is over; the age of democratic revolution will dawn... Then we shall think specifically of a socialist dictatorship of the proletariat and talk about it in greater detail.'[13] Even *The State and Revolution* (August-September 1917) devoted little space to the nature and the functions of the dictatorship of the proletariat. On the other hand, following the triumph in October 1917 and right up to a few days before his death, Lenin was to write and say so much about the dictatorship of the proletariat, its character and peculiarities, its forms and functions, that several anthologies running to hundreds of pages have been compiled from these statements alone. After his death, Lenin's closest allies and disciples took it upon themselves to systematize the ideological and theoretical legacy of their leader. Our theoretical literature rang with controversy over what really mattered about Leninism. This discussion eventually reached a measure of agreement. What mattered was not so much the peasant question, as some people had thought, but the dictatorship of the proletariat and the conditions under which it might be attained and then consolidated.[14]

Let us limit outselves to one or two typical and fairly exhaustive pronouncements made by Lenin on this subject. In 1919 he wrote as follows: 'The dictatorship of the proletariat means the merciless use of severe, swift and decisive violence in order to put down opposition from the exploiters, capitalists, landowners and their hangers-on. Anyone who fails to see this is no revolutionary; he should be removed from any position as leader or adviser of the proletariat. However, proletarian dictatorship does not depend on violence alone, or even principally on violence. Its essence is to be found in the organization and discipline of the forward troops of the working people, their vanguard, their one and only leader, the proletariat itself. Its goal is the establishment of socialism, the elimination of class divisions in society, the conversion of all members of society into workers and the removal of all possibilities for the exploitation of man by man. This goal cannot be achieved instantaneously, it calls for a substantial period of transition from capitalism to socialism since the reorganization of production is a complex matter and radical change in any walk of life takes time. ...Throughout this transitional period opposition to reform will come equally from the capitalists and their many stooges among the bourgeois intelligentsia, all of whom will show conscious opposition, and also from the vast masses of working people, including the peasantry, all of them downtrodden by petty-bourgeois customs and traditions. In most cases these latter workers will show unconscious resistance... What is needed is the dictatorship of the proletariat, power in the hands of a single class, the strength of their organization and discipline, their centralized might, resting on all the achievements of culture, science and technology under capitalism, their proletarian closeness to the psychology of every working man, their authority over scattered, underdeveloped, politically uncertain country folk and those involved in petty-bourgeois production, so that the proletariat may lead the peasantry and all the different levels of the petty bourgeoisie... Among the oppressed classes only one has the capacity to use its dictatorship to eliminate all classes, the one which has been educated, hardened, united and brought up on decades of industrial and political warfare against capital. Only the class which has taken over the whole of urban, industrial, large-scale capitalist culture has the courage and the capacity to stick it out, to consolidate and develop further every last gain, to make these available to all the people, all the workers. This can only be achieved by a class able to bear every hardship, trial, adversity and great sacrifice visited by history on those who break with the past and boldly cut themselves a path to a new future...'[15]

In another article, Lenin wrote: 'The "dictatorship of the proletariat". If we translate this scientific, historical, philosophical Latin term into plain language this is what it means: only one particular class of people, the urban workers—especially those in plants and factories, those in industry—have the capability to lead the great mass of toilers and exploited working people in the battle to throw off the yoke of capital, in the actual process of throwing it off and the struggle to maintain and consolidate victory, in the business of creating a new socialist form of society, in the whole battle for the elimination of all classes.'[16]

Lenin often repeated that the dictatorship of the proletariat was more than the use of power to defend the interests of the urban workers: it extended to workers of all kinds, it must be realized in conjunction with workers of all kinds, including, above all, the peasantry. On another occasion he wrote: 'The dictatorship of the proletariat is a special form of class unity between the proletariat, the vanguard of the workers and the numerous strata of working people outside the proletariat—the petty bourgeoisie, smallholders, the peasantry, the intelligentsia, etc., (or most of them), it is a unity created to oppose capital ... a unity aimed at the irreversible creation and consolidation of socialism.'[17] The aim of the dictatorship of the proletariat was the education and *re-education* of all these groups in the socialist spirit. The process of education itself must be based on persuasion, instruction and the strength of example. Not that Lenin had any illusions—in some cases the proletariat might have to use violence and compulsion since all the classes and groups referred to would be susceptible to various vacillations and therefore unstable. This was crucial, since their vacillations and instability might ruin the whole cause of socialist revolution. 'It is essential for the proletariat to exercise governmental authority, centrally organized power and organized violence in order to quell opposition from the exploiters and to lead the vast mass of the population, the peasantry, the petty bourgeoisie, semi-proletarians, throughout the process of "getting the Socialist economy going".'[18]

The Russian experience makes it quite clear that the socialist revolution could never have triumphed without the dictatorship of the proletariat. Without it, no base could have been laid for the socialist economy. By the end of 1917, it was obvious that the overwhelming majority of the proletariat stood behind the Bolsheviks and supported the measures they were taking. Workers formed the first detachments of the Red Guard and then of the Red Army and its command. Workers formed the basic corps of food requisitioners. In 1917 and 1918, workers filled the ranks of the Bolshevik Party, and the better educated and more politically-minded among them formed the nucleus of the new governmental apparatus. The peasants and the petty bourgeoisie, on the other hand, did not support all the measures taken by the Soviet government; they were indeed subject to vacillation and their moods and political attitudes varied a good deal. These people, moreoever— the petty-bourgeois masses—accounted for the great majority of the population, the working class forming a very small minority. In 1917, the industrial proletariat, plant and factory workers, those in mining and metallurgy, numbered approximately 3,500,000[19]. In order to lead and rule, the small Russian proletariat had to set up a special government invested with extraordinary powers, particularly since the country lacked a solid tradition of democracy and even a well-developed social system. This was also a country of many nationalities, with Russians supplying less than half the population, and its centripetal tendencies were strong. It was, in addition, the first country to take the path of socialist revolution, and, predictably, would before long find itself surrounded by international hostility. It is scarcely surprising that, when in 1917 the enormous, centuries-old machinery of autocracy was suddenly destroyed, the resulting conditions were favourable not to the peaceful development of democracy but to a disorganized, anarchic outburst of age-old grievances. We must also remember that this same country was now in its fourth year of wars, with an army of fifteen million, most of whom were peasants, longing to get back to their villages and hamlets. Dissension, the destruction of private estates, countless acts of uncontrolled violence multiplied throughout the land. An enormous, multinational empire had begun to disintegrate in a process accompanied by violence and devastation. The task of uniting, organizing and, to some extent, restraining these outbursts of pent-up disaffection and violence, in the Russia of 1917, was within the capabilities of only one group—the Bolshevik-controlled industrial proletariat. Only the dictatorship of the proletariat could have staved off total ruin for the country and its economy.

It is useful in this context to consider the itinerary of one of the most prominent Menshevik leaders, A.S. Martynov. In 1905, this man had been one of Lenin's chief opponents; in his book *The Two Dictatorships,* he had condemned Bolshevik tactical thinking and Lenin's conception of the dictatorship of the proletariat, both *per se* and in relation to the impoverished peasantry. Naturally enough, Martynov took an extremely hostile view of the October Revolution and the first measures taken at that time. Politically disillusioned, he went down to the Ukraine and began working as an ordinary engineer in a sugar refinery. However, in the period 1918-20, the towns and villages of the Ukraine changed hands many times with nationalist and anarchist-communist groups and armies springing up everywhere and simply taking over what territory could be seized and held for a time. Seeing no possible end to this sanguinary, semi-anarchic breakdown of law and order, with all the accompanying destructive enmity, Martynov surprised himself by coming to the conclusion that, given the present conditions in Russia, only the dictatorship of the proletariat, as outlined by Lenin and once bitterly opposed by himself, could save society from itself and avert the total destruction of the economy. He decided to return to political life, not now as a Menshevik but as a Bolshevik. In the early 1920s, he published two booklets, *My Ukrainian Impressions and Reflections* and *The Great Test.* In 1923, he was accepted into the Party and worked until his death later that year on the editorial staff of the journal *Communist International.*

Lenin had a good opportunity to take stock of all that occurred during the Russian Revolution. He did not, however, conclude from this experience that the dictatorship of the proletariat was exclusively relevant to Russia's particular conditions. On the contrary, he felt certain that some of the measures taken during the Russian Revolution would be equally necessary in any other revolution: one of these was the dictatorship of the proletariat. On a number of occasions, he claimed that, given conditions in the West, the proletariat should be able to come to power without armed conflict, as, for instance, in Hungary in 1919, and also that socialist revolutions in the better developed capitalist countries would take place without any degeneration into civil war and without violence or terror on anything like the scale experienced in Russia. Lenin did not believe that armed insurrection, mass 'Red Terror' or Civil War were necessities in every socialist revolution and transitional period. But the dictatorship of the proletariat was a different matter. On this subject, he wrote: 'International unity in the tactical thinking of the Communist working-class movement in all countries does not presuppose that diversity must be eliminated or that national differences be destroyed... it requires only the adoption of the fundamental principles of Communism (soviet power and the dictatorship of the proletariat) which may then be altered appropriately in their details, adjusted and adapted to suit national and national-governmental variations.'[20] Earlier he had claimed that 'the transition from capitalism to communism must naturally allow for an enormous abundance and diversity of political forms, but one essential feature must necessarily remain throughout: the dictatorship of the proletariat.'[21]

It comes as no surprise, then, that the dictatorship of the proletariat was retained as a requirement not only in the new programme of the Russian Communist Party adopted at the Eighth Congress, but in all the important documents of the Third (Communist) International. Twenty-one conditions were laid down for the acceptance of a party into that organisation and the *very first* of these required acknowledgement of the need for the dictatorship of the proletariat. The necessity for this no doubt stemmed from the fact that Lenin's understanding of the dictatorship of the proletariat was currently coming under fire from socialists of many different complexions. Many Social Democrats were claiming that in most capitalist countries the state was gradually evolving into a mechanical system of regulation no longer based on class. Anarchist theoreticians, on the other hand, were calling for the dismantling of all government machinery following the triumph of the socialist revolution, leaving only a free federation of industrial associations and agricultural communes. But within the Communist movement, Lenin's formulation of the need for the dictatorship of the proletariat remained an indisputable postulate until the Comintern was disbanded in 1943.

Lenin's Errors

Lenin is widely acknowledged to have made a singular contribution to the development of Marxist thinking on government. This does not mean, however, that we have to ignore the various errors and inconsistencies in his numerous statements on problems of government and the dictatorship of the proletariat. Let us consider, for example, his certainty, some months before the October Revolution, that, given the dictatorship of the proletariat, it would be a straightforward matter to organize government affairs, including the running of a nationalized economy, and that no particular capabilities, no special skills or training, would be called for:

'During the transition from capitalism to communism, "government" will still be required, but ... the subjugation of the minority of exploiters by the majority of yesterday's hired slave labour ... will be a comparatively simple matter, a straightforward and natural process... The exploiters will be in no position to suppress the people without the complex machinery necessary to do so, whereas the people can suppress the exploiters with only the simplest of machinery, or almost none at all, without any special apparatus, just the simple organization of armed mass strength.'[22]

'We are not utopian. We do not indulge in fanciful dreams of getting by immediately without any form of government... We want the socialist revolution with people as they are today who cannot manage without subordination and control. But no one will be able to resist... the armed proletariat. The specific "bossing" of civil servants can and must be replaced immediately, *overnight,* by the introduction of the simple functions "supervisors and accountants", functions *well within the grasp of the general run of citizens* and worth "a worker's salary".'[23]

'Capitalist culture has created heavy industry, factories, railways, a postal system, telephones and the like and thus the vast majority of functions performed by the old "state power" have become greatly simplified and can be reduced to such simple systems as registration, records and checking procedure, systems which will become increasingly accessible to all literate people.'[24]

'The development of capitalism creates the preconditions for literally "everyone" to participate in the government of the state... Accounting and control—these are what matter in "getting things going", starting off the correct functioning of communist society in its first phase ... Accounting and control of production have been reduced by capitalism to a series of incredibly simple operations, within the grasp of any literate person, a matter of observing, recording and knowing your three R's.'[25]

All of this was clearly utopian in the extreme, as Lenin was soon to discover; the running of the state and its nationalized economy retain a good degree of complexity even under socialism. In order to administer and dynamize the Soviet state, the Red Army, the Cheka, and the Soviets running the national economy, and also to organize accounting and control (including the control of the activities of the state apparatus itself), it turned out that mere literacy and knowledge of the three Rs were not enough. Lenin realized that it was essential to retain a system of high salaries for 'bourgeois specialists' and impractical even to introduce equality in pay for different categories of workers and officials, and this applied also to workers within the Party apparatus itself.

Further substantial errors occurred in Lenin's definition of the state and state power in general, and the dictatorship of the proletariat in particular. The concept of 'dictatorship' arose in antiquity and was taken to indicate an exceptional form of authority that assumed particularly wide-ranging special powers and depended directly on armed superiority and violence rather than on laws passed by the state concerned. Dictatorial powers could be assumed by an individual or by a whole government. At the same time, the concept denoted a *temporary* regime instituted for a specific period, after which the dictatorship would be replaced by normal forms of government. The word 'dictatorship' itself is Latin in origin. In the Roman Republic, a 'dictator' was an official (usually a consul) invested by Senate decision with extraordinary powers *for a specific period*. A suitable pretext for the establishment of a dictatorship might have been an outbreak of war or a revolt by the slaves. The Roman military commander and ex-consul known as Pompey the Great (Gnaeus Pompeius, 106-48 BC) was appointed dictator in 67 BC in order to do battle with the pirates who were disrupting trade and the flow of supplies into Rome. He was invested with extraordinary powers for a three-year period, with full authority over the Mediterranean area including the shore-line up to seventy kilometres inland. As it happened, he saw off the pirates in a matter of months. The decisions and sentences handed down by Roman dictators were not contestable in the courts, their actions were not subject to complaint or appeal, and on the expiry of the period of extraordinary powers the dictator could still not be called to account for his actions *during the dictatorship*. The normal term for a Roman dictatorship was six months.

Extraordinary power unlimited by time or by law was generally referred to in antiquity as 'tyranny' or 'despotism'; even in those times, there were numerous forms of hereditary monarchy, but these had nothing to do with the Roman concept of 'dictatorship'. There were indeed occasions when individual military leaders were given the title and authority of a dictator for an unspecified time. One such dictatorship was accepted, or more probably seized with the help of the army, by Lucius Cornelius Sulla (138-78 BC), on whose orders thousands of Roman citizens were liquidated. Even so, after three years of power, Sulla abdicated voluntarily and died soon afterwards. Julius Caesar also received dictatorial powers from the Senate. These were renewed on several occasions and in 44 BC Caesar was appointed Dictator for life. At the same time, he was appointed Consul for a ten-year period and made Censor for life; that, however, was the very year of his murder by Cassius and Brutus. After his death the Roman Senate voted to abolish for ever the institution of dictatorship, though this decision could not prevent the fall of the Roman Republic or the formation of the Roman Empire.

In the Middle Ages, all forms of republican and democratic government died out virtually everywhere; their survival is recorded only in individual cities and communities in Europe. The concept of 'dictatorship' ceased to be used, since the unlimited power exercised over their subjects by the monarchs of Europe and Asia was anything but *temporary;* it was centuries-long, passing through inheritance from one king, shah, emperor or khan to the next. Only in the eighteenth and nineteenth centuries, along with the revival of republican forms of government, was the ancient concept of 'dictatorship' itself resurrected. The English Revolution produced its own dictator, Oliver Cromwell, a man who, in the words of Friedrich Engels, 'combined in one personality Robespierre and Napoleon'.[26] The French Revolution produced dictators like Robespierre himself, and his closest allies in the Committee of Public Safety. Robespierre not only facilitated the replacement of a constitutional regime in France by a revolutionary-democratic dictatorship; he also attempted to enforce acknowledgement that the dictatorship should be a *temporary* measure. His claim was that 'Revolution is warfare between Freedom and her enemies; Constitution is a regime of victorious and peaceful freedom'.[27] The European movement of counter-revolution also gave rise to a number of dictators, such as General Louis Cavaignac, who wielded full executive power over the French Republic for several months during 1848, after his brutal suppression of the June revolt of the French working class.

When Marx and Engels spoke of the 'dictatorship of the proletariat', they were using the term 'dictatorship' in its ancient Roman sense. They were at pains to stress not only the exceptional nature of this form of authority, its assumption of extraordinary powers and its violent character, but also its necessary limitation in time and therefore the fact that it was transitional in character. Dictatorship would be necessary for the proletariat only for a period of time during the transition from capitalism to socialism. Outside this period, there would be no need for it, particularly since the argument of Marx and Engels presupposed that once socialism proved victorious not only would the proletariat cease to exist, so would the state itself, as a political institution irrelevant to a classless society.

We cannot doubt that the concept of 'dictatorship' entails direct violence, the assumption of extraordinary powers, and the dictator's flouting of the laws and constitutional safeguards in a given country. An equally essential, though less obvious, characteristic of a dictatorship is its transitional nature, the time limit imposed upon it. It is not surprising that, in current political literature and in the political practice of the last hundred years, the distinctions between the terms 'dictatorship', 'tyranny' and 'despotism' have been eroded. Nowadays they are virtually synonymous expressions. The various regimes of Mussolini, Hitler, Salazar, Franco, Somoza, Duvalier and Stroessner are referred to not by the name of tyranny, despotism or fascism but as 'dictatorships'. All of these, incidentally, avoided any time limit. Some of them were transferable by heredity from father to son, and, although the dictatorships of Hitler, Mussolini, Salazar-Caetano and Somoza did not go on forever, they came to end not because the dictator himself abdicated 'on the expiry of the specified period' but because he was overthrown by war or revolution.

Contemporary political literature and political practice have, however, preserved rather than eroded the distinctions between 'dictatorship' and 'democracy', or a 'dictatorial' and a 'democratic' regime, a 'dictatorial' or 'democratic' state. In fact the distinction between 'dictatorship' and 'democracy' has now acquired a sharper definition than it had at the beginning of the century. In relation to a country with a solidly *democratic* political system, we avoid, when defining its method of government, any mention of a 'dictatorship' or 'dictatorial regime' or, to use the now fashionable expression, 'totalitarian regime'. Each democratic country, of course, does possess government apparatuses, including a vitally important army, political force, judicial system, prison service, counter-intelligence network and secret police, all of them organizations using violence in one form or another. In the first place, however, this kind of violence is employed as a rule within the existing framework of law and constitutional safeguards of that country, therefore the violence cannot be described as *direct,* as it is under a dictatorship. Second, in democratic countries, violence is far from being the *main instrument* by which government is carried on and a particular class retains power. Argument and propaganda in their various forms, the exploitation of the media in every possible way, the voices of religious ideologies, the democratic machinery of general elections, the existence of different political parties, parliament and many other kinds of local and national representation —these are the essential means by which a given class attempts to retain power. Even so, in any democratic country, various abuses of power and illegal violence may still occur. At any moment of deep crisis, the ruling classes may, for a short time or an indeterminate period, suspend all constitutional guarantees, prevent the activity of the various democratic institutions and introduce unlimited authoritarian government without the sanction of law—in other words, dictatorship. Nevertheless, the possibility of such a contingency is no reason for confusion over the concepts of 'democracy' and 'dictatorship', no reason for describing any such state as 'dictatorial'. If we describe all power and all systems of government as dictatorial, we are guilty not only of a logical error but a political one too. By doing so, we reduce the value for working people of those democratic institutions and safeguards in law which they have by no means always enjoyed but which have resulted from prolonged, bitter and often bloody struggle conducted by working people themselves in the name of democracy.

It must be said that in many instances Lenin did draw a clear distinction between dictatorship and democracy. For example, he wrote that 'anyone who has failed, when reading Marx, to understand that, in a capitalist society, *in any crisis, in any serious class confrontation*, the dictatorship of the bourgeoisie and the dictatorship of the proletariat are equally feasible has failed to understand anything at all in the economic and the political teaching of Marx.'[28] Here, Lenin is clearly associating the concept of dictatorship—direct violence, unlimited by any laws or constitutional guarantees—with occasional 'crises' and 'class confrontations'. In times of more tranquil and peaceful capitalist development, the proletariat, he suggests, must endeavour to exploit to the full all existing democratic institutions and freedoms, particularly the freedom of assembly, legalized party activities, general elections, the various forms of popular representation and parliamentary structures, all of which represent an enormous step forward from feudal-aristocratic and autocratic forms of government. On other occasions, Lenin makes it clear that a dictatorship is a temporary form of power born of peculiar circumstances. He asserted, for instance that *'during a civil war*, a victorious power can only be a dictatorship.'[29] The concept of dictatorship is once again associated with a temporary phenomenon, a period of civil war, rather than with the whole period of the existence of capitalist society. The words used clearly recall a statement made by Marx to the effect that 'any temporary governmental structure following a revolution requires a dictatorship, and an energetic one'.[30]

Unfortunately, however, it was much more common for Lenin *not* to draw any clear distinction between the concepts of 'democracy' and 'dictatorship', *not* to limit the term 'dictatorship' to an association with one specific period in the life of a bourgeois or proletarian state, perhaps a time of civil war or violent class confrontation. It was Lenin's regularly expressed opinion that democracy was but one of the forms assumed by dictatorship; there were only two possibilities—the dictatorship of the proletariat or the dictatorship of the bourgeoisie. This is clear from *The State and Revolution*, in which he wrote: 'Democracy is one form of the state, one of its various guises. Consequently it represents, like every state, the organized and systematic use of violence against the people.'[31] This imprecise definition, which leaves out of account the essential difference between the use of violence in a democracy and under a dictatorship, led on to another imprecise and false assertion, to the effect that power, any kind of power, amounts to dictatorship. In other words, any kind of government must ultimately be considered dictatorial government. Direct violence, unconstrained by any law, becomes for Lenin the inevitable and obligatory token of any government. The concepts of 'political power', 'the state' and 'dictatorship' blur into synonymy. Again, in 1917 Lenin wrote: 'The different forms taken by bourgeois states are extremely varied but the essence of them all is the same: one way or another all of these states are ultimately and necessarily a dictatorship of the bourgeoisie.'[32] On another occasion, he referred to Engels's assertion that 'the state is nothing more or less than machinery for the suppression of one class by another and this applies to a democracy just as much as a monarchy'.[33] He had this in mind when, in the course of a polemic with Kautsky in 1918, he wrote: 'Every little boy knows that a monarchy and a republic are two different forms of government. What Mr. Kautsky needs to remember is that both these governments... like all such "forms of government" under capitalism are in essence simply different guises of the *bourgeois state,* i.e. *the dictatorship of the bourgeoisie.*'[34] He said more or less the same thing in 1919: 'The most democratic of bourgeois republics has never been and could never have been anything other than a machine for the repression of the workers by means of capital, a weapon of capitalist political power, the dictatorship of the bourgeoisie.'[35]

Statements like these abound in Lenin's work, although he did sometimes take note of a difference between 'open' and 'hidden' dictatorship of the bourgeoisie—'thousands of facts testify to the truth, which the bourgeoisie tries vainly to conceal, that even the most democratic of republics are ruled by terror and a dictatorship of the bourgeoisie that emerges quite clearly every time the exploiters get the impression that the power of capitalism is wavering.'[36]

Lenin's definitions, which are often as imprecise as they are categorical, sometimes prove embarrassing for today's Soviet sociologists and political commentators. Some of them attempt to 'touch up' what he said by using other quotations from his writings.

For example, in a collective work entitled *Lenin's Theory of Socialist Revolution and the Present Day,* there is a passing reference to the effect that dictatorship is the political rule of one specific class. Alongside this generalized and therefore inexact formulation we read the following: 'Speaking of dictatorship as a special form of power not bound by former laws and directly dependent on the use of violence, Marxism-Leninism emphasizes that it is a temporary structure inextricably bound up with the conditions of bitter class warfare and civil war, i.e. not with the entire history of class formation..., but only with certain periods when a practical solution is being discovered to the question of replacing the rule of one class (or classes) by another (or others). Substantiating the inevitability of this period *in certain conditions,* Lenin wrote that 'history teaches us that no oppressed class has ever come to power, and could not ever come to power, without going through a period of dictatorship, i.e. the seizure of political rule and the violent suppression of the most desperate, most furious opposition which stops at nothing and which has always been provided by the exploiters.'[37] In this utterance by Lenin what stands out with particular clarity is his understanding of dictatorship as class rule and as a *special temporary regime* in the period of the seizure of political power and suppression of desperate opposition by the class enemies which have been overthrown.'[38]

This is all very well, but it is more common in our literature to encounter quite different definitions. An example may be taken from a book by V.E. Guliyev, *Democracy and Contemporary Imperialism.* 'Class dictatorship, especially that of the bourgeoisie is a complex, many-sided phenomenon of political life. The study of it is very much in the interests of the working class, of all workers, since this very class dictatorship is the essence, the true nature and at the same time the precious secret of any bourgeois state, be it a fascist regime, a semi-fascist one built on the military and the police, a constitutional monarchy or any other bourgeois-democratic republic. Like any other political form, bourgeois democracy is, in its own particular way, a form by which capitalist dictatorship organizes (and protects) itself.'[39]

Here the author misleads us by confusing several terms, *political power, the state, democracy* and *dictatorship.* The plain fact that in a bourgeois-democratic republic power belongs ultimately to the capitalist class does not necessarily imply that this power must be *dictatorial*. In a number of bourgeois republics, the observance of laws, the constitution and other judicial standards is by no means an empty formality. Confusion of such concepts as 'political power' in general, 'the state' and 'dictatorship' can only hinder the development of sound strategy and tactics for the Communist parties. It will cause us to ignore differences in principle existing between states such as Chile, Paraguay or Guatemala, where vicious dictatorial regimes do exist, and places like England, France, Italy, Spain or Japan where there is no regime of political dictatorship. Even in the Russia of 1917, there were weeks and months when Lenin seriously considered the possibility of a peaceful course of development for the socialist revolution. Although government was transferred after the events of February to the middle class, the Russian bourgeoisie was as yet in no position to impose violence upon the masses; it wanted, but was unable, to assert itself as a dictatorship. Naturally, in all the developed capitalist countries, reasonably strong apparatuses of government, with all their ramifications, have long histories. Nevertheless, the political set-up in a number of them is such that the working class and its parties know there is a possibility of peaceful progress to revolution. The analysis and exploitation of possibilities like these derive no benefit at all from an inordinate extension of the meaning of the word 'dictatorship'.

It must be accepted, then, that by no means all political power and every form of state government may be described automatically as a dictatorship and that democracy is more than simply one of the manifestations of 'hidden' dictatorship. The hallmarks of a true dictatorship are direct violence and the setting aside of the rule of law in a given country. Although Lenin made the mistake of equating all government and political power with dictatorship, nevertheless he did believe that the proletarian state would be short-lived in Russia. It was his conviction that revolution in Russia would soon be followed by socialist revolutions in the main countries of capitalism. It followed that, as revolution spread throughout the world and socialist societies became established, the state would begin to atrophy as a political entity and its functions, including that of suppression, would diminish steadily.

It turned out that the state was still with us in the USSR twenty-five to thirty years later and remains with us today, sixty-odd years after the Revolution. It shows no sign yet of atrophy. On the contrary, the Soviet state has turned into an extraordinarily wide-ranging government apparatus embracing every aspect of life in our society. On a world scale, proletarian revolution has proceeded only at a snail's pace since 1917, and not one of the major capitalist countries has followed Russia's example. For the time being, we shall not go into the legality of the state's involvement in all spheres of social life in the USSR. Let us merely note in passing that very few of our political commentators, sociologists and lawyers draw any distinction between the concepts of 'the state' and 'dictatorship'. Most Soviet theorists continue to adhere to Lenin's principle. Yu. Volkov, for instance, writes as follows: 'Lenin's works consistently advance the idea that any form of state power, at all times, irrespective of the particular form of government or political regime in which it is embodied—monarchist, republican, aristocratic or democratic, etc—represents the dictatorship of a certain class.'[40] In the latest edition of the *Great Soviet Encyclopaedia,* the word 'state' is defined as follows: 'However varied the different historical forms of the state, state power and organized state apparatus, in their essential character and the nature of their relations with society, these amount to political power wielded by a ruling class (class dictatorship).'[41]

Soviet theorists are particularly embarrassed today by Lenin's assertion that dictatorship is power based *directly* upon violence and divorced from *any rule of law*. This formula is frequently repeated in our propaganda when dealing with bourgeois states or semi-feudal monarchies. It is, of course, avoided in relation to the Soviet Union or the other countries in the Soviet bloc. Not uncommonly, Soviet theorists attempt to 'touch up' Lenin's comments and give a new interpretation to his statements about the dictatorship of the proletariat. The usual approach is for them to suggest that, on these occasions, Lenin had in mind the old laws, that is the laws of a bourgeois society now destroyed by socialist revolution—not the new laws passed by the proletarian state itself. G.N. Shakhnazarov for instance, explaining Lenin's utterances on the dictatorship of the proletariat, states categorically that 'there are no circumstances at all, however exceptional, which justify uncontrolled dictatorial power or despotism. Even when conditions call for a limited concentration of power and extreme measures to be taken against the enemies of revolution it remains essential that Soviet legality be observed.'[42] This idea has been developed by Yu. A. Krasin, who writes: 'The dictatorship of the proletariat does not mean the liquidation of the rule of law, which would place society in a state of total anarchy. It is not limited by laws which express the will of a minority of exploiters and was established by an age-old system of oppression and violence towards the people. It could not have solved the problem before it without departing from the framework of bourgeois legality, bourgeois law. The dictatorship of the proletariat itself sets forth a new revolutionary legality which is the expression of the interests of the working class, the toiling people, and is a defence against the arbitrary misuse of power.'[43]

Naturally Lenin did not preclude the necessity to establish and develop a new revolutionary, socialist form of legality after the revolution. But this would be a matter of years rather than days. What was clear was that there would be a period in post-revolutionary Russia when the ruling power would not be able to use existing laws because the *old* laws were invalid and the *new* ones were not yet in existence. Apart from this, the main point about dictatorship was that it was an exceptional use of power which in the particular circumstances was not to be closely limited even by the new laws. Lenin did not leave this open to doubt. As he insisted to Kautsky: 'Dictatorship is power directly dependent on violence and bound by *no* laws. The revolutionary dictatorship of the proletariat is power seized and maintained by the violence exercised by the proletariat on the bourgeoisie, a power bound by no laws.'[44] In a speech to the All-Union Assembly of Soviets on June 5, 1918, he said: 'A revolutionary who has no wish to be hypocritical will not shrink from capital punishment. There has never been a revolution or an age of civil war that has not known executions... We have reached a stage which is the most critical period in our revolution... References are made to decrees abolishing capital punishment. But he is a bad revolutionary who stops in the moment of bitter struggle, faltering before the inflexibility of the law. In the transitional period, laws take on a temporary significance. And if the law stands in the way of revolution it gets repealed or amended.'[45]

These statements are fairly precise, and they refer not only to the old laws of tsarist times but to the laws and decrees promulgated under Soviet power itself. Even at a time when the basis of law in the

Russian Federation had been established, and Lenin was insisting on the strictest observance of legality, he nevertheless continued to accept the possibility of adopting extreme measures necessitated by the struggle against counter-revolution and outside the framework of existing law, on the one condition that the Council of People's Commissars, or a similar institution or official person, must be informed immediately. As he put it, 'people must learn how to battle for legality in a cultivated way without ever forgetting the limits of legality in revolution'.[46]

A dictatorship must therefore be considered only a temporary institution and a new proletarian power must not become reconciled for long to the conditional and temporary nature of its laws. Lenin's mistake was not that he actually vacillated, in conditions of bitter civil war, 'before the inflexibility of the law.' If he had, there would have been neither a revolution nor a civil war. But by blurring the distinctions between concepts such as 'the state', 'political power' and 'dictatorship', he made it much easier for his successors to extend their extraordinary and unlimited power indefinitely. In our country, as long as thirty years after the October Revolution, the government headed by Stalin went about its business unconstrained by any rule of law and in defiance of all constitutional guarantees and Soviet civil rights. Lenin's mistake was to keep on strengthening, needlessly, the already clearly defined meaning of dictatorship. In the course of one of his arguments with members of the Constitutional Democratic Party in 1906, he wrote: 'The scientific concept of dictatorship denotes nothing less than power which is unlimited, unconstrained by laws or by *any kind of rules* and directly dependent on violence. This is what "dictatorship" entails, no more and no less—and don't you forget it!'[47] Then, recalling the example of the spontaneous confrontations during the 1905 Revolution between the masses of the people and the police, Lenin explained that dictatorship comes into being 'when the people, the mass of the population...comes directly on to the scene itself, carries out judgment and reprisal, uses power and creates a new revolutionary legality... For revolution, in the narrow, direct meaning of the word, is that period in the life of a people when age-long enmity... bursts forth in actions rather than words, and that means the actions of millions of the masses, not a few individuals. The people awaken...the people employ violence, they take power...'[48]

These words could be corroborated by any number of episodes from the history of Russian revolution in the 1905-7 period and the February Revolution of 1917. However, this kind of outburst—spontaneous, violent action taken by the people against the police, attacks on departments of the Secret Police, the releasing of prisoners, the murder of particularly odious officers and generals by soldiers and sailors—this generally lasted only for a few days. Then the revolutionary government and party saw immediately that they had a duty to restore organization and revolutionary order to the actions of the popular masses. Otherwise that 'age-old enmity' would repeatedly impel the masses towards acts of senseless brutality contrary to the interests of the revolution. It is now well known, for example, that in thousands of villages and settlements all over Russia the peasants in 1917 did not stop at seizing and sharing out private lands, and destroying all receipts; they went on to burn down the manor-houses and farm buildings, slaughter the livestock, wreck the machinery and kill off the landowners themselves and their families. It was, of course, extremely difficult in a country like Russia to prevent such outbursts of popular anger, which really was unbound by any law. Nevertheless, the revolutionary powers considered it their duty to introduce rules of some kind and certain fairly reliable standards even into this process of direct violence. Even if Lenin's words about dictatorships being 'unconstrained by any laws' necessarily applied to the mass of the people, rising up spontaneously, and to individual outbursts of popular anger, they could not be said to apply to the activities of the organizations, parties and government of the revolution.

Long after the 1905 Revolution, with the Russian Civil War at last waning, Lenin seems to have wished to summarize his ideas on the dictatorship of the proletariat and to draw some general conclusions from three years of Soviet power. He therefore wrote an article entitled 'A Contribution to the History of the Dictatorship Question' for the journal *Communist International,* in which he not only quoted from his 1906 article but once more confirmed all the definitions and arguments that it included. This time his argument was not with the Russian Constitutional Democrats but with 'Messrs Dittman, Kautsky, Crispien and Hilferding in Germany, Longuet & Co. in France, Turati and his friends in Italy, MacDonald and Snowden in England'.[49]

It is no coincidence that, of all Lenin's utterances, Stalin was particularly fond of citing the definition of dictatorship as power unlimited by law and 'absolutely unconstrained by rules'.[50] Where is the error in this definition? It consists in the failure to allow for any difference between spontaneous, often anarchic actions by the popular masses or by small groups of the population and the activities of the organs of revolutionary power and government. The error is both logical and political and it was to lead to much abuse of power, particularly during the Civil War in Russia. Such abuses were unfortunately no rarity, not only among the counter-revolutionary forces ranged against the Bolsheviks, but in the activities of the Bolsheviks themselves. It is sufficient to recall the policy of 'Cossack Liquidation' carried out on the Don and in the Urals (Orenburg province) early in 1919 in accordance with a Party directive, the mass executions of hostages in Petrograd in the autumn of 1918, the countless acts of violence by the local authorities against the middle peasants, indignantly condemned by Lenin himself on several occasions, a number of instances when prisoners of war were subjected to torture, the bombardment of churches, and the widespread elimination of families of the nobility. Abuses of this kind seriously undermined the authority and influence of the Soviet government and the Red Army, and thus hindered and delayed the eventual victory of the Bolsheviks in the Civil War.

The definition of dictatorship no doubt must include a reference to direct violence, but it ought to exclude mention of power 'unconstrained by any rules'. After all, even the Cheka and the NKVD were set up not only in order to deal with counter-revolution and sabotage but also to eliminate the hitherto frequent incidence of mob law by the 'mass of the population' when dealing with undesirable elements. The Bolsheviks themselves introduced clear-cut and very strict rules for the activities of military and civilian personnel, revolutionary committees and organs of the Cheka. A whole series of decrees forbade the torture and taunting of prisoners. In the military zones, there were numerous executions of captured officers and of individual peasants who refused to obey orders on mobilization and the surrender of arms but, equally, many Red Army officers and men found guilty of theft, the massacre of civilians and unauthorized requisitioning were also executed for their crimes. One example is the execution of a large group of military commanders and commissars in a division of the Red Cavalry that had taken part in a pogrom against the Jews in a small town in the Ukraine. The Soviet Government was compelled on another occasion (January 1918) to issue a public condemnation of the actions of a group of sailors who had taken the law into their own hands and killed two prominent Kadet leaders, A.I. Shingarev and F.F. Kokoshkin, in hospital. Lenin immediately sent a note to the Commissariat for Justice: 'Urgent investigation to be started immediately... Sailors guilty of murder to be arrested'.[51] Lenin was much displeased when hearing after the October Revolution of occasions when 'the mass of the population... itself takes the law into its own hands'. He insisted, on the contrary, that the 'dictatorship of the proletariat is possible only through the Communist Party'.[52] He it was who, once the Civil War was over, demanded a severe curtailment of powers assumed by the organs of the Cheka, the strict observance of Soviet law, the introduction of universally applied powers of procurator and the strengthening and reorganization of Party organs and state control. In other words he recommended the institution of all manner of rules and constraints designed to regulate and organize the dictatorship of the proletariat in practice. It is true that he was not wholly consistent. For instance, he never revoked—indeed he confirmed—his earlier reference to violence 'unlimited and absolutely unbound by any laws or any kind of rules'. Thus it is not surprising to discover that, when the first Russian Federation Criminal Code was being framed in the spring of 1922, Lenin insisted on the inclusion of several extremely imprecise formulations allowing for a wide range of arbitrary interpretation. He wrote as follows to the then People's Commissar for Justice, D.I. Kursky: 'The court must not claim to eliminate terror—to promise that would be self-deception or deceit—but should institute it and legalize it in principle, for all to see, without pretence or embellishment. The formulation must be kept as broad as possible, since only a revolutionary sense of justice and a revolutionary conscience will lay down conditions for implementation of it in practice.'[53]

There can be no doubt that this inconsistency on Lenin's part, taken together with the imprecise definitions of 'dictatorship' discussed above, made it much easier at a later date for Stalin to construct a basis in theory for his own dictatorship of terror. As early as 1900, at the outset of his revolutionary career, Lenin had written: 'Terror can never become a commonplace act of war; at best it is fit for nothing more than use as a device of sudden assault.'[54] Sadly, in the history of our country, not only did terror indeed become 'a commonplace act of war' for decades on end; it was actually turned by Stalin against the personnel of the Communist Party itself and the Soviet State.[55] It would be a strange thing if the Communist parties of other countries failed to take account of this lesson in the evolution of Bolshevism in their day-to-day activities and the preparation of their policy documents.

Extracts from Russian History: The Victory and the Crisis of the Dictatorship of the Proletariat.

Lenin's general definition of 'dictatorship' did not change substantially over the years. His views on the practical forms and functions of the dictatorship of the proletariat, however, and the range of its violent activities, varied considerably from one stage of the Revolution and the Civil War to another. After ultimate defeat in the revolutionary period of 1905-1907, Lenin formed the opinion that the battle against the Russian autocracy would be long and hard. 'There was no need to take up arms', was Plekhanov's conclusion; the Bolsheviks thought otherwise. Lenin's attitude was expressed as follows: 'We can see that the weakness of the workers consisted in the fact that they lacked decisiveness, breadth and speed in resorting to the aggressive economic and armed political warfare that arose from the whole course of events.'[56]

However, much to the surprise of supporters and opponents alike, the colossal and seemingly all-powerful state machinery of autocracy crumbled and disintegrated in the spring of 1917 in a matter of days, as a result of a general strike in Petrograd and the desertion of soldiers of the Petrograd garrison to the side of the workers who had come out on to the streets.

Victory over autocracy gained so rapidly and with comparative ease, the dismayed confusion of the bourgeois parties and their leaders who had proved so inept at controlling the situation in the country or creating some kind of apparatus of rule, the sudden expansion of the revolutionary mood, not only among the workers but out among the peasantry, including those peasants who had been in uniform—all of this created an impression that the revolution, including socialist measures like the nationalization of all means of production and the banks, would advance without too much trouble. At the time, Lenin was heard to say that the Russian revolutionaries would hardly need to have recourse to the guillotine. All they would have to do would be to 'arrest the chief magnates and bigwigs in banking, the leading knights of embezzlement and bank robbery, and then only for a week or two'. After that it would be an easy matter 'to place under the workers' control all the banks, capitalist syndicates and contractors "working" for the war effort'.[57] Lenin wrote this in June 1917, but within a month his views on the prospects for the Russian Revolution had undergone considerable change. His appraisal of the situation in the country was even more pessimistic than the circumstances warranted. However, a movement to the left was occurring deep within the mass of the Russian population both in June and August, making it possible quite quickly to quell Kornilov's counter-revolutionary revolt. In those days of crisis, the main industrial centres of Russia witnessed a spontaneous and informal union between all the country's socialist parties, since Kornilov's victory was seen as a threat not just to the Bolsheviks but to the Mensheviks, Anarchists and Socialist Revolutionaries. This turn of events caused Lenin to revive his hopes of a peaceful course for the Revolution. In early September he wrote: 'If there is one absolutely indisputable lesson taught by the revolution, absolutely proven by the facts, it is this—that only the union of Bolsheviks, SRs and Mensheviks, only the immediate transfer of power to the Soviets could make civil war an impossibility. Against that kind of union, against the Soviets made up of deputies of workers, soldiers and peasants, any civil war started by the bourgeoisie would be unthinkable, a "war" like that would not get as far as the first battle. After Kornilov the bourgeois would not get a second chance, they would not have a "savage division" or any Cossack echelons to move against the government!'[58]

Events were moving swiftly, however, and they were soon to indicate that there was no possibility of a union between the SR-Menshevik camp and the Bolsheviks. Now came the question of a possible transfer of power to the Bolshevik party alone. Lenin, not one to vacillate, wrote as follows: 'My opinion remains unchanged. No political party—especially no party of the leading class—would have any right to exist... if it were to refuse power once the possibility of it exists.'[59] He did not exclude the possibility that, once power had been seized, it would be necessary to endure a period of brutal civil war. 'If the revolution began under seemingly rather straightforward circumstances, revolution itself, as it develops, always creates complex situations. For real, profound revolution, "a people's revolution"—to use Marx's expression—is an unbelievably complicated and painful process involving the death of a social system belonging to tens of millions of people and the birth of a new one. Revolution means the most bitter, furious and desperate class warfare and civil war. No great revolution in history has passed without civil war. And to think that a civil war is conceivable without "exceptionally complex circumstances" is impossible unless you are (as in Chekhov's story) a man locked in a case... If you don't like wolves keep out of the forest!'[60] Nevertheless, the swift, almost bloodless success of the military coup in Petrograd that October, the fall of the Provisional and the establishment of the Soviet Government, the victory of the Bolsheviks in the Soviets and the 'triumphal procession of the Soviets' throughout the country, the relatively easy defeat of the centres of counter-revolution on the Don and elsewhere—all of this revived hopes of a more or less peaceful development of socialist revolution in the country. This accounts for the comparative leniency shown by the victorious Bolsheviks to their recent enemies: for their decision to free the Kadets and Cossacks who had organized an armed revolt against Soviet power, to parole General Krasnov, leader of the attack of Cossack units on Petrograd, and to release most of the ministers of the Provisional Government; for the legal sanctioning of the activities of the Mensheviks and SRs, and the preservation of press freedom for many of the newspapers and journals that had been stridently anti-Bolshevik.

The attitude and policy of the Bolsheviks hardened quickly following the dissolution of the Constituent Assembly in January 1918, a further hardening occurred in February with the repelling of the attack by the German army, and again in March on the signing of the Peace of Brest-Litovsk. However, only in late spring 1918, when the position in Russia had taken a sharp turn for the worse because of counter-revolutionary activities and a number of serious errors committed by the Bolsheviks, did it become clear that there was no possibility of avoiding Civil War and 'the most desperate class warfare'. In contrast with his rather unconvincing suggestions in 1917 that the 'capitalist bigwigs' would bend obediently to the will of the proletariat after a week or two in prison, Lenin now proposed a new idea that was by no means certain and in any case was not universally accepted: that the capitalists and landlords, stripped of their political and economic power, would be more dangerous now to the working class than they had been during their own rule. 'After their first serious defeat the overthrown exploiters who did not anticipate their overthrow, did not believe in it, would not even think about it, now with tenfold energy, with impassioned fury, with a hatred a hundred times greater than before, rush into battle to regain their lost paradise, fighting for their families who used to have such a sweet existence but who are now doomed by the "common herd" to ruin and penury (or else "common labour"). And behind the capitalist exploiters stretches the great mass of the petty bourgeoisie, shown by decades of historical experience to be vacillators and waverers.'[61]

In late May and June 1918, when starvation began to threaten the industrial centres of Central Russia, Lenin called the workers forward 'into the last, decisive battle,' claiming that the Soviet Republic had entered the stage of its harshest suffering. Two or three months later, when Civil War had broken out on all sides and with Soviet power routed in Siberia and the Urals, all along the Volga and the Don, with battles lost in the Caucasus and retreat unavoidable in Northern Russia, Lenin was claiming that never before had the Russian Revolution endured so difficult and dangerous a period. He had to repeat these words in the spring of 1919 when Kolchak's troops were recording their greatest successes, and again in the autumn of that year when Denikin's armies were approaching Moscow from the south and Yudenich was nearing Petrograd from the west. Then, in the autumn of 1920, during the confrontations with Wrangel's forces in the south and Pilsudki's Polish army in the west, Lenin called on the commanders and commissars of the Red Army to defeat the enemy by the end of that autumn for, as he openly admitted, Soviet Russia might not survive another winter campaign.

The Red Army did defeat the forces of Pilsudski and Wrangel by the end of November 1920. It is widely believed that 1920 was the last year of the Civil War, an idea which, although well established both in Soviet and Western historiography, is wrong. The Civil War continued in Russia almost throughout 1921. Moreover the Soviet government was now confronted by an enemy far more dangerous, according to Lenin, than any number of Denikins, Kolchaks, Wrangels and their forces put together. This was the broad policy adopted throughout the country under the name of 'War Communism'. In the southern Ukraine, the Red Army committed large sections to fight the forces of the Anarchist Nestor Makhno, which consisted predominantly of peasants from the province of Yekaterinoslav. Another wave of Cossack revolts had begun on the Don, and now the largest Cossack sections were being directed by the recent commanders of the Red Cavalry (order of the Red Banner), Maskalov, Vakulin and Popov. In the vast territories of the Tambov, Saratov and Voronezh provinces, the peasant uprising incited in the summer of 1920 and led by the Socialist Revolutionary A.S. Antonov was still under way. At the beginning of 1921, he had at his disposal and army of 30,000 men made up of twenty-one regiments and a brigade. This uprising was not put down until August 1921, when massive sections of the Red Army were moved into the Tambov province. That year also saw the famous sailors' revolt in the fortress-town of Kronstadt the quelling of which also proved costly in effort and in lives. Dozens of other, smaller uprisings occurred in the North Caucasus, the Urals and Siberia. Victory was finally achieved by the Bolsheviks in this last phase of the Civil War only because, over and above its military strength, the Soviet government saw the need to make a number of substantial concessions to the peasants, one of which was the Lenin-inspired temporary strategic 'retreat' known to history as the New Economic Policy.

Thus it was that the 'gentle' dictatorship of the proletariat and relatively 'easy' victory for the Bolsheviks, hoped for and predicted by Lenin in the summer of 1917, failed to materialize. As he put it himself 'in Russia it became necessary to establish the dictatorship of the proletariat in its severest form.'[62] From all points of view, the Russian Revolution turned out to be one of the harshest cataclysms in Russian history.

The New Economic Policy, the ending of the Civil War and the international situation in late 1921 gave the Bolshevik Party a breathing space. At last there was a chance to begin laying the foundation of economic and cultural life in the socialist state. However in 1922-23, at the outset of this programme, the Party ran straight into a series of grave political problems that, taken together, amounted to a crisis in the establishment of the dictatorship of the proletariat in Russia.

The position with regard to production at that time may be described in two words: economic ruin. The largest plants and factories were not working, there was a shortage of raw materials, fuel, electrical energy, skilled workers and management personnel. Transport had virtually stopped, most of the coal mines, oil installations and iron mines were virtually in ruins. According to later estimates, the output from heavy industry in the early 1920s was a fifth of the total for 1913.[63] Agricultural production was down by forty per cent on pre-war figures. The world revolution so eagerly awaited by the Bolsheviks was late in coming. In fact, the revolutionary movement in Europe was winding down. The capitalist countries had retained control of their colonial empires and in one or two places had even expanded them. There was still some hope of a socialist revolution in Germany but even this began to fade in 1923 after a series of defeats had been inflicted on the German proletariat.

In letters and conversations off the record, Lenin showed great alarm over the current position. In public, he was more optimistic and expressed confidence in the triumph of socialism in Russia. But even he could now see that the transition from 'NEP Russia' to 'socialist Russia' would call for greater efforts, and take longer, than he had hoped in 1917. To judge by his notes and articles of 1920-22, he saw this transitional period as lasting for fifteen or twenty years. Lenin remained convinced that, under NEP conditions and the revival of some forms of capitalism in town and country, there was a particular need for the dictatorship of the proletariat, including its harshest methods, such as terror. In March 1922, he wrote to Kamenev, one of his deputies in the Council of People's Commissars: 'It is the greatest mistake to believe that NEP means the end of terror. We are going back to terror, and economic terror too. Foreigners are suborning our office workers and exporting "the remains of Russia". And they'll get away with it. Monopoly is a polite form of warning: my dear sirs, when the moment comes I'll hang you for it'.[64]

The greatest danger for the dictatorship of the proletariat, however, was the weakness of the proletariat itself and the lack of tried and trusted staff to run the country. Hundreds of thousands of the finest workers had died at the front in the Civil War. Hundreds of thousands of proletarians had perished from sickness and starvation. Not less than a million working people had left the starving cities for the countryside. The numbers of plant and factory workers in the country had fallen from 3,500,000 to 1,300,000, and that in a country with a population of 135,000,000.[65] Even among the workers remaining in the cities, many were unemployed or engaged in casual labour. The working class was physically and spiritually exhausted. Strikes were commonplace. Many workers were giving full vent to their dissatisfaction at the state of affairs, and their mood was reflected within the Party where opposition groups like 'democratic centralism' and the Workers' Opposition were formed.

The working class, in any case, cannot establish a dictatorship of the proletariat just like that. A whole state apparatus must be set up, and this was proving to be a difficult task. Lenin's hopes of the *State and Revolution* period that a state apparatus could be set up simply and cheaply were not being vindicated. During the Civil War, a massive government machine had been set up, but it was totally alien to the people and consisted of the same former officials. Even before the transition to NEP, during a bitter exchange in one of the current Party debates, Lenin exclaimed: 'It is clear from our Party programme that we now have a workers' state with *a bureaucratic perversion*. We ought to hang that sad label on it too. This is the reality of the transition for you. With the state as it now is in practice do you tell me that our trade unions have nothing to defend, can they be dispensed with for the defence of the material and spiritual interests of the proletariat which is now properly organized down to the last man? That is an entirely theoretical proposition. Our state as it now exists is such that this well-organised proletariat must defend itself and we must use these workers' organizations for the defence of the workers against the state and the defence of the state by the workers.'[66]

Two years later, with the experience of the Civil War and the first NEP period behind him, Lenin referred to the Russian state apparatus and the economy in even harsher terms. In a note intended only for Central Committee members, which remained unpublished until 1956, he wrote: 'Conscience decrees that we describe as "our own" an apparatus which is alien to us throughout. It is a bourgeois and tsarist shambles which, in five years, lacking any outside help and "preoccupied" as we have been with military affairs and the war against famine, we have had no opportunity to reform... Under these conditions the derisory proportion of Soviet and Sovietized workers are going to drown in that sea of chauvinist, Greater Russian swill, like flies in milk.'[67] An attempt to control this unwieldly apparatus by means of a specially created People's Commissariat of Inspection, by workers and peasants, ended in failure. Lenin was soon to admit that the apparatus of this Commissariat turned out to be worse than many of the institutions it had been set up to investigate. The Party itself was the only organization that could guarantee some form of control over the activities of all the state institutions. Thus it happened that all the key positions in every branch of the state came to be occupied by members of the Bolshevik Party, and the upper strata of the state organization necessarily began to coincide with the upper strata of the Party. This is how the Communist Party became the prime instrument in the system of the dictatorship of the proletariat, and how, in the conditions of a one-party state, the supreme Party institutions gradually became also the supreme institutions of state.

Lenin had expounded, explained and defended his concept of 'the dictatorship of the proletariat' without identifying it with 'the dictatorship of the Party', a phrase he used only rarely. He did not totally repudiate this latter concept, however, and he did not use the idea only in a figurative sense, as Stalin was at pains to suggest in an argument with Zinoviev.[68] In 1919, Lenin said in one of his speeches: 'When we are reproached for allowing dictatorship by a single party and proposals are made, as you have heard, for a single socialist front, we reply, "Yes, dictatorship of a single party! We do insist on this and we're not going to be moved from this ground, because it's that same party which for decades has been fighting to gain a position in the vanguard of the industrial proletariat toiling in plants and factories...".'[69] Then, a year later, speaking to a Comintern Congress: 'By dictatorship of the proletariat we understand actually dictatorship by its organized and politically conscious minority... A political party can unite only the minority in a class since in any capitalist society the proportion of workers who really are politically enlightened is bound to be a minority of all the workers.'[70]

At the same Congress, Zinoviev spoke as follows, with no objection from Kautsky or Lenin: 'People like Kautsky tell us: in Russia you don't have a dictatorship of the proletariat, you have a dictatorship of the Party. This is meant as a reproach. It is nothing of the kind. We do have a dictatorship of the working class and, for that very reason, we also have a dictatorship of the Communist Party. The dictatorship of the Communist Party is but a function, a token and expression of the dictatorship of the working class.'[71]

There were many such references. What did Lenin really mean by Party 'dictatorship'? He meant the monopoly of state power enjoyed by the Bolsheviks in Russia and the USSR. A unified socialist front had simply not come about in Russia, union with the Mensheviks or the Socialist Revolutionaries had proved impossible, though some attempts in this direction had been made (which explains the brief appearance of left-wing SRs in the Soviet government). In any case, as Lenin explained to the 10th Party Congress, this form of dictatorship reflected the catastrophic situation of Russia's proletariat following the Civil War. They had been the leading class in 1917 and 1918, but in 1921 this was no longer true. 'Our proletariat has been largely declassed... There have been unprecedented catastrophes—the closing of factories, people running away from starvation, workers abandoning the factories and having to settle down in the countryside, ceasing to be workers. We have seen all this and watched it happen—unprecedented crises, the Civil War, the break-down in proper town-country relations, a halt to the transportation of bread, all of it leading to small factory-made products—cigarette-lighters—being bartered—for bread... This is all happening in the economy and it means a declassing of the proletariat, and that leads inevitably and necessarily to the appearance here of petty-bourgeois and anarchist tendencies...'[72]

It is clear that Lenin was speaking of the 'dictatorship of the Party' as a peculiarly Russian phenomenon arising under specific and concrete circumstances created in the course of the Russian Revolution. In other words, Stalin was probably nearer to the truth of the matter than Zinoviev, in theory at least. In practical terms, the situation in the country was such that in the early 1920s we really did have Party dictatorship. Lenin did not even balk at the phrase 'dictatorship of the leaders'. At the beginning of 1918 he wrote: 'The indisputable experience of history tells us that the dictatorship of individual persons has often been the expression, the bearer, the conductor of the dictatorship of the revolutionary classes.'[73] Lenin went on to defend this idea later in 1918, with a proposal that certain leaders of the economy, and, in particular, the railway chiefs, should be invested with 'unlimited' and 'dictatorial' powers. Then, in 1921-22, Soviet Russia arrived at a position in which this became reality for the whole Party and the whole nation. At the time Lenin had no great regard for the Party. He saw it as overmanned and infiltrated by the non-proletarian and careerist elements that all ruling parties attract. Staffed as it was, the Party was in great danger of evading any reform and it thus threatened the whole system of the dictatorship of the proletariat. Lenin proposed a great purge in which workers from outside the Party were to be involved. Party numbers fell by thirty per cent following the purge of 1921, but he was still not satisfied with its membership. In a note to the Central Committee Chairman, Molotov, again intended only for members of the Committee, he wrote: 'If we are to accept the evidence of our own eyes we have to admit that at present the proletarian policy of the Party is determined not by its membership but by the enormous, monolithic authority of that wafer-thin stratum which can be called the Party's Old Guard. The slightest in-fighting within this stratum and its authority will be, if not undermined, then at least sufficiently weakened to deprive it of decision-making power.'[74]

Lenin was by no means exaggerating the danger to the Party. It was this concern for Party unity that accounted for his own proposal for a temporary ban on the creation of sub-groups and factions within it. Naturally, he saw the need for free discussion throughout the Party and an extension of inner-Party democracy, but all this was impossible without retaining the broad freedom to set up groups and factions that did not infringe the principle of democratic centralism. Even during the months of crisis following the Peace of Brest-Litovsk, Lenin did not object to our Party including factions of 'left-wing communists'. However, in 1921-22, he came to the reluctant conclusion that, given the unwieldy and largely alien state apparatus, the 'clogged state' of the Party itself, the absence of any firm proletarian base, and considering the famine conditions, the poverty and the express dissatisfaction of Party members, those freedoms were 'an impermissible luxury'. Even so the abrogation, temporary though it was supposed to be, of democratic centralism in the Party and its replacement by direct, almost military, centralized control, was a risky business. This was the point at which Party dictatorship was actually converted into the dictatorship of the ruling faction. The danger of in-fighting in the thin stratum of the 'Party's Old Guard' had not disappeared, it had merely receded a little. Although the authority of this 'wafer-thin stratum' really was enormous, it lacked cohesion. Lenin, whose task it was to adjudicate in many a bitter conflict arising between his closest assistants, knew this only too well. He was well aware, for example, of the antagonism between Stalin and Trotsky, the enmity between Trotsky and Zinoviev, not to mention lesser-known figures in the ruling layer. A situation was arising in which the whole fate of the Party and the dictatorship of the proletariat depended largely upon Lenin himself, his health and ability to keep working. He was the only person in the 'Old Guard' who enjoyed undisputed authority. At that very juncture in 1922, Lenin's health began to crack.

Lenin knew there was no one to replace him in the Party leadership, and he spent the last months of his life wondering how to prevent a schism in the Party in the event of his departure. He looked urgently for new ways and means of controlling the activities of the vast state apparatus, but, more significantly, he also sought methods of controlling the ruling layer of the Party in whose hands (especially Stalin's) was concentrated 'infinite power'. Lenin therefore proposed not only a substantial expansion of the Central Committee in favour of the workers but also a reorganization of the Commissariat of Inspection and the setting up of a controlling body invested with the power to intervene in the activities of the Politburo, and even those of the Party's General Secretary. This particular task was never carried out, though some of the proposed measures were put into practice. It was not that the Politburo rejected the majority of Lenin's proposals (who was now effectively removed from leadership). The task itself was akin to squaring the circle. The Party leadership, in whose hands rested supreme power over the Party and the state, was incapable of setting up machinery for control with sufficient power actually and effectively to direct its own activities. Inevitably, things worked out differently: the organs of supreme Party control were in practice subordinate to the control exercised by the Politburo and the Secretary of the Central Committee. How could any other result have been expected when 'powerful' and 'authoritative' ruling organs of the Party were set up at the outset and then an attempt was made to place 'above them' some kind of controlling body consisting of Party members with less authority? There remained, in the last analysis, only one guarantee that a genuine Communist policy would be maintained in the leadership—this lay in the actual people involved in it, their personal qualities, their convictions, their individual commitments to Communism, their fundamental political and moral values. This means of influencing the ruling members of the Central Committee was not neglected by Lenin who, in his 'Testament', asked the 'future Party Congress' to give consideration to the qualities and deficiencies of the leading politicians in the Party: Trotsky, Stalin, Kamenev, Zinoviev, Pyatakov and Bukharin. Lenin himself, however, had had occasion more than once in the past to indicate that in politics the personal qualities of individual leaders are not entirely reliable. 'History,' as he put it, 'knows various kinds of transformation'.

Lenin's proposal to enlarge the Central Committee and the Central Control Commission of the Party in order to limit dissent between the leaders was meant to benefit not workers within the apparatus of the Party or the state but the ordinary politically-minded workers from the shop floor. An article by him was published in *Pravda*, but his wishes were never carried out. He was now ill and almost all the members of the Politburo and the Central Committee spoke out in one way or another against his proposals. This did not mean merely that they distrusted Lenin. The implementation of Lenin's proposals could never have had much effect on the situation in the upper ranks of the Party. Rank-and-file workers were incapable of exerting any authority or influence simply because they came from the ordinary proletariat. Lenin's new proposal in 1922-23 had the same naïve ring as his ideas for a proletarian state in the summer and autumn of 1917. Besides, he himself knew only too well that membership of the working class alone was no guarantee against either 'transformation' or the 'communist pride' he found so hateful. Only recently, in September 1922, Lenin had reprimanded Bukharin for publishing in *Pravda* some vulgar, philistine thinking by V.F. Pletnyov, chairman of Proletkult.[75] The Prolekult movement was one that Lenin had deeply distrusted since its very inception. Gorky's attitude to it was similar; in a letter to Gladkov (1926) he wrote: 'I cannot feel "at one" with people who turn class truth into caste truth; I cannot be "at one" with people who say, "We are proletarians" with the same feeling as people before them used to say "We are noblemen". I no longer see "proletarians" in Russia. I see the faces of our workers as the true guardians of the Russian land and the teachers of all her inhabitants. First, we must see this and take pride in it; second, it means we must be careful in our attitude to anyone so that not "anyone" has the right to say that the worker is not the organizer and leader of the new life but is just as tyrannical as any other dictator and stupid into the bargain.'[76] Lenin's misgivings concerning the possible 'transformation' of the dictatorship of the proletariat were expressed with particular acuity in his statements about another political tendency of the early 1920s, the so-called 'Smenovekhovstvo' (volte-face) movement, which had arisen among anti-Bolshevik *émigrés* and staked everything on the regressive transformation of the dictatorship of the proletariat under NEP conditions. One of the movement's leaders, N. Ustryalov, ridiculed appeals issued by the SRs, populist Socialists and Kadets for a new revolution to be mounted in Russia or, to put in another way, for some form of counter-revolutionary uprising. Lenin completely rejected the claim in the *émigré* press that the Bolsheviks were incapable of evolution, insisting that 'any hopes for the transformation of the existing power are vain'.[77] Ustryalov wrote an article for the *émigré* journal *Novosti zhizni* (News of Life) in November 1921, in which he listed three methods of attack considered by the various *émigré* circles as effective ways of bringing down the Bolsheviks: intervention by the West, incitement to popular revolution within Russia, and the organization of a total boycott. He went on as follows: 'So, all three forms of attack are at the present time anachronisms at best. All of them, wishing to serve the God of patriotism, are capable only of pleasing the devil of anarchy and groundless revolutionism. Our homeland can do without them. However, it does not follow that the foreign press must use its freedom only to be mealy-mouthed about Soviet power. There is no reason to hide the countless inadequacies of that power. We must roundly condemn ghastly atrocities (on the basis of facts and figures), specific defects or crimes perpetrated by government agents. It is essential for us to formulate serious, businesslike criticism of the various aspects of government activity. We must list our questions about imminent reforms, while ensuring consistency and sober realism (pie in the sky is no use). This kind of loyal criticism will be in the country's interests and will prove to be a factor working towards the transformation of the revolution which is already under way.'[78]

It is known that, before the Revolution, Lenin tried to read newspapers and journals of every political persuasion that could be got out of Russia. After his return to Petrograd in 1917, he spent some time each day reading the local press, absorbing the moods and opinions of the various political groups and levels of society. During the Civil War he asked to be supplied with as many different publications as could be arranged from territories under White control. In 1921-22 he followed the émigré press closely. He used to read the articles written by Ustryalov, an ex-Kadet leader, once chairman of their eastern section, and editor of the Omsk newspaper *Russkoye Delo* (Russian Affairs). By 1921 Ustryalov had emigrated to the Chinese city of Harbin where he wrote for the local newspaper, and for the journal *Smena vekh* (Volte-Face) which had first appeared in Prague in June of that year, for the newspaper of the same name issued in Paris, and for another by the name of *Nakanune* (On the Eve). In his report to the Eleventh Party Congress, Lenin said: 'We hear a lot of sweet-sounding Communist nonsense nowadays—I do, it's part of my job. And it makes you feel sick, murderously sick. Then instead of this "Communist nonsense" here comes a copy of *Volte-Face* and it says straight out, "Things aren't what you say, you're just imagining it. Actually you're just rolling down into the same bourgeois marsh and you'll find little Communist pennants dangling about there with all sorts of writing on them. This is all very useful because here we have not just a chorus of what we keep hearing all round us but just the class truth from the class enemy…it really is the class truth crudely and frankly spoken by the class enemy. "I support Soviet power in Russia," says Ustryalov, despite his having been a Kadet, a bourgeois, a supporter of intervention. "I support Soviet power, because it has now taken a path down which it will roll back to the usual bourgeois power... He doesn't agree with his friends. He says, "Do what you want about Communism. What I say is—there aren't any tactics over there, only evolution." ... Now this is very useful and I think we ought to keep it in mind... The sort of thing described by Ustryalov is possible—let's face it. History has seen every kind of transformation; it's no use relying on conviction, devotion and other such admirable spiritual qualities—this is politically ridiculous. Admirable spiritual qualities are the property of very few people, whereas historical issues are decided by gigantic masses who, if there are one or two people who don't suit, behave towards these one or two people in a manner which is not very polite... The *Volte-Face* group is expressing the mood of thousands, tens of thousands of bourgeois or else of Soviet officials, participants in our new economic policy. This is a radical and very real danger... This question deserves our closest attention: in reality, who is going to win?"[79] It is clear that Lenin did not reject the possibility that Soviet power might be transformed, and, along with it, the Bolshevik Party and its individual leaders. He did not repudiate the statements and hopes expressed by the Volte-Face movement as slanders—he called them 'class truths'. He gave the Party a warning but could issue no valid guarantee against what he called this 'very real danger'.

Was there, in fact, any 'happy' way out of the current situation? Was it possible to make progress without veering into a 'right-wing' or 'left-wing' one-man dictatorship? Was there any way of avoiding the transformation of the dictatorship of the proletariat into the dictatorship of the Party, which meant the dictatorship of its strongest faction, the dictatorship of a group of leaders followed by the one-man dictatorship of a single member of that group? Without doubt such a solution did exist, and it would have consisted in the understanding that the Party had survived the critical period of 1921-22 and should now begin to put in hand not only the industrial and cultural development of the country but also the broadening of democracy within the Party and outside it in Soviet society. But the Bolsheviks in 1922-3 were afraid of this course of action. A resolution adopted at their conference in August 1922 announced point-blank that the Volte-Face group, the Mensheviks and the SRs were fostering vain hopes in anticipating that 'economic concessions would be followed by political ones leading in the direction of bourgeois democracy'. In addition, the conference called for an end to the right of anti-Bolshevik parties to enjoy legality within organizations like agricultural co-operatives, workers' unions, schools and institutions of higher education, the trade-unions, and any cultural, educational and publishing enterprises. 'Given proper tactics', the conference concluded, 'the Russian Communist Party in this case will be able quite soon to eliminate the SR and Menshevik Parties as political factors.'[80]

However, by 1924-25 the political crisis was over. The position of the Communist Party had been strengthened and the economy had been stabilized. It was now essential to embark on a course by which inner-Party discussion could be extended; it was time to revoke the resolution of the 10th Party Congress banning factions and subgroups within the Party. There was a need to broaden Soviet democracy and at the same time create possibilities for a renewal within the Soviets of activity by other socialist parties. Political history knows of no true means of establishing control over the activities of the leaders of a party other than the right of the members in that party to criticize those leaders freely and to set up opposition groups within the party. Similarly there exists no reliable mechanism for controlling the activities of a ruling party other than the possibility of setting up opposition parties and political groups.

Whether Lenin himself could ever have introduced such radical changes into our social and political system we have no means of knowing. What we do know is that his successors took a different route. Instead of broadening democracy within the Party and throughout the state, they chose to restrict it, limiting any kind of opposition within the Party and even more so outside it. The results of this are now widely known. In the 1930s, the USSR saw the establishment of an absolute, one-man dictatorship, that of Stalin, and the 'Party Old Guard' was not only removed from power but in most cases physically exterminated. This involved the simultaneous loss of a number of the achievements of the October Revolution. As we have seen, Stalin was actually assisted in his struggle for power by a number of errors in the theory of the dictatorship of the proletariat. If nowadays some Western Communist parties are reluctant to use the term 'dictatorship', no doubt they have in mind not only the associations that arise in the minds of working-class people at the mention of the dictatorships of Hitler, Mussolini, Franco and Salazar, but also Stalin's dictatorship.

Communist Parties in the West and the Dictatorship of the Proletariat

We have already seen that, until 1943, all the fundamental policy documents of the Comintern, and therefore those of all Communist parties, retained the concept of the dictatorship of the proletariat. The question of excluding this concept from policy documents arose for the first time after the Second World War when Communist parties had actually come to power in the countries of Eastern and South-Eastern Europe, even though the governments of many of them still included certain ministers from socialist, populist or even bourgeois parties. The countries of Western Europe, once freed from German occupation, returned bourgeois parties to power, though a number of them also allowed some Communists into their first post-war administrations.

Although Stalin himself preferred not to make a public statement on this issue, matters were being taken out of his hands. At a plenary session of the Czechoslovak Communist Party Central Committee, Klement Gottwald announced to the audience that during an informal conversation in Moscow Joseph Stalin had given it as his opinion that now, following the defeat of Hitler, a new road to socialism was opening up—bypassing soviets and the dictatorship of the proletariat.[81] Stalin had not insisted on his keeping this secret. Word of Stalin's new opinion spread to other Communist parties and naturally influenced their thinking. The leadership of Poland's Communist Party also declared in 1946 that in their country the road to socialism did not necessitate a violent revolutionary upheaval and that therefore the need for the dictatorship of the proletariat was obviated. The Hungarian Party leadership took the same view and stressed that their position should not be construed as merely tactical. They explained that conditions in their country and in Europe, viewed subjectively and objectively, made it possible for socialism to be achieved there without the dictatorship of the proletariat.[82] In France, Maurice Thorez told the 11th Congress of the French Communist Party in 1947 that he too considered the transition to socialism to be feasible without the dictatorship of the proletariat.[83]

A new *type* of state, a 'people's republic', was described in 1947 by A.A. Zhdanov, in an address to the First Information Conference attended by representatives of several Communist Parties. 'In Yugoslavia, Bulgaria, Romania, Poland, Czechoslovakia, Hungary and Albania...a new type of state has been set up, *a people's republic*, in which power belongs to the people, heavy industry, transport and the banks belong to the state, and the strongest force is a bloc of the toiling population headed by the working class. As a result not only have the people of these countries evaded the clutches of imperialism but they are also laying the foundations for the transition to socialist development.'[84] In that year, 1947, I was a philosophy student at the University of Leningrad. I have a clear recollection that Zhdanov's speech, together with a number of occasional articles in the Party press concerning this new type of state, not a dictatorship of the proletariat and yet capable of building socialism, caused a great deal of embarrassment and confusion among our lecturers on Party history and historical materialism. These statements by Zhdanov and Thorez contradicted not only explicit and unambiguous pronouncements made by Lenin himself but, what was even more embarrassing, explicit and unambiguous pronouncements made by Stalin and also, for good measure, a number of basic principles in our *History of the CPSU(B)—Short Course*, which was a set book. The confusion was short-lived, however. In 1948, almost all the people's democracies suffered a sudden change in their development, involving the expulsion from government of all the bourgeois parties. Before that, in 1947, Communist parties had been excluded from the government of the Western European countries. After the break with Yugoslavia, every country in Eastern and South-Eastern Europe was hit by a wave of repression affecting not only bourgeois and petty-bourgeois circles but Communists as well. The formula of a 'people's republic' remained part of the theory of Soviet and foreign Marxists, but now it was supplemented everywhere by a new statement to the effect that 'the state in a people's republic is one form of the dictatorship of the proletariat'. No one was embarrassed by the fact that in the governments of the people's democracies, Communists as a rule sat alongside representatives of other parties. The Czech theoreticians I. Goushka and K. Kara were quite open about this: 'the governments of states now at the second stage in the development of people's democracy have virtually everywhere retained some features, even if they are only formalities, of coalition, since, at present, side by side with representatives of the Communist Parties sit representatives of other parties. This, however, most emphatically does not disrupt the functioning of the dictatorship of the proletariat, the undivided leadership of the masses by the Communist Party...Leadership of people's democracies by the Communist Party is becoming exclusive...the remaining political parties no longer pursue a particular individual political line but accept as part of their general line the building of socialism as seen by the Communist Parties. These parties have set themselves the task of facilitating the introduction to the building of socialism of the specific social strata on which they exercise an influence...'[85]

In the 1950s, the international Communist movement did not undertake any serious discussion of the dictatorship of the proletariat. In the 1960s, however, prominent theoreticians in foreign Communist parties did begin to take issue with several of the commonly accepted assertions and dogmas of Marxism-Leninism, including this concept. Almost all of them were branded as 'revisionists' and expelled from their parties, of which they claimed membership going back for decades (Garaudy, Fischer, Marek, Šik, Petkov and others). The opinions and expressions of these 'revisionists', including their observations on the dictatorship of the proletariat, are still subjected to barrages of hostile criticism in the Soviet press. In one recent book, for instance, we read the following: 'The revisionist dread of the dictatorship of the proletariat certainly does not stem from democratic traditions in the capitalist countries of Europe, as is claimed by right-wing revisionists. How can we speak of democratic traditions in Spain today, a country which has only just begun to emerge from the political torpor of forty years' duration and fascist dictatorship? And the present political set-up in Italy, France and other capitalist countries can scarcely be taken as a democratic ideal. The dread of the dictatorship of the proletariat stems actually from a dread of all dictatorships irrespective of class which is commonly expressed in petty-bourgeois circles. The defenders of bourgeois democracy cultivate this fear in every possible way as a useful device. Social reformers long ago stopped seeing the true bourgeois dictatorship behind its facade of bourgeois democracy.

They have long since been transformed into apologists for the bourgeois state and its political machinery. Right-wing revisionists are slipping into the same ways, and are being deflected from the battle for socialism.'[86]

Despite all this, however, it remains true that the phrase 'dictatorship of the proletariat' has come to be used less and less in policy documents of the Communist parties in capitalist countries and, more significantly, in those of the international Communist movement. The concept was not mentioned at all in the final resolutions drawn up by the International Conference of Communist Parties held in Moscow in 1969, which speak only of 'the power of the working classes and their allies'. The Conference of European Communist and Workers' Parties held in Berlin in 1976 likewise omitted any mention of the 'dictatorship of the proletariat'. It has been estimated that, at present, sixty of the world's ninety Communist and workers' parties have stopped using the term.[87]

In the 1920s the 'dictatorship of the proletariat' was one of the most popular phrases used by Communist parties. Lenin could say, with satisfaction, that 'Bolshevism has popularized the idea of the "dictatorship of the proletariat" the world over; it has translated the words first from Latin into Russian and thence into every language in the world'.[88] How are we to explain its loss of popularity since then? Sometimes the phrase is avoided for straightforward tactical reasons. It may have been omitted from policy documents, but it is still used in various forms of propaganda. The General Secretary of the Communist Party of Canada has said more than once that he does not foresee the triumph of socialism in his country, even given a peaceful revolution, without the dictatorship of the proletariat; but the concept is omitted from the programme of the Canadian Communist Party, *The Road to Socialism in Canada*, which limits itself to mentioning 'the political power of the working class'. This false identification between 'the dictatorship of the proletariat' and 'the political power of the working class' is repeated in the documents of the Communist Party of Greece (Exterior). One of its leaders, G. Farakos, writes: 'Our programme, now as before, takes the scientifically based view that a socialist state, whatever specific form it might assume, must by its class nature amount to the revolutionary power of the working class in union with other strata of working people capable of building and defending Socialism. In other words it must be the dictatorship of the proletariat.'[89] The leader of the Portuguese Communist Party, Alvaro Cunhal, speaking at its 7th Congress, announced the need for changes in the Party programme:

'We are changing some of the terms used—correctly—in Marxist terminology. This is of no ideological significance. The main reason for the changes is that some of the terms are not comprehensible in Portugal in the sense normally intended. One example is the use of the term "dictatorship of the proletariat". In Marxist terminology, dictatorship denotes the power of one class, or several classes, over others. The most liberal bourgeois democracy is a dictatorship of the bourgeoisie. The dictatorship of the proletariat, under which the proletariat and its allies retain power, may take many forms. It may even be multi-party. It may assume a wide variety of forms of state organization. The dictatorship of the proletariat is a most democratic order compared with the most democratic of bourgeois democracies. However, the actual expression "a dictatorship", which has been used for fifty years in Portugal to describe a fascist dictatorship, creates an extremely delicate situation which does not promote the understanding of our policies or the achievement of our tasks. We are changing no part of our doctrine, none of our conceptions. Let this be made clear in order to avoid any wrong interpretation of the changes which are now being made.'[90]

There are, however, some parties in which the abandonment of the phrase goes beyond tactics, reaching out into considerations of principle, with particular reference to the new circumstances obtaining in their particular countries. This new approach was perhaps most clearly demonstrated by the General Secretary of the French Communist Party, Georges Marchais, at the 22nd Party Congress on February 4, 1976. 'In the conditions of Russia in 1917 and of the young Soviet Union, the dictatorship of the proletariat was essential in order to guarantee the building of socialism. It is fair to say that without it the working class and the Soviet people could not have begun or defended the unprecedented work of liberation that was undertaken. This is why the Communist parties, laying the foundations of a new society at that time and under those conditions, and learning from the weakness of international Social Democracy and from the triumph of the October Revolution, were fully justified in adopting this slogan. The world has changed. In the recent period of history, the world has changed profoundly. The alignment of forces has changed, and continues to do so, in the direction of independence and freedom for the people, in the direction of democracy and socialism. Peaceful co-existence is affirmed. In the course of a bitter and complex struggle, moving to and fro, reaction and fascism are at last beginning to yield to democracy, which—as events in Greece, Portugal and Spain prove—is making progress. It is undeniable that never before have the people had as much chance to decide their own destiny, to move forward along the road to national and social liberation. These new possibilities are based on the existence and the progress of the socialist countries, on the developing struggle of the working class and the masses of the people in capitalist countries, on the broad sweep and lift of the movement towards national liberation, and on the solidarity of all revolutionary powers.'

In the new circumstances, Marchais considers, the slogan 'dictatorship of the proletariat' has lost all relevance to the French Communist Party, since the people of France can proceed towards socialism by a different means from that of the existing socialist countries. While avoiding a direct clash with Lenin, Marchais proposes that the French workers themselves must be the ones to mount a decisive defence of the country's existing democratic institutions, which guarantee the working class and its allies the possibility of coming to power via the ballot box. At the same time they must stop 'all possible attempts by reaction to infringe the law, subvert the movement and use violence... The dictatorship of the proletariat does not appear in our draft document designating the kind of political power for which we are fighting because it does not essentially apply to our policy, what we are really saying to the country. What do we say in our document? We say this: "The power that will bring about the socialist reconstruction of society will be the power of the working class and other classes of toilers labouring with body or mind in town and country, i.e. the overwhelming majority of the people". This power will take shape and will operate electorally, by the freedom of expression provided by the ballot box, and it will aim to introduce the most perfect form of democracy into the whole of the social and political life of our country. It will respect as a matter of duty the democratic choice of the people and will compel others to respect the same. By contrast, the word "dictatorship" automatically evokes memories of Hitler, Mussolini, Salazar, Franco, etc., the very denial of democracy. This is not what we want. As to the word "proletariat", this now evokes an impression of a nucleus, the core of the working class. If that small section is given a fundamental role, of supreme importance, this will not represent the whole of what we propose and, moreover, it will fail to represent the all-round solidarity of all the workers which will lead to the socialist power under discussion. It therefore follows that what we are offering to the workers, and to all our people, cannot be called the "dictatorship of the proletariat".[91]

The leadership of the Spanish Communist Party shares a similar attitude to the dictatorship of the proletariat. In his book *Eurocommunism and the State,* Santiago Carrillo writes: 'The dictatorship of the proletariat is a concept from which a significant proportion of Western Communist Parties have dissociated themselves. The term *dictatorship* has itself taken on odious connotations this century which has seen the most repulsive Fascist and reactionary dictatorships, including Franco's, and experienced the crimes of Stalinism, a phenomenon caused by the disintegration of the dictatorship of the proletariat. This is quite sufficient to justify repudiation of that expression. ... Naturally the reasons for repudiating the expression are much more serious and entail far-reaching consequences, ... but, in my experience, they have not been adequately explained from the serious Marxist viewpoint. I must admit that in addressing myself to this problem in all its enormity I have a sense of my own inadequacy. I don't consider myself in any way a theoretician. I consider myself a modest Marxist political worker. But actually because I am a *Marxist political worker* I cannot feel happy and satisfied if I fail to work out a political platform which I can consider *not only more useful but also more correct,* and if I don't give it a good grounding in Marxist principle ... This is the question: can the proletariat in countries of developed capitalism establish their hegemony without having recourse to dictatorship? The concept of the dictatorship of the proletariat is not merely a synonym for the hegemony of the proletariat; it presupposes also the means by which hegemony and social superiority are achieved. In the countries of developed capitalism the workers constitute a majority of the population—the centres of cultural power are getting nearer and nearer the position of the proletariat.

This situation differs from the one in which Marx, Engels and Lenin examined the need for the dictatorship of the proletariat. In their conditions the dictatorship of the proletariat was a historical necessity, as was also revolutionary violence. Under modern conditions in the countries of developed capitalism the dictatorship of the proletariat is not a means of consolidating the strengths of the working class ... In the struggle against fascism, we Communists, along with other people, have confirmed that democratic freedoms, for all the limitations imposed on them by bourgeois society, do have real value which should not be underestimated. Perhaps it was oy by enduring those sad experiences that we have begun to arrive at a better understanding of the fact that democracy *is not a historical phenomenon created by the bourgeoisie,* as we used to think when our first aim was to establish a dividing line between ourselves and "bourgeois democracy" ... It must be said that the struggle against fascism has also caused us to react all the more critically to that degenerate form of the Soviet system which bears the name of "Stalinism" and to all its consequences, and also to treat with some scepticism the practical implementation of what might be called "socialist totalitarianism" ... The question is now whether power can ever be won without infringing the rules of democracy by changing the content of traditional democratic institutions, supplementing them with new forms which will broaden and strengthen political democracy. We, the Communists of Spain and other countries of developed capitalism, now declare that *this is possible.* The argument that *there never has been a single example of working class hegemony in this form* is without scientific foundation. It amounts to a dogmatic, conservative idea that the same must always be.'[92]

After the publication of his book, Carrillo confirmed in an interview that the concept of a democratic road to socialism had no logical connection with the concept of the dictatorship of the proletariat. This latter, according to his claim, could not serve as a proper definition of the kind of state that was essential for the transition to socialism in countries of developed capitalism. In answer to the charge that his views did not coincide with statements made by Lenin, he drew attention to a central and crucial aspect of Marxist method frequently referred to by Lenin—for 'a specific analysis of a specific situation.'[93] Many leading theoreticians in the Italian Communist Party have expressed similar views. Luciano Gruppi wrote: 'Compulsion will not disappear, of course, because democracy cannot be made to develop in the direction of socialism without decisive and consistent action, *within the framework of state legality,* directed against the reactionary and subversive forces of large-scale capitalism. Against such forces, compulsion will be undertaken by a coilition or power bloc which will go on to direct the socialist transformation of society and the state.'[94]

It is not open to doubt that statements differ substantially from those of Lenin on the same question. It is a well-known fact that Lenin did not allow for the possibility that a new socialist society could be built without the dictatorship of the proletariat, and he certainly never confused this with the question of the peaceful or violent development of the dictatorship. In 1919, he acclaimed the victory of soviet power in Hungary and observed with satisfaction that it had been achieved by peaceful means and with support from the Social Democrats. He went on to comment that Hungary had given the world 'an even better model than Soviet Russia' but also added: 'The form of transition to the dictatorship of the proletariat in Hungary has been quite different from the one in Russia: the voluntary withdrawal of the bourgeois government, the instantaneous restoration of working class unity, the unity of socialism in a Communist programme. The true nature of soviet power now stands out all the more clearly: no other power supported and headed by the proletariat is now feasible anywhere in the world except soviet power, the dictatorship of the proletariat.'[95] In *The State and Revolution* he had been more specific: 'A Marxist is by definition one who extends recognition of the class struggle to recognition of the dictatorship of the proletariat. This is what distinguishes a Marxist from a run-of-the-mill petty (yes and even big) bourgeois. This is the touchstone of a correct understanding and recognition of Marxism.'[96]

It is therefore easily established that the statements of Marchais, Carrilo, Gruppi and other prominent Western European Communists on the subject of the dictatorship of the proletariat, the value of democratic institutions in Western countries, the use of violence 'within the framework of state legality', and also concerning problems of the state, the political power of the working class and the peculiar characteristics of the transitional period, all differ to a significant degree from the views expressed by Lenin. This fact has not passed unnoticed or undiscussed by the theoreticians of the Western Communist parties themselves. A French Communist, Etienne Balibar, has written a book entitled *On the Dictatorship of the Proletariat*,[97] which is highly critical of Georges Marchais and the line of argument which was approved by the 22nd Congress of the French Party. The theoretical weakness, superficiality and inadequate historical substantiation of a number of Marchais's proposals is exposed there. Balibar shows convincingly that Marchais's ideas on the dictatorship of the proletariat are substantially different from those of Marx, Engels and particularly Lenin. He believes that the road to socialism in France today, and also in the other developed capitalist countries, leads through the dictatorship of the proletariat. His book has one major drawback, however: it relies far more on an analysis of texts and statements from classical Marxism than on a comparative study of conditions in Lenin's Russia and contemporary Western Europe. Criticism of this kind is commonly encountered in the Soviet press. Soviet commentators have, so far at least, stopped short of branding the prominent leaders of the Western Communist parties as 'revisionist' or 'opportunist.' They seem not to have noticed for example, resolutions passed by the 22nd Congress of the French Communist Party, or a number of other policy documents issued by the Communist parties of France, Italy, Spain or Britain. References are made only to the Social Democrats or, more generally, to the 'revisionists' of the 1960s. Thus, in a recent article published in *Pravda*, 'Lenin and the Socialist State', V. Zotov writes: '"Revisionists and opportunists making every effort to dissociate themselves from revolution" (Lenin) have been treating the dictatorship of the proletariat not as a new type of state but like a single form of government which, as a consequence, might exist under some historical conditions, but not under others. But Lenin stressed that "the dictatorship of the proletariat, the proletarian state, is not a form of government but a different kind of state."'[98] Criticism of this kind, regrettably, lacks any specific analysis of specific historical situations. Most of the arguments of Soviet theoreticians are based not on any analysis of the new situation that has evolved in the capitalist countries but on quotations from Marx and Lenin. Such an approach to the solution of theoretical problems can properly be condemned as dogmatic, a charge often levelled by Western Communist parties at Soviet theory. After all, the countries of developed capitalism now exhibit political and social conditions that did not exist anywhere in the world during the lifetimes of Marx, Engels or Lenin. These have opened up new possibilities for Communist activity and require a new analysis.

The concept of the 'dictatorship of the proletariat' is doubtless not yet obsolete or outmoded. It remains relevant for dozens of countries which in 1917 were much more backward than Russia and which, for a number of reasons, social, economic and political, are now comparable with Russia at the beginning of the twentieth century (the 'middle' stage of capitalism, with its deep dependence on foreign capital, large numbers of peasants and petty bourgeois, a weak national bourgeoisie, an impoverished working class and the peasantry, but also a militant working-class party and revolutionary parties of the middle class). In most such countries, class contradictions are rife, since, under the conditions of fierce international competition on world markets, the economies of these countries can only survive or make slow progress at the cost of increasing exploitation of the working masses. Cases in point are Turkey, South Korea, Mexico, Argentina, Brazil, Egypt, Portugal and the Philippines. There is another numerous group of Third World countries which might look upon the socialist road to development as the only one possible—those in which capitalism has begun to develop only after they have gained national independence and still remains well short of the 'middle' stage. Some of these countries have retained a feudal or semi-feudal system. Their middle classes lack the means to set up large-scale industrial enterprises and this calls for an extension of state control over the economy of the attraction of foreign capital investment. We are thinking of Algeria, Nigeria, Sri Lanka, Burma, Thailand and, to some extent, India, Tunisia, Bolivia and Peru. The problem of the dictatorship of the proletariat is a very real one also for countries that have yet to embark on capitalism and which are attempting to broaden their economic potential in other ways: Angola, Mozambique, Ethiopia, Tanzania and a few others. The overwhelming majority of all these countries depend politically on an authoritarian regime; they have only the weakest forms of democratic tradition, or none at all.

Things are entirely different in those twenty-five to thirty countries of highly developed capitalism—most of Western Europe, the USA, Canada, Japan and Australia. For these countries the question of the means of transition to socialism is posed in relation to their own special circumstances. Recognition of this fact and the development of a corresponding political attitude ought not to be considered some sort of 'revisionism' or 'opportunism'—it is the inescapable duty of all Communist parties. What are the factors, the new political, economic and social developments, in these countries that permit a change of attitude both to the 'dictatorship of the proletariat' and the whole range of problems connected with working-class power? Let us consider some of the most important among them.

1. Perhaps the most important single new factor that has to be reckoned with by Communist parties in Western countries is the change in the social structure. Nowadays, the intelligentsia and students outnumber agricultural workers by a large margin. Farmers and smallholders account for not more than ten per cent of the population, and most of the families in this group are comparatively prosperous, many of the poorer peasants having sold off their plots and moved into the cities. Agricultural production is now based on a wide and varied range of machinery; it is quite common for a farmer in the West to exceed a modern factory worker in level of mechanization and energy use. In these countries, the working class, together with adjacent groups of hired workers (in trade, service industries and the lower levels of the intelligentisa), constitutes a large majority. This was not the situation anywhere in the West in 1917, except perhaps in England, and present-day conditions make the Western world a very different place from the Europe and Russia known to Marx, Engels and Lenin. This circumstance is not to be ignored.

An analysis of Lenin's statements not merely about the dictatorship of the proletariat but about the problems arising from the class struggle and the state will show that his central and main argument in favour of the dictatorship of the proletariat was not based on the inevitability of opposition from a bourgeoisie deprived of power and determined at all costs to regain it. Much more significant for Lenin were the instability and vacillations of the petty-bourgeois majority of the population in capitalist countries, and, particularly in Russia, the instability and vacillations of the peasantry. The sober politician in Lenin saw clearly that the enemies of the working class, the enemies of revolution and socialism, would never enter into conflict with a new proletarian state if they had not the slightest hope of emerging victorious. For the bourgeoisie and landowners, this hope depended on the disillusioned petty-bourgeois masses who considered themselves let down by the workers' state. Without help from the ordinary ranks of the army and the police, the Cossacks, the lower-ranking civil servants and sections of the peasantry, the bourgeoisie would be in no position to wage war against the power of the working class supported by the poorest of the peasants. Although the working class itself was a minority group, the bourgeoisie and landed class was much smaller still in numbers; and in the countryside, poverty held sway over prosperity. All of this made it possible for Lenin to assert that 'the Bolsheviks will retain state power' in Russia, but this would not have been feasible without the dictatorship of the proletariat.

In 1902, in a discussion document on Plekhanov's second draft Programme for the RSDWP, Lenin had written: 'The draft omits mention of the dictatorship of the proletariat, which was included at first. This may have happened by accident or oversight, though it remains beyond doubt that the concept of "dictatorship" is incompatible with positive recognition of outside support for the proletariat. If we knew really positively that the petty bourgeoisie would support the proletariat in a revolution conducted by that same proletariat then *there would be no need for any talk of "dictatorship" since we should be guaranteed such an overwhelming majority that we could easily get by without it*... Acknowledgment of the need for a dictatorship of the proletariat is linked indissolubly with the principle outlined in the *Communist Manifesto* that the proletariat is the one and only revolutionary class.'[99] But Communist parties in the West are now operating under circumstances in which they are able to count on support for socialist reforms from the overwhelming majority of the population. For this reason they are able to exclude the concept of 'dictatorship' from their policy documents.

2. In the course of his ongoing argument with Kautsky about the dictatorship of the proletariat, Lenin frequently claimed that the

value of democratic institutions in capitalist countries was limited since the middle classes could easily abrogate them if they saw in them a threat to their own power. At the slightest suggestion of this kind of threat, the bourgeoisie would go over immediately to direct dictatorship, declaring a state of emergency and abolishing all constitutional guarantees. The proletariat needed to act accordingly in its struggle for power. This reasoning is undoubtedly correct in every case so far as the *wishes, interests and intentions* of the bourgeoisie are concerned. It is not so certain in relation to the actual possibilities open to them. Even the Russian experience does not quite square with Lenin's argument. In 1917, the bourgeoisie and the landed class were very anxious to declare a state of emergency, to abolish the hated Soviets and usher in a direct dictatorship. The short-lived Kornilov revolt had this as its aim. The Provisional Government doubtless wished to prevent the Bolsheviks from using the democratic institutions and the democratic atmosphere of the country in 1917 to set up organizations and raise a political army for socialist revolution, but it was too weak to do so. This is applicable also to contemporary Western Europe and Japan. The power of the bourgeoisie in these regions was under severe threat in the 1920s and 30s when the world capitalist economy underwent an extremely severe crisis, and in many countries the Communist and working-class movements were strengthened. In these conditions, the bourgeoisie in several countries did embark on an assertion of their own direct dictatorship, involving the abolition of various democratic institutions, particularly the parliamentary system. This was to lead ultimately to the rise of fascism and the Second World War.

However, following the military and political defeat of fascism, democratic regimes were re-established in the Western countries and Japan. The 1970s saw the liquidation of the last of the fascist regimes, in Portugal, Spain and Greece. This struggle, with its many victims, has made the democratic institutions of Western Europe and Japan much stronger than in the pre-war period and much stronger and more varied than the ruling classes would have wished. In the countries of highly developed capitalism, democracy is anything but a sham; the popular masses and the political parties representing the working classes in them make wide use of democracy in their own interests. Thus the constant linkage of the epithet 'bourgeois' to the concept of 'democracy' is not only inappropriate, it is actually wrong. The situation in many Western countries today is such that, even during a political crisis, the bourgeoisie might well find itself incapable of abolishing constitutional guarantees and declaring a state of emergency and then a dictatorship, a form of power based on direct violence. Thus it remains perfectly possible that a left-wing coalition might come to power by peaceful means and, moreover, that social and socialist reforms might be carried through within the present-day framework of legality rather than through the dictatorship of the proletariat. In the formulation of his ideas on the dictatorship of the proletariat, Lenin said, ' "Freedom" in a bourgeois-democratic republic has meant in practice freedom for the rich. As a general rule the proletariat and the toiling peasantry have not had any real opportunity to use democracy.'[100] This 'general rule' no longer applies in most capitalist countries, where the workers and the toiling peasantry have now actually become the main defence and guarantee of democratic institutions.

3. When defining the means and problems of the transition to socialism after October, Lenin pointed as a first priority to the economic and cultural backwardness of Russia. The proletarian state had been created there in advance of the economic development necessary for socialism. There was, of course, some heavy industry and monopolies, which were readily convertible to socialism. For, as Lenin wrote, 'socialism is nothing more or less than a monopoly of capital and state power for the benefit of all the people... State-monopoly capitalism is the fullest material preparation for socialism, it is its threshold, it is that rung on the ladder of history which comes immediately before the one called socialism.'[101] These monopolies and corporations, however, and more so the elements of state-monopoly capitalism, existed in Russia like tiny islands in the vast ocean of the natural economy and trade within the country. Lenin wrote in 1921: 'Take a look at a map of the Russian Federation. North of Vologda, South-East of Rostov-on-Don and Saratov, South of Orenburg and Omsk, North of Tomsk there are unimaginably vast open spaces, enough room for dozens of enormous civilized states. All of them are ruled by an outdated patriarchal spirit, semi-barbarism and barbarism itself in an extreme form. What about the peasant backwoods in the rest of

Russia? Everywhere miles and miles of track, or more accurately no road surface at all, separate the countryside from the railway, in other words from a material link with culture, capitalism, heavy industry, the big city. Don't these places also abound with the patriarchal spirit, Oblomovism and semi-barbarism? Can we even think of managing a direct transition from this situation, which exists virtually throughout the whole of Russia, to socialism? Yes, we can to an extent, but only under one condition known to us at present. ... This condition is electrification ... But we know full well that this "one condition" requires at least ten years' work in the first instance...,[102] Hence a transitional period between capitalism and socialism was essential economically as well as politically. And the state, which was to bring about the economic reform of Russia on the basis of electrification and socialism must, according to Lenin, be a dictatorship of the proletariat and nothing else.

It is obvious that this argument scarcely applies nowadays to the countries of developed capitalism, the economies of which are in fact *highly* developed. In these countries, the monopolization of means of production has reached a level that could scarcely have been envisaged at the beginning of the century. A significant proportion of their GNP depends upon international or multinational monopolies and, in the countries of Western Europe, since the war a substantial amount of industrial production has been transferred to the state, which denotes an increase in the role and significance of state capitalism. Even here, difficulties will arise when the basic means of production are transferred to the working class and its allies, but not the difficulties that Soviet Russia had to cope with. In economic terms, the developed capitalist countries have matured sufficiently for a smoother transition from capitalism to socialism.

4. The development of monopolistic capital in Western countries and the growth of state capitalist undertakings have weakened the economic and political status of small-scale or average capital. The socialist revolution in Europe can thus be limited to the expropriation of large capital undertakings; there is no need to touch most of those average or small-scale operations which, given a sensible policy on the part of the new workers' state, might even go on to experience an improvement in their conditions. This allows for the political neutralization of many such enterprises and the isolation of

the most active enemies of socialism. As to the large-scale enterprises, the economic potential of the West should make it possible to 'buy out' the owners and without disturbing the interests of small shareholders. This will probably make it possible to undermine opposition to the projected reforms. Marx and Engels did allow for the possibility of a workers' state, under certain circumstances, 'buying out' the capitalists. Lenin too never considered it essential that the radical methods of economic reform undertaken in Russia must apply to other countries; on the contrary he insisted that such reforms would be bound to be effected differently in Western countries. He also predicted that in future socialist revolutions in the better developed countries of Europe, the bourgeoisie would retain many political rights including the vote.

5. For all the contradictions and vacillations, temporary backsliding and defeats, a gradual shift to the left has been witnessed in Western countries over the last twenty years. Changes in the mood of the population in favour of structural reform have been observable not only in Western Europe and Japan but even in the USA. In many countries, the influence of the Communist Party has increased rather than diminished, a process which has been assisted by a state of permanent economic crisis, with mounting unemployment and rising inflation. Nevertheless, not one of these countries of advanced capitalism has yet arrived at what Lenin called a revolutionary situation. Although the ruling classes can no longer cope with problems of increasing severity by re-using yesterday's methods, and a considerable majority of the population is dissatisfied with the old way of living, this desire for change has its limitations. The great majority of workers in Western Europe and in Japan have no time for violent upheaval, preferring gradual reform, in other words, a more gentle and peaceful transition to socialism. Communist parties must take into account the mood of the broad masses of working people. The only people in those countries who favour more radical and violent methods are the comparatively small groups of the 'far left' whose influence is as minimal as those on the 'far right'. The despair that arises at the most oppressed levels of society out of extreme poverty and deprivation, and occurs also within groups of fascist inclination when they become aware of their own impotence, combines brutality with stupidity and nurtures

terrorism on the left and the right. But the wave of terrorism that has engulfed the Western countries has had the effect of alienating the working masses even further from violence and dictatorship.

All these circumstances create conditions suitable for a *rapprochement* between Communists and Social Democrats. Without going into the complex history of the relations between these two groups, it is safe to say that the left-wing camp in the West today does not suffer from the bitter conflict that divided Communists from Social Democrats in the Russia of 1917. Given goodwill, concessions in both directions and plenty of effort, the Western countries and Japan might well see unions of the left not unlike the French. Italy might welcome a union including both the Socialists and the left-wing Christian Democrats or even a general coalition of all the democratic parties. The basis of this union of the left could be preserved after the assumption of power, as a powerful instrument for the gradual reform of Western society. Both Socialists and Social Democrats, not to mention the left-wing Christian groups, have been emphatically opposed to the slogan 'dictatorship of the proletariat'. The refusal of the Communist parties in France, Spain and Portugal to retain the term is more than mere tactics, for a union of left-wing forces in Europe opens up the possibility of radical reforms without any kind of dictatorship, that is, without any need of a power based on direct violence and extra-legal measures. It is less easy to assess the situation of the Communist Party in a country like Austria, where the demand for a dictatorship of the proletariat persists, and is included in the Party's policy documents. Perhaps this explains why it has failed to grow over the past sixty years! In 1921, the Austrian Communist Party could count on a membership of 25,000: now it is down to about 20,000, most of them over forty. During the same period the Austrian Social Democratic Party's membership has grown from 600,000 to about 700,000, most of them from the working classes. In their eagerness to follow Lenin's demand for the establishment of a dictatorship of the proletariat, some leaders of Western Communist parties have overlooked another, perhaps more significant, demand from the same source: 'gain a close knowledge of the moods of the toiling masses and take them into account.'

6. One of Lenin's strongest arguments in favour of the dictatorship

of the proletariat was that even after the transfer of power to the working class or to a coalition of workers' parties (as in Hungary in 1919), and even after the expropriation of the main means of production, the bourgeoisie would hang on to political and economic influence for some time, not only through their connections with the petty bourgeoisie and the peasantry but also because of their contacts with the world of international capitalism. International capital would provide enormous sustenance to any overthrown bourgeoisie in its attempts to regain state power. This argument has probably retained its validity to the present day, though the possibilities open to international capital have been much reduced since Lenin's time. A balance has now been struck between the influence and power of the capitalist camp and those of the socialist countries. In addition, the entire collapse of the colonial system has undermined the international strength of capitalism. The most furious opposition of French capitalism could not prevent Algeria from gaining independence. The entire might of US imperialism could not prevent the victory of the Viet Cong in Vietnam, or the fall of the pro-American monarchy in Iran, or the defeat of the Somoza dictatorship in Nicaragua. Support from the most reactionary circles in international capitalism could not long delay the collapse of the white minority in Rhodesia (now Zimbabwe). There are many such examples.

We know that Lenin had little belief in the possibility of the working class's ever coming to power through parliamentary elections. He was equally convinced that, in the event of victory by the Communists and their allies in such elections, the ruling classes would disregard the results and usurp power. Today, however, the possibility of victory for the left in a general election is a real one that exercises the minds of all the enemies of socialism. However, events in Chile have shown clearly that the friends of socialism must exercise their minds over the possibility of a fascist military coup. Attempts at military take-over did occur in the 1960s in Italy and France, and in Greece they met with temporary success. The right is making every effort to regain power in Portugal. There are many examples of this too. The lessons of recent and not so recent history show clearly that left-wing forces even in the most democratic of Western countries must not allow themselves to rely on the moral strength of a general election. Their parliamentary activities must be supported outside parliament by agitation among the masses of the people and a strengthening of their influence not only among the workers but in the army and other key sectors of the state apparatus. This agitation, before and after victory, can be made within the framework of existing laws and any new ones adopted by a newly elected administration. Even if the forces of reaction should turn to violence, the response of the popular government ought to be within the bounds of legality.

Events may, of course, develop in many different ways, and there is no possibility of foreseeing every possible variant and turning point. There were striking differences between the democratic revolutions of the 1970s in Portugal and Spain and it is clear, incidentally, that the sudden and stormy course of revolution in the former country stimulated and accelerated the gentler, more gradual, though determined transition to democratic forms of government in the latter. This may recur during similar transitions in other Western countries. The French Communist Party has issued repeated warnings that the French bourgeoisie has a 'Versailles mentality', that is, a tradition of bloody suppression of all demonstrations by the workers that threaten bourgeois privilege and power. In the post-war period, England has undertaken a relatively tranquil though not entirely voluntary withdrawal from colonial power. France, by contrast, spent almost ten years fighting a ferocious colonial war in Indo-China and followed this up with a similar period of no less ferocious fighting in Algeria. Portugal's colonial wars lasted even longer. These examples suggest that, however identical the class nature of the various bourgeois countries might seem, reactions to similar sets of circumstances may vary. And although the possibility of creating a socialist society without a dictatorship of the proletariat does exist in many countries of advanced capitalism, the realization of this possibility depends not only on the working class but also on its political adversaries.

7. How are we to explain the fact that the great majority of workers in the developed capitalist countries nowadays condemn violent methods in the class struggle, and particularly the dictatorship of the proletariat? This is surely determined by their present situation in society. There may be some controversy as to the meaning of the second half of the phrase 'dictatorship of the proletariat', but

writers of every hue agree that the working class today in the Western countries is very different from the nineteenth-century proletariat. Speaking of hired labour in that period, Marx and Engels used to refer to the 'outlawed proletariat' for whom 'every freedom disappears in law and in practice', 'a class ousted from society', 'reduced by capital to the status of beasts of burden'. It was described as a class that 'loathed its toil' and was 'broken down by introduction of women and children into production', a people 'with no country', and so on. These expressions scarcely apply nowadays; it would clearly be an exaggeration to reiterate the idea of a class 'ousted from society'. But it is hardly less of an exaggeration to claim, as has been done by Herbert Marcuse and other left-wing theorists, that the workers form a class 'fully integrated' into modern bourgeois society and interested in its survival. During the past decade, practice as well as theory has made it clear that the Western working class is a long way from full integration into capitalist society. Its potential for revolution remains strong. However it does not consist of 'outlawed beasts of burden'. The prolonged working-class struggle for democratic and other rights has brought significant results. Trade-union freedoms have been acquired and the unions themselves have become a force to be reckoned with. Working-class living standards have risen, on the whole, considering the long intervals of time involved. Child labour has been abolished by law or severely restricted and most working-class children go on into some form of secondary education, which raises the educational standards of the whole class. The workers have their own political parties which function legally in most western countries. They have their own press and educational organizations. The proportion of skilled and semi-skilled workers has risen markedly so that the overall percentage of workers without any qualifications is now quite low. There have been many other such changes.

However, some important characteristics of the nineteenth-century proletariat have been retained in latter-day capitalist society. The working class continues to exist without ownership of the means of production; its labour is sold to those who do own them, the capitalists. In other words, modern workers remain even today a class of legally free, hired labourers opposed to the capitalist class in the process of production. Thus, although in most cases the concept of a 'proletariat' has given way to that of a 'working class', in the right context there is nothing wrong with continuing to use the former expression.

Can a Communist or Workers' Government Ever Resign?

One of the chief objections voiced by those who oppose the introduction of Communist governments in Western countries, and especially the formation of a leftist government with Communist participation, is the claim that Communists never give up power voluntarily, even when the majority of the population loses confidence in them. Among our Soviet theorists today, there are some whose reasoning bears out these accusations. For instance, Krasin and Leybzon write as follows: 'Communists cannot give an unequivocal answer to the question of the rotation of parties in power. Are they to go through the motions of democracy by giving way to a reactionary government whose aim it will be to drown democracy in a bloodbath?'[103] Why must it be that any government succeeding a Communist one must inevitably aspire to 'drown democracy in bloodbath'? When seeking examples, why do our authors turn only to such events as the military coup in Chile, which was certainly not carried out by 'going through the motions of democracy', or the assumption of power in Germany by the Nazis, which was not replacing anyone resembling Social Democrats or Communists at the head of the state. In his book *Three Revolutions in Russia and Our Time*, K.I. Zarodov goes into this question in closer detail. His defence of the dictatorship of the proletariat includes this statement: 'One of the characteristics of a socialist revolution consists in the very fact that it opens up the possibility of an absolute guarantee against the restoration of the previous, i.e. bourgeois, order. This possibility is finally realized by the dictatorship of the proletariat.'[104]

It is natural enough for any party in power to be reluctant to be removed from it. This eventuality may be prevented in several ways, however: by foreseeing the correct policies and making sure that they are in the interests of the mass of the people, through demagogy and deceit, or by direct violence, that is, dictatorship. Zarodov is not one to exlude at least the first and third of these options: 'Let us take, for instance, the variant by which a party of the working class wins power by achieving an electoral majority. If at the same time the bourgeois socio-economic bases of society are preserved, then the bourgeois parties retain great advantages which they will no doubt attempt to exploit in order to win the next election. This is why the dictatorship of the proletariat, born of the will of a popular majority, immediately comes up against the need to reckon with inevitable changes in the disposition of class power, with the fact that groups and sections of society allied to the working class are bound to display their inconsistency, that some of them will go over to the bourgeoisie and that, in general terms, the majority of the population will for some time ahead continue to vacillate significantly before coming down firmly on the side of revolutionary power. A Marxist-Leninist understanding of the role of the proletariat as a class, the only class capable of consistent struggle for the transition from capitalism to socialism, therefore provides the theoretical foundation on which is constructed the idea that the dictatorship of the proletariat is essential for the defence and consolidation of the first victory of the revolution.'[105]

This form of reasoning—and other arguments along the same lines, though less precisely formulated—must be regarded as irrelevant to present conditions in the West. It is quite clear that, even if working-class parties come to power by 'winning an electoral majority' and not by armed revolution, they will not use their mandate simply to lounge in the armchairs of parliamentary ministers and delegates. With a parliamentary majority and other, non-parliamentary organizations behind them, these parties will proceed to carry out an agreed programme of socio-economic measures and pass laws actually aimed at undermining the 'bourgeois socio-economic bases of society.' Given this, the possibility of the bourgeoisie's exploiting these 'bases' and any other advantages at the next election will be much reduced.

Zarodov does not make it clear why, after the victory of the workers' party and a series of profound social and economic reforms, 'groups and sections of society allied to the working class are bound to display their inconsistency', 'some of them going over to the bourgeoisie'. Is there no possibility that a leftist alliance might, after a period of successful governmental activity, actually gain strength? Of course it is feasible that, once in power, the Communists or the coalition of workers' parties might prove incapable of solving a number of vital problems, or working out the proper timing and order of their reforms, and might thus lose the confidence of the voting majority. What should they then do—attempt to prolong their stay in power by the use of direct violence, or follow the wishes and will of the electorate and resign? Many Western Communist parties have made it clear that in that situation they would prefer the latter alternative.

The behaviour of a workers' or a Communist government is usually related to the circumstances in which it came to power. In Russia, the Bolsheviks came to power by armed revolution, supported only by an active revolutionary minority. Thus, the only way to remove them from power was to use force. When the results of the elections to the Constituent Assembly showed that Russia's petty bourgeoisie and peasantry had given a majority not to the Bolsheviks but to the Socialist-Revolutionaries, and when the Assembly was actually convened in Petrograd and began to lay claim to supreme power over the country, the Bolsheviks had no hesitation in dissolving it. For the maintenance of power, they went over to the more flexible, and for them more favourable, system of election to the Soviets. Even then they showed a cavalier attitude to the results. The history of the celebrated Baku Commune is particularly instructive in this respect.

In Baku, and also in many regions of Azerbaijan, the elections to the Soviets in late 1917 and early 1918 were won by the Bolsheviks, who went on to convene the Soviet of People's Commissars in the spring of 1918. However, at the end of July, with Civil War and intervention under way, the same Baku Soviet passed a narrow vote of no confidence in the Bolshevik government. The Bolsheviks debated the issue among themselves and there were calls for the abolition of the Soviet. In the event the decision went the other way; the Baku Soviet of People's Commissars accepted Shaumyan's proposal and resigned. Elsewhere the Bolsheviks refrained from this kind of 'liberalism'. On discovering that the population had turned against their Party, they frequently did without any elections to the Soviet and appointed a *revkom* (revolutionary committee). When it came to elections to the All-Russian organs of Soviet government, they used an unequal electoral system whereby one worker's vote was deemed equal to five countrydweller's votes, or even more.

Whatever our attitude to those events, we must not forget that in the brutal Civil War conditions from June 1918 onwards, the fight to retain power meant for the Bolsheviks more often than not a fight for life. The first priority of their opponents, on coming to power, was to arrest all Bolsheviks and commissars and usually to eliminate them. The Baku commissars were to pay dearly for their liberal attitude; they were arrested and exiled to Turkestan where almost all of them were shot.

It is worth repeating that conditions today in the developed capitalist countries are quite different from Russia in 1917. Even there, of course, the situation outlined by Zarodov might well come about. It is not inconceivable that, after introducing radical reforms, the putative left-wing coalition might fall into disagreement and the alliance might collapse. How should the Communists then behave? That would depend on the disposition of power in parliament and the results of new elections. If they were returned with a majority then they would form another government with any allies who were prepared to honour previous obligations. If another party, say the Socialists, gained a majority, then the Communists would have to follow the wishes of the people, resign from their ministerial posts and return to the status of a party in opposition. There would be no question of using violence in order to hang on to power. Violence would be acceptable to left-wing governments, Communist ones included, only as and when the bourgeoisie and its parties themselves turned to violence or other illegal means in order to facilitate their own return to power. In this event, working-class parties would have to utilize all possible governmental power within the law and, only on certain occasions, say in the case of foreign intervention, would it be proper to declare a state of emergency and thus establish a dictatorship of one form or another. It is to be hoped that such extreme measures as these never have to be taken.

3
Soviets as a Form of Revolutionary Power

Marx and Engels on the Forms of Revolutionary Power

As early as 1847-50, Marx and Engels posed the questions of how political power was to be transferred to the proletariat in the countries of Europe and how the proletariat should be organized to form the ruling class. The authors of the *Communist Manifesto* set out in some detail the main tasks to be undertaken by the proletariat once political power had been achieved. What they did not discuss at that stage were the different forms this political power might take. We now see the nineteenth century in Europe as a period of developing bourgeois democracy, with the advent of various kinds of parliamentary representation, universal suffrage, trial by jury and a relatively free press. Marx and Engels were rarely disposed to praise the forms of democracy of their day; they were much more inclined to criticize the limitations of what they described as 'democratic swindling'. They castigated the hypocrisy and false promises of contemporary democratic institutions, though, significantly enough, they called not for the destruction of these institutions but for changes in their social composition. Democracy was not only an essential condition for the organization and development of the political power to be wielded by the proletariat over the bourgeoisie, it could actually become the form of government assumed by the proletariat.[1]

The nineteenth century was, however, not only a period of developing bourgeois democracy. It was an age that also saw the evolution in most European countries of the unwieldy apparatus of bureaucratic executive power. This was seen by Marx and Engels as a parasitic growth to be eliminated in the course of proletarian revolution. In his analysis of the lessons to be learned from the French revolution and the experience of the Second Republic, Marx wrote in 1852: 'The executive power possesses an immense bureaucratic and military organization, an ingenious and broadly based state machinery, and an army of half a million officials alongside the actual army, which numbers a further half million. This frightful parasitic body, which surrounds the body of French society like a caul and stops up all its pores, arose in the time of the absolute monarchy, with the decay of the feudal system, which it helped to accelerate. The task of the first French revolution was to destroy all separate local, territorial, urban and provincial powers in order to create the civil unity of the nation. It had to carry further the centralization that the absolute monarchy had begun, but at the same time it had to develop the extent, the attributes and the number of underlings of the governmental power. Napoleon perfected this state machinery. The Legitimist and July monarchies only added a greater division of labour, which grew in proportion to the creation of new interest groups, and therefore new material for state administration, by the division of labour within bourgeois society. Every *common* interest was immediately detached from society, opposed to it as a higher, *general* interest, torn away from the self-activity of the individual members of society and made a subject for governmental activity...Finally, the parliamentary republic was compelled in its struggle against the revolution to strengthen by means of repressive measures the resources and centralization of governmental power. All political upheavals perfected this machine instead of smashing it.'[2]

Although Marx did call on the proletarians of Europe to destroy the organs of executive power perfected by the bourgeoisie, his reference to a 'ghastly parasitic organism' included an element of journalistic hyperbole. He saw clearly that, in a class-ridden society, government control was essential, and not only in order to suppress the lower orders and defend the privileges of the upper classes, for the activity of the state embraces both the conduct of general affairs arising from the nature of any society and certain specific functions arising from the opposition between government and the mass of the people.[3] It follows naturally that Marx did not propose that the proletariat should repudiate the state and government immediately after the victory of proletarian revolution. Neither he nor Engels, however, was in a hurry to deal with the question of the precise forms to be assumed by the new proletarian state. They went into greater detail on this account in their works written in the early 1870s, having learned a great deal in the interim from the experience of the revolutionary movement in France and particularly from the Paris Commune of 1871.

Naturally Marx did not regard France as an absolute example. It was clear to him, for example, that unlike continental Europe, England and the United States had not yet established any significant apparatus of executive power. For this reason it would be possible for the proletariat in these countries to gain power by peaceful means, by availing themselves of existing democratic institutions. In a speech in Amsterdam in 1872, Marx said: 'The worker must in time seize political power ... But we have never asserted that in order to achieve this end identical methods are necessary in all places. We are aware that the institutions, manners and traditions of different countries must be taken into account; we do not deny that there are countries like America and England—and if I knew more aobut your institutions I might well be able to add Holland—in which the workers might achieve their ends by peaceful means.'[4] Continental countries like France were quite different. After 1871, Marx considered that the optimum form of state power in these countries would be not a parliamentary republic but a state organized on the lines of the Paris Commune....The Commune was formed of the municipal councillors, chosen by universal suffrage in the various wards of the town, responsible and revocable at short terms. The majority of its members were naturally working men, or acknowledged representatives of the working class. The Commune was to be a working, not a parliamentary, body, executive and legislative at the same time. ... Its true-secret was this. It was essentially a working-class government, the product of the struggle of the producing against the appropriating class, the political form at last discovered under which to work out the economic emancipation of labour.'[5]

One of Marx's most important works, *The Civil War in France*, was devoted to a detailed analysis of the Commune. Unfortunately, however, the Commune lasted for no more than ten weeks and its power never extended beyond a single city. It failed, or else it never aspired, to penetrate deeply into questions of property-owning. Paris did pass a decree dealing with the transfer to workers' cooperative associations of businesses abandoned by their owners, but the Commune, despite enormous financial difficulties, never voted to take over management of the French bank and thus make use of its three billion francs. Thus Marx and Engels did not regard it as an absolute example and, when speaking in general terms of proletarian power in the future, they continued to use the concept of a 'democratic republic' (which was not the same as a 'parliamentary republic'). Referring to the Erfurt Programme of the German Social Democratic Party (1891), Engels wrote: 'If one thing is beyond doubt it is that our party and the working class can achieve power only under a political system like a democratic republic. This latter is even to be considered the one specific system for the dictatorship of the proletariat, as the great French revolution has shown.'[6]

The Origin and Structure of the Soviets

In 1904-1905, it was the working class that emerged as the leader and the driving force of the first Russian Revolution. At the beginning of the twentieth century, Russia had virtually no democratic institutions. The newly formed working-class party operated illegally and the trade unions embraced only a small number of workers. These conditions of revolutionary creativity led to the formation of the first Soviets of Workers' Deputies, the earliest of which sprang up in the spring of 1905 in the Urals and in Ivano-Voznesensk as organs for directing strike action. By the autumn of that year, Soviets of Workers' Deputies had been established in more than fifty towns and working communities in Russia. In some instances, Soviets had been formed by workers and soldiers, and there were one or two Soviets of peasant deputies. These directed not only strikes but all the other forms of revolutionary activity. In Moscow, they actually prepared and led the armed uprising in December 1905. Nevertheless the Soviets remained, in 1905-1907, nothing more than an embryonic form of revolutionary power. There was no 'dual power' at that time. The Russian autocracy may have been forced into one or two concessions, including the formation of the State Duma, but it was still the Tsarist government and all its localized organs that ran the country, quelling any attempt to create genuine government by the people. Once the revolution had been put down, therefore, the Soviets ceased to exist.

Circumstances were quite different in the spring of 1917. Although the mass demonstrations of workers in Petrograd were accompanied by occasional bloody clashes with the police, once the Petrograd garrison had gone over to the side of the rebels a speedy victory for the revolution was assured. The system of autocratic government was collapsing in full view; the mere announcement of Nicholas II's abdication and the victory of the revolutionaries in the capital led almost automatically to the fall of the old regime in the other cities, provinces and regions of the vast Russian Empire. The Council of Ministers scattered, and many Tsarist ministers were placed under arrest. The corps of gendarmes collapsed and the Secret Police and Police Department were wiped out. The prisons were opened and Tsarist sentences of hard labour and exile were revoked. Practically all the military garrisons in the cities of Russia and all army units serving at the front joined the revolution. After the fall of the monarchy, then, whose hands held the reins of political power?

The only institution of the old regime that enjoyed some influence and survived the first days of the revolution was the State Duma. This was, however, not a truly representative organ. Elections to it were neither universal nor equal. The workers, peasants, landowners and urban bourgeoisie chose their own electors separately, and the rules of representation in the various 'curiae' were such that the working class had only a small number of representatives. The working peasantry was no less under-represented. In the fourth and last State Duma, elected in 1912, the majority of the deputies came from bourgeois and landowners' parties (the Octobrists, Kadets and 'moderate' right-wing groups). Under the autocracy, the functions of the Duma were really no more than consultative, and Nicholas II had rejected all demands for the creation of a government responsible to the Duma. This possibility now re-emerged, but only in the circumstances of a revolution that had instilled in the leaders of the Duma a fear amounting to panic. During the February Revolution, the State Duma did manage to form the Provisional Committee, soon to be converted into the Provisional Government, the ruling majority of which was at first provided by the Kadets, the Constitutional Democrats who constituted the most influential party of the Russian bourgeoisie.

The driving force of the revolution was provided, however, by the workers and the other ranks in the military garrisons, none of whom could consider the State Duma an expression of their own interests. Thus it became necessary, immediately after the beginning of the revolution, to establish representative organs capable of reflecting immediately the interests and the will of the workers and soldiers. As under the Paris Commune, these organs must represent and at the same time lead and direct the mass of the people. These conditions were satisfied by the Soviets of Workers' and Soldiers' Deputies. Thus the Soviets originated as a kind of extension of the existing State Duma, a unique form of 'lower house', part of an imaginary parliament. The 'upper house' (the Duma and the Provisional Government) represented the 'qualified' elements, or ruling classes of society; the 'lower house' (the Soviets) represented the workers. A compromise between the two was possible only by creating a quite new system of representative government reflecting the will of the whole nation. A suitable title for such an organ was proposed almost immediately after the Revolution—the Constituent Assembly—but the feeble Provisional Government kept postponing its convocation with a view to underpinning and extending its own power the better to control elections to it.

The Soviets were not the only workers' institution brought into being by the February Revolution. Many workplaces set up sections of the Workers' Militia and the Red Guard, and committees sprang up everywhere, formed in factory workshops or by peasants and soldiers. However, it was the Soviets and their executive committees that became the main organ of the revolutionary masses, and their decisions and resolutions were taken up with incredible alacrity by the rebellious people. Without their voluntary co-operation, neither the Provisional Government nor their affiliated organs of power—the town dumas, the district councils *(zemstva)* and the provincial commissars who had replaced the pre-Revolutionary governors—could have carried out their functions.

The structure of the Soviets as an organ of revolutionary government in 1917 was simple in the extreme. Each Soviet consisted essentially of authorized representatives from the main businesses in a particular town and the military units stationed in it. The representatives were selected as a rule by a show of hands at a workers' meeting in a plant, factory or military unit. They generally turned out to be activists from the various parties who had some influence over the people, though sometimes they were just effective speakers and a number of them seemed to have got in by accident. Not that this mattered—at a time of almost daily gatherings and meetings, there was no difficulty in electing authorized representatives or recalling them. In any case, a new meeting of the Soviet would frequently elect new representatives. It was a time when people were projected into sudden prominence—and, on many occasions, lost their political reputations with equal rapidity. Another consideration was the return to Petrograd and other cities in March 1917 of political prisoners, some of them from nearby prisons, others from distant exile or labour camps. Many of these people were immediately elected to their local Soviets, as were, naturally enough, most of the political émigrés who returned in April and May. At this early stage, there were no stringent norms of representation; only later were the ground rules for this sort of thing worked out. A meeting of the representatives, once elected, comprised the *Soviet* (of a region, town, or district) and it had two functions, to discuss and settle any questions brought before it and to elect an executive committee, known as the *Ispolkom*. This was a standing committee, though its constitution changed rapidly as the revolution progressed. After a general meeting, the members of the Soviet went about their ordinary work in the factory or unit. In many cases so did the members of the Ispolkom. This had the right to convene a meeting of the whole Soviet when necessary, by which time its membership had often changed considerably, so fickle were the workplaces and military units in their political moods. Any particular workplace could call for a meeting of the Soviet. Any member of the Soviet or the Ispolkom, as a representative of one particular workplace or unit, could be recalled or replaced at any time, though the Executive Committee members were re-elected at ordinary meetings of the Soviet. The simplicity and flexibility of this system of popular representation were the strength of the Soviets, and the closest possible contact with the working masses was guaranteed by them.

In 1917, almost every town saw the creation of United Soviets with workers' and soldiers' deputies; only here and there were the two kinds of Soviet kept separate. There was a war on and military personnel were everywhere. Large garrisons were stationed in the towns, there were troops home on leave, new units were being formed, the hospitals were overflowing with wounded soldiers and many academies were set up for the training of command staff. At the front, and in the front-line zone, military committees were elected at general meetings to carry out the functions of Soviets in the army, at first on a regimental basis and then to serve a division, a corps, the armed services and the front-line troops. At the front itself there existed a kind of dual authority; alongside the ever-weakening power of the officers a new power began to operate, that of the military committees whose first obligation was to represent the other ranks. It was not long either before Soviets of Peasants' Deputies began to be formed in districts and provinces all over the country.

In the spring of 1917, the ubiquitous Soviets and committees worked without any overall leadership or general centre. In practice, however, they followed the acknowledged 'leadership' of the Petrograd Soviet, the decisions of which were commonly accepted as exemplary. A good example of this was the celebrated 'Order No. 1' issued by the Petrograd Soviet which revolutionized the entire army and was immediately adopted by all the other Soviets and military units. Gradually, however, the Soviets became systematized to form one of the parallel authorities in a system of dual government. In May 1917 the First All-Russian Congress of Peasants' Deputies met and elected a Soviet Central Executive Committee. Only a month later, in June, the First All-Russian Congress of Soviets was held and this too elected an Ispolkom. In the course of events, the Soviets came to act as a government authority, solving problems of the economy and settling disputes between workers, bringing in an eight-hour working day, helping to supply the army and even arresting people (one or two policemen and provocateurs). What were the main qualities of the Soviets as a governmental authority? One indisputable advantage was the simplicity of their organization, to which we have referred. In the situation of revolutionary crisis, the political life of our nation was proceeding with remarkable and alarming speed. Individual politicians came and went very rapidly, as did whole political parties. No parliamentary system with elections every four or five years could have served as an adequate reflection of the will of the people who were in a state of revolutionary ferment. One prominent member of the State Duma, V.V. Shulgin, has left a set of impressive descriptions of just how quickly the moods of the people could change in the days of the February Revolution. 'I remember a right-wing nationalist being sent to one of the regiments, a man with sincere views and a barrel-chest with bass voice and persuasive music to match. He came back and said, "That's all right then ... fine. I spoke to them, they cheered. I said we can't do without officers, our country's in danger. They cheered. They promised everything would be all right, they trusted the State Duma..." No problems there? Suddenly the phone rang. "Where are you calling from? Hello? What's that? Yes but I've just come from your place ... everything finished up all right ... What, they're getting restless again? Who? Someone a bit more left-wing? Right, we'll send someone." Miliukov was sent. Miliukov came back, very pleased, within the hour "Yes, they are a bit restless. I think the right chord wasn't struck with them... I spoke to them in the barracks on a sort of scaffold. The whole regiment was there and some men from other units ... Anyway, the mood's all right now. They carried me out shoulder-high." But soon afterwards the telephone rang again and a desperate voice spoke. "Hello. Yes. Such-and-such a regiment. Not again! Well, what more do they want? Someone further to the left. Yes, right, we'll send a Trudovik." I think we sent Skobelev. He calmed them down for a while. Then we sent them an SD... Who could we send after that?'[7] There was no one in the State Duma more left-wing than the Trudoviks and Social Democrats (Mensheviks). This kind of fickleness in the political mood of the working masses, soldiers, workers and peasants, recurred at every crisis point in 1917, in April, June-July and at the end of August, and made the Soviets an indispensable instrument of revolutionary power.

In the Russia of 1917, the Workers' and Soldiers' Soviets were also the best means of uniting the working class and the peasantry. The soldiers were, after all, predominantly revolution-minded peasants who had been organized and armed by the Tsarist state apparatus. In the situation of revolutionary crisis, the Soviets acquired particular strength and flexibility from the fact that the election of authorized representatives took place directly on the factory floor, on the railways, at workplaces and in the military units. This allowed them to mobilize the masses quickly and effectively to carry out any particular revolutionary measures, and it also enhanced the authority of the deputies since behind each one of them stood a workers' or soldiers' collective. Moreover, these deputies were, in their great majority, workers, peasants and soldiers themselves; civil servants, lawyers and professional politicians were few in number, most of them belonging to the leadership of the political parties.

Like the Paris Commune, the Russian Soviets were both legislative and executive organs. Once a session of the Soviet was declared closed, its delegates personally saw to the implementation of policies decided upon. From their inception, the Soviets had assumed the functions of government, even though they formed only one of the important links in the diarchic system which had arisen. It was obvious at the outset that the Soviets carried greatest authority in local matters: law and order in the towns, relations between workers and bosses, administration of supplies to the urban population, and so on. When it came to matters of state—waging war, supplying the army, diplomatic relations, law-making, and so on—the Provisional Government came into its own. Most of the Soviets, headed by a Menshevik bloc, supported the Provisional Government; they were, nevertheless, both an opposition and a controlling force affecting the government. The Soviets had the backing of the working masses and the Provisional Government could not take any important measures without assuring themselves of at least their tacit support. This fact was to be cleverly exploited by the Bolsheviks to increase their own influence and representation in the Soviets.

The problem was that, after the February Revolution, the life of our nation and the whole body of Russian society, far from settling down to normality, continued to be disrupted. The Provisional Government could not bring itself to undertake any of the necessary large-scale reforms. It was procrastinating on land reform and forever postponing elections to the Constituent Assembly; it pursued a policy of continuing the war and even tried to stimulate the military effort. There had been no real change in government policy towards the country's outlying national minorities. As a result the authority of the Provisional Government declined steadily. All over the country industry and transport were in ruins, and food-supplies for the cities were running low. Efforts by the Provisional Government to mount a large-scale attack on the South-Western front ended in total defeat and infuriated the war-weary army. The military defeat caused an outburst of spontaneous insurrection at home. Mass demonstrations were held at the beginning of July 1917 in Petrograd; the Provisional Government decided to put them down by force, and the SR-Menshevik leadership of the Soviets came out in its support of the Provisional Government, putting an end for the time being to the system of dual government. Even during these critical days, however, despite mass persecution of the Bolsheviks, some of whose leaders were arrested while others were outlawed, the Bolshevik presence was maintained in the Soviets and they never stopped working to win over the mass of the people. The July crisis did not lead to victory for counter-revolution or a complete transfer of power to the bourgeoisie and the officer corps, as the Bolsheviks had first thought likely. In the popular mind, this crisis was yet another shift to the left and it was soon reflected as such in the constitution of the Provisional Government. A new government was formed on July 24, with Kerensky at its head. The fifteen-strong group was made up of seven Mensheviks and Social Revolutionaries, two members of the Radical Democratic Party, four Kadets (Constitutional Democrats) and two unaligned members. The inclusion of Menshevik and SR leaders in the government did not indicate an alliance with the Soviets. The Provisional Government, while able to count on majority support from the Soviets, bore no responsibility towards the Central Executive Committee. In July and the first half of August, the Bolsheviks managed to increase their representation in many regional and city Soviets. A shift in the balance of power within the Soviets occurred when left-wing tendencies and groups arose within the Social Revolutionary and Menshevik parties and began to vote for Bolshevik proposals on a number of issues. The Bolshevik newspaper *Proletarian*, assessing the outcome of the sessions of the Petrograd Soviet on August 18 and 21, was thus able to conclude that the Soviet was moving to the left with each passing day.[8]

The leftward movement of the masses, reflected as it was in the activities of the Soviets and even the composition of the Provisional Government, caused consternation in the counter-revolutionary camp and accelerated preparations for Kornilov's ill-fated coup attempt. The battle against counter-revolution dynamized the Soviets and strengthened the authority and stature of the Bolsheviks within them. On August 31, the Petrograd Soviet passed a Bolshevik resolution, prompting the resignation of its SR-Menshevik Praesidium. However, at an ordinary session of the Soviet on September 9, the Bolshevik resolution was once again carried by a large majority. Leadership of the Petrograd and then the Moscow Soviet passed into Bolshevik hands. The whole country was being converted to Bolshevism, which renewed the possibility not only of restoring the slogan 'All power to the Soviets' but actually of making practical preparations, with the support of the majority of the Soviets, for armed insurrection and the overthrow of the Provisional Government. Acting according to resolutions passed by the Bolshevik Party's Central Committee, the Petrograd Soviet set up a Military Revolutionary Committee, and it was with the very active participation of this body that the government was brought down on October 24-25, 1917. At that very moment, the Second All-Russian Congress of Soviets was convened in Petrograd and it provided the Bolsheviks with a majority mandate. The Congress proclaimed the transfer of power to the Soviets and a new Soviet government was established to conduct affairs of state: the Soviet of People's Commissars headed by Lenin. Control over the activities of the new government was entrusted to the re-elected Central Executive Committee consisting of Bolsheviks, some left-wing Social Revolutionaries, Menshevik-Internationalists and one or two Ukrainian Socialists.

Lenin on the Significance of the Soviets

The formation of the Soviets during the revolution of 1905 attracted Lenin's closest attention. 'The Soviets of Workers' Deputies', he wrote, 'arise spontaneously from the soil of mass political strikes as the non-party organizations of the broad working masses.'[9] 'The Soviets of Workers' Deputies', he explained elsewhere, 'are not a workers' parliament, not an organ of proletarian self-government, not any kind of organ of self-government, but a battle formation for the achievement of certain aims.'[10] In March 1906, that is after the armed uprising in Moscow and other cities, Lenin observed that the 'revolutionary whirlwind' in Russia had led to the creation of 'new organs of revolutionary power', namely the Soviets. He went on to say: 'They were indeed organs of government, for all the rudimentary character, spontaneity, informality and diffuseness of their composition and functions. ... They behaved like a government ... yes, they were without doubt the embryo of a new popular, if you like revolutionary, government. Their socio-political attitudes gave them the character of an embryonic dictatorship of the revolutionary elements of the people ... since this government power recognized no other, no law, no rules proceeding from any other source.'[11]

Much later on, analysing the experience of the first Russian Revolution, Lenin invariably pointed up the importance of the activities of the Soviets. At a meeting of Swiss youth on January 9, 1917, for instance, he made a broad survey of the 1905 Revolution. It included this comment: 'Some of the towns of Russia were experiencing at that time a period of various little "republics" in which government power had been displaced and a Soviet of Workers' Deputies functioned in practice as a new state power.'[12] Some two months later, on March 7, 1917, in his first letter from Switzerland to Party comrades in Russia, Lenin hailed the new revolution and the new Soviets. In an assessment of the dual power then existing in the country, he wrote: 'Alongside this Provisional government...a new one has arisen, the main one, an unofficial workers' government, as yet undeveloped and relatively weak, which expresses the interests of the proletariat and all the most impoverished sections of the urban and rural population. This is the Soviet of Workers' Deputies up in Petersburg.'[13]

The Russian Social Democratic Workers' Party, at its Second Party Conference, adopted a programme that foresaw that, at a certain stage in the democratic revolution, it would be necessary to create a legislative body 'consisting of representatives of the people and comprising a single chamber'. This body was to be formed by means of universal suffrage by secret ballot.[14] This amounted in essence to the creation of a parliamentary republic in Russia—the programme actually mentioned the subsequent establishment in the country of 'biennial parliaments'. The Bolsheviks never revised these policy decisions either after the division of the Party or after the debacle of the first Russian Revolution. It came as no surprise, then, that, after the victorious February Revolution, many Bolsheviks began to repeat the catch-phrases calling for the setting up of a parliamentary republic as soon as possible, this being the responsibility of the Constituent Assembly. However, Lenin returned to Russia on April 3 and on the very next day, addressing a large meeting of Bolsheviks, made public his 'April Theses' calling for a general transfer of power to the Soviets and the establishment of a 'republic of Soviets'. What he called for was 'not a parliamentary republic—to return to that from the Soviets of Workers' Deputies would be a retrograde step—but a republic of Soviets of Workers', Agricultural Labourers' and Peasants' Deputies throughout the country, from top to bottom.'[15] This did not mean that Lenin was opposing the then popular idea of a Constituent Assembly. Lenin's argument was that only the transfer of all power to the Soviets would facilitate early elections to the Constituent Assembly, and he took it for granted that this Assembly would approve and support a republic of Soviets.

When Lenin was defending his 'Theses', most of the Soviets were under the influence and control of Mensheviks and Social Revolutionaries. In the Petrograd Soviet, only sixty-five of the 2,500 deputies owed allegiance to the Bolsheviks. But Lenin did not doubt that, as circumstances developed and also as a result of agitation and propaganda, the Bolsheviks would succeed in winning over the Soviets. The bourgeois revolution, Lenin believed, had already been won. Now it was time for the socialist revolution in Russia, the main part in which would go to the Soviets, which would themselves come to be controlled by the Bolsheviks. Lenin's prediction did not begin to come true until the beginning of September 1917, when the largest and most influential of the Soviets in Russia, including those of Petrograd and Moscow, began one after the other to pass Bolshevik resolutions. It was now, as we have noted above, that the Bolsheviks restored the temporarily abandoned slogan, 'All power to the Soviets!'. One month before the October Revolution, in a long article entitled 'Can the Bolsheviks Retain State Power?', Lenin answered this question in the affirmative. Among the factors that would allow the Bolsheviks to retain power, perhaps the most important was the existence of the Soviets, in which the Bolsheviks by now enjoyed a majority influence. He put it as follows: 'The Soviets are a new state apparatus, which, in the first place, provides an armed force of workers and peasants; and this force is not divorced from the people, as was the old standing army, but is fused with the people in the closest possible fashion. From a military point of view this force is incomparably more powerful than previous forces; from the point of view of the revolution it cannot be replaced by anything else. Second, this apparatus provides a bond with the masses, with the majority of the people, so intimate, so indissoluble, so readily controllable and renewable, that there was nothing remotely like it in the previous state apparatus. Third, this apparatus, by virtue of the fact that it is elected and subject to recall at the will of the people without any bureaucratic formalities, is far more democratic than any previous apparatus. Fourth, it provides a close contact with the most diverse occupations, thus facilitating the adoption of the most varied and most radical reforms without bureaucracy. Fifth, it provides a form of organization of the vanguard, i.e. of the most class-conscious, most energetic and most progressive section of the oppressed classes, the workers and peasants, and thus constitutes an apparatus with the help of which the vanguard of the oppressed classes can elevate, educate and lead *the gigantic masses* of these classes, which hitherto have stood remote from political life and history. Sixth, it proves the possibility of combining the advantages of parliamentarism with the advantages of immediate and direct democracy, i.e. of uniting in the persons of the elected representatives of the people both legislative and executive functions. Compared with bourgeois parliamentarism, this represents an advance in the development of democracy that is of historical and worldwide significance.'[16]

The victorious October Revolution served merely to confirm Lenin's view of the enormous, even unique significance of the form of revolutionary power embodied in the Soviets. Early in 1918, he wrote: 'If the creativity of the people during the Russian Revolution, along with the great experiences of 1905, had not established the Soviets in February 1917, in no way would it have been possible for them to seize power in October, since success depended entirely on the existence of readymade, organized forms of a movement embracing millions. This readymade form was provided by the Soviets, because of which in the sphere of politics we proceeded to those brilliant successes—that triumphant procession—that were awaiting us. A new form of political power was ready and all we had to do was issue one or two decrees in order to transform the power of the Soviets from the embryonic condition in which they existed during the first months of the revolution into a form legally acknowledged and confirmed by the Russian state, into the Soviet Russian Republic. This was born immediately, and so easily, simply because in February 1917 the masses created the Soviets before any of the parties had a chance to come out with the same slogan.'[17] Lenin's comments on the Soviets reveal increasingly positive assessments of their significance and their advantages over all other forms of democratic power. When, in January 1918, he recommended the dissolution of the Constituent Assembly, because it reflected only 'yesterday, before the revolution', he remarked that the Soviets were 'a form of democracy unequalled in any other country...the organization of these Soviets helps create something great and new, unprecedented in world revolutions'.[18] Comparing the Soviets with various forms of parliamentary democracy, he claimed on a number of occasions that Soviet power was a much higher form of democracy than the bourgeois republics of the West. 'Only Soviet Russia has given the proletariat and the whole gigantic working majority of Russia a kind of freedom and democracy unheard of, unthinkable and impossible in any bourgeois-democratic republic...by substituting for bourgeois parliamentarism the democratic organization of the Soviets which are a thousand times nearer to the "people" and more democratic than the most democratic of parliaments.'[19]

It was natural that Lenin should have compared the Soviets with the Paris Commune. He considered that the Commune belonged to the same type of workers' state organization as the Soviets, though the latter represented a great step forward from the former. 'There can be no doubt that in our Soviets there is much that is crude and unfinished. This is clear to anyone who takes a close look at the work they are doing. But what is important about them, what is of historical value, what represents a step forward in the world-wide development of Communism is that here we have created a new kind of state. In the Paris Commune it lasted for a few weeks in a single city and without any real awareness of what was going on. The Commune was not understood by those who created it, they did it with the brilliant sense of the awakened masses and not one of the French Socialist factions was aware of what they were doing. We are in a position where, thanks to our ability to stand on the shoulders of the Paris Commune and the years of experience of German Social

Democracy, we can see quite clearly what we are doing in creating Soviet power. The masses of the people, despite the crudity and indiscipline that do exist in the Soviets, left over in our country from the character of the petty bourgeoisie, have created a new type of state. It has lasted not weeks but months and not in one city but in a vast country and several nations.'[20]

In one of his many polemics against Kautsky, answering the latter's charge that the Bolsheviks had infringed democracy, Lenin admitted that the Bolsheviks had not been 'all that democratic' in their treatment of the old clerks of justice and the Constituent Assembly. However, he went on to claim that the Bolsheviks 'have given the workers and peasants a much more accessible form of representation, replaced the clerks by *their own* Soviets, or put *their own* Soviets in charge of them, made *their own* Soviets the electors of judges. This fact alone is sufficient for all the oppressed classes to recognize that Soviet power, this particular form of the dictatorship of the proletariat, is a million times more democratic than the most democratic of bourgeois republics.'[21] In 1917 Soviets existed only in Russia. By 1918, the revolutionary movements elsewhere in Europe had also given rise to Soviets that in many ways resembled those which existed in Russia after the February Revolution. This fact met with Lenin's fervent approval. At a meeting of Party workers in late November 1918, he said: '...now all the revolutions which have begun in the West have adopted the slogan of Soviet power and are creating Soviet power. Soviets—these are characterizing revolution everywhere. They have spilled over from Austria into Germany, Holland and Switzerland... This means that the defeat of bourgeois democracy was not something dreamt up by the Bolsheviks but an absolute historical necessity. It means we have taken true account of reality.'[22] Some months later, at a meeting of the Petrograd Soviet, he repeated the message. 'Before the revolution in Germany we kept on saying that the Soviets were the most appropriate organs for Russia. At that time we could not claim that they would to the same extent prove to be appropriate for the West, but life has taught us differently. We now see that the Soviets in the West are gaining popularity—people are fighting for them in America as well as Europe. Everywhere Soviets are being set up and sooner or later they will assume power. America is going through an interesting phase with the creation of Soviets there. It is possible that the movement there will take different paths from ours but what is important is that even in that country the Soviet form of organization is winning widespread popularity.'[23]

At this same time—that is, before the Soviet victory in Hungary—Lenin drew up the draft of a new programme for the Russian Communist Party, during which he formulated his conclusions on the overall significance of the Soviets as a form of revolutionary power. He called upon the Party to 'strengthen and develop the federal republic of Soviets as an immeasurably more elevated and progressive form of democracy than bourgeois parliamentarism and as the *only type of state* corresponding...to the transitional period between capitalism and socialism, i.e. the period of the dictatorship of the proletariat.'[24] This idea runs like a red thread through many of Lenin's speeches and articles. By creating Soviet power, he believed, the workers and peasants of Russia had initiated a worldwide change between 'two epochs of world-wide historical significance: the epoch of the bourgeoisie and the epoch of socialism, the epoch of capitalist parliamentarism and the epoch of Soviet state institutions of the proletariat'.[25]

Nowadays, some Soviet critics attempt to expound Lenin's views on the Soviets by re-editing them. Let us consider, for example, the following extract from *Revolutionary Theory and Revolutionary Practice* by Yu. A. Krasin and B.M. Leybzon: 'The Communist parties of the developed capitalist countries advocate not the breakdown of their electoral organs but filling them up with genuinely democratic content... V.I. Lenin considered that, although future revolutions might not necessarily repeat exactly the Soviet form of organization of workers, these revolutions would include the main thing, that which was characteristic of the Paris Commune and the October Revolution—the replacement of the organs of bourgeois democracy by genuinely democratic organs of government. In connection with the preparatory work for the platform of the first Congress of the Cominterm, the theses "The Bases of the Third International" were produced. At one point in the draft it was stated that the natural organs of the mass revolutionary struggle, to be converted upon victory into the organs of government, were the Soviets of Workers' Deputies. Lenin wrote: "Of the Commune or Soviet type (Soviets not essential)".'[26]

This is an incorrect interpretation of Lenin's views. In the first place, even in the example quoted Lenin's note concerns organs of power of the Commune and Soviet *type*; and it is quite clear from the many preceding quotations from Lenin (which could be multiplied without difficulty) that he regarded contemporary parliaments and municipalities as a quite different type of organ of power from the Soviets. Second, Lenin considered that the Commune represented, albeit in embryo, that very organ or form of revolutionary power which would manifest itself, fully matured, in the Soviets. In other words the Commune and the Soviets were two stages in the development of one and the same form, one and the same type of state. Third, the note referred to by Krasin and Leybzon remained unpublished until 1970, when it appeared for the first time in the penultimate volume of a new edition of Lenin's works.[27] It is easy enough, on the other hand, to point out many well-known statements in which he declares openly that not only the dictatorship of the proletariat but also Soviet power itself are among the general principles of Communism, which may be varied only 'in particular details' relating to 'national and national-state differences'.[28] These are the statements always referred to by the many interpreters of Lenin who have regarded his declaration that the Soviets are the *only form* of government capable of guaranteeing the transition to socialism as one of the most important principles or basic tenets of Leninism.[29] In the fourth place, Lenin's note, which seems to hold such profound significance for these two authors, was ignored in the revised version of the *Manifesto of the Comintern* and the *Platform of the Comintern*. These documents of the Comintern's First Congress refer clearly and unambiguously to the universal applicability of the Soviets as a new form of revolutionary power opened up by the Russian Revolution.[30] Moreover, Lenin personally wrote down his theses for the opening of the Congress, and they include the following reference to the Paris Commune: 'At this very time, just as the Soviet movement, embracing the whole world, can be seen to be continuing the work of the Commune, there are traitors to the cause of socialism who forget the real-life experience and real-life lessons of the Paris Commune and repeat the old bourgeois rubbish about "democracy in general". The Commune was not a parliamentary institution.'[31] There was an even clearer reference to the role of the Soviets at the Second Congress of the Comintern, which was held in the summer of 1920, with Lenin actively involved in it. This

Congress passed a special resolution, 'On the Conditions for the Creation of Soviets of Workers' Deputies', which included the following recommendation: 'Communists can and must systematically and urgently advertise the idea of the Soviets and popularize it for the masses by demonstrating to the broadest levels of the population that the Soviets are the only expedient form of state during the transition to complete communism.'[32] Even more specific references were contained in another resolution, 'Communist Parties and Parliamentarism'. 'Parliamentarism cannot be a form of proletarian government during the transition from the dictatorship of the bourgeoisie to the dictatorship of the proletariat. At the moment of intensified class struggle merging into civil war the proletariat must inevitably construct its state organization as a fighting organization from which representatives of the former ruling classes must be excluded; all fictions concerning the general will of the people are a danger to the proletariat; the proletariat has no need of a parliamentary division of power that can only harm it; the form of proletarian dictatorship is to be found in the Soviet Republic. The bourgeois parliaments, which comprise one of the most important pieces of apparatus in the bourgeois state machine, cannot be conquered, just as the bourgeois state itself cannot be conquered by the proletariat. The task of the proletariat is to explode the state machine of the bourgeoisis, to destroy it and along with it the parliamentary institutions whether they be republican or those of a constitutional monarchy... Consequently Communism repudiates parliamentarism as a form of the future society, repudiates it as a form of the class dictatorship of the proletariat; it repudiates any possibility of conquering parliaments in the long term; it aims for the destruction of parliamentarism. Thus we can only speak of using bourgeois institutions of state with the aim of destroying them'.[33]

Lenin's undoubted overestimation of the potential of the Soviets as a form of revolutionary power is perfectly understandable. Victory in revolution almost always creates an impression for many of the revolutionaries that the particular forms used in their own case *must* guarantee success in other countries. It was no accident that a demand for the establishment of Soviets was included not only in the basic documents of the Comintern but also in the policy documents of the Communist parties formed under the influence of the October Revolution. From the standpoint of the Communist parties formed during the past forty or fifty years, many of the statements made by Lenin and quoted above, and the resolutions passed by the first congresses of the Comintern might well be diagnosed as instances of the 'infantile disorder' of 'Left-Wing Communism', the dangers of which were pointed out by Lenin himself for the benefit of young Communist parties. As things turned out, the Soviets of Workers', Soldiers' and Peasants' Deputies were far from being universally applicable instruments of revolutionary power and the perfect form of the revolutionary state. And it must be added that the shortcomings of the Soviets emerged not only from the experience of other countries and other revolutions; they were soon to show themselves in Soviet Russia itself. Under the conditions of acute political and economic crisis in the Russia of 1917, the Soviets really did prove to be the best form through which to prepare the masses of the people, to organize and unify a political army for socialist revolution, but the same Soviets were anything but the best form of government for the country as far as the Bolsheviks themselves were concerned. For this reason it seems important to examine briefly the evolution of the Soviets after the October Revolution.

The Difficulties of Soviet Power and the Disadvantages of the Soviets

The first hundred days after the victorious October Revolution saw a triumphal procession of the Soviets through our country. Soviet power had conquered virtually throughout the entire territory by the beginning of 1918, and the occasional attempts at counter-revolution were soon put down. The reinforcement of this power was assisted by the unification of the Soviets of Peasants' Deputies with those of the Soldiers' and Workers' Deputies, which had been functioning independently throughout 1917. Among the peasant population, the influence of the SRs lasted longer than in the cities, and they used the peasant Soviets as a means of exerting pressure on the Bolsheviks. After October, even these peasant Soviets began to feel the growing impact of the Bolsheviks and left SRs. On January 13, 1918, the Third All-Russian Congress of Peasants' Deputies was held in Petrograd, having been convened by the Bolsheviks. At its first session, this Congress resolved to join with the All-Russian

Congress of Workers' and Soldiers' Deputies which had begun to operate on January 10. This speeded up the merger of the two systems of Soviets in the provinces—a process completed by March 1918. It was at this early stage, however, that some of the disadvantages to the Bolsheviks themselves of the Soviets as a form of power began to appear.

At the Second Congress of Soviets, which opened in Petrograd a matter of hours after the start of the armed insurrection in October, the Bolsheviks received more than fifty per cent of the votes. This made it easier for them to announce Soviet power to the country and to form a new government comprised at first of Bolsheviks alone. However, the Bolshevik influence was spread very unevenly over the country. They enjoyed overwhelming influence in the main industrial centres, but elsewhere, not only in some peasant regions but in entire provinces, their political position was extremely weak. In the grain-producing areas of the Volga region and the black earth centres, the SRs, of left and right, held sway; Georgia was under Menshevik influence, and in other Caucasian regions the bulk of the population favoured the various nationalist parties. The province of Yekaterinoslav in the Ukraine was witnessing a steady growth in the popularity of the Communist Anarchists, who were later to organize the resistance to German occupation in 1918. Theoretically, all the local organs were obliged to carry out the decrees and instructions handed down by the higher authorities of the Central Executive Committee headed by Sverdlov and the Council of People's Commissars headed by Lenin. In practice, the acceptance by local Soviets of the decisions of these bodies could not always be taken for granted.

From the outset, the Soviets had arisen not as generally representative organs; they were created by the workers themselves as a counterpoise to the State Duma and the Provisional Government. Hence there was no representation in the Soviets of the centrist or right-wing parties. Most of the monarchist parties of the right had collapsed long before October. The main bourgeois party, the Kadets, was declared illegal after the October Revolution. The Russian bourgeoisie dreaded the convocation of the Constituent Assembly since they were worried about strengthening the power of the SRs, but, by rejecting this Assembly, all radical agrarian reform, and peace talks with Germany, they insured that within a few months they would be faced not with an SR-Menshevik government but with the Bolsheviks.

The Soviets excluded from representation not only the bourgeoisie but all other sections of the 'non-working' population. Housewives and senior citizens went unrepresented, elections taking place only in workplaces and military units. The workers themselves were represented unevenly, to the disadvantage of the Bolsheviks. In Petrograd, for instance, huge factories elected only one person to represent thousands of workers on the Soviet whereas small businesses also had one representative, who might represent a work-force of only two or three hundred. This meant that the large works, accounting for eighty-five per cent of the workers in Petrograd—including the Bolsheviks' strongest supporters—had the same number of deputies as the small businesses employing only fifteen per cent. On the other hand, a large number of very small enterprises and tradesmen's workshops had no representation at all.

Before the Revolution, it had seemed to Lenin that in the Soviets the proletariat had a ready-made and simple state apparatus equipped to run the country *without a bureaucracy*. The Soviets did deal effectively with a string of local problems, guaranteeing law and order and reallocating living space in favour of working-class people. They were also adept at legislation, and in a very short time had passed a large number of normative acts that would form the basis of the new Soviet law. In this respect there was no friction between the Central Executive Committee and the Council of People's Commissars. As a matter of expediency, it was decided that any decrees passed by the latter body, which provided most of them, would become law before being confirmed by the CEC. Many of them, dealing with very urgent matters, needed no ratification. In any case the CEC was an unwieldy organ with representatives of more than one party and it could not be convened as rapidly as the CPC. However, although the Soviet executive committees, including the CEC, could get by with a minimum of supporting apparatus, the Council of People's Commissars could not, since this body carried the whole weighty burden of governing a huge country. The People's Commissariats needed civil servants and a large army of officials with administrative experience. Such people did not exist among the proletariat, so the Bolsheviks were compelled to offer employment in Soviet enterprises to large numbers of specialists and officials who had worked in the departments of the old regime. The apparatus of the Commissariats had constantly to be expanded since the new government was having to deal with problems that in capitalist countries were settled without government interference. The nationalization of industry and finance, for instance, necessitated the setting up of innumerable complex organs to control the various sections of the economy; these included Councils of National Economy, Central Directorates and Industrial Trusts. The slogan calling for armed insurrection was now replaced by a demand for a centralized Red Army, the leadership and provision of which required not only its own special Commissariat but a High Command and a Supreme Revolutionary Military Committee. The people's militia, responsible both to the local Soviets and the Commissariat for Home Affairs, soon needed assistance in the form of a special body to deal with the struggle against counter-revolution and speculation; this was the special commission known as the Cheka. Institutions that began as small concerns in the new government indulged in empire-building and their procedures began to smack of the red tape that Lenin abhorred. Although he did all he could to overcome these deficiences in the new executive machinery, he was later to admit that in the first five years of their power the Bolsheviks had not achieved much in the battle to defeat the 'fundamental internal evil' of bureaucracy.

The main disadvantage of the Soviets, however, arose from what had been their finest quality during the period when the Bolsheviks had been fighting for influence in these bodies and for power in the country. This was their ever-changing composition, their direct and strong dependence on the moods of the masses, which allowed the workers of a particular region or town when they felt like it to bring about substantial changes in the composition of the party and the leadership of the local Soviet. This turned out to be both the strength and the weakness of the Soviets. Under a parliamentary system, an assembly is elected for a four or five-year period and the electorate cannot recall any individual member before the completion of the term. Local authority organs are elected for a two-, three- or four-year period. The victorious party or coalition, with a mandate extending for several years, can set about its reforms and other measures, progressive or conservative, without worrying too much about the short-term impressions or discontent of the electorate. Not so the Soviets. The ease with which the masses could recall any deputy and call for new elections led to instability in their composition and leadership. Every Soviet had to maintain continuous popularity with the electorate or face the threat of dismissal.

For some weeks and months after the October Revolution, this did not worry the Bolsheviks. It was a time when their popularity, and that of the left SRs was increasing rapidly and perceptibly. The SRs and Mensheviks walked out of the Second Congress of Soviets as a protest against the overthrow of the Provisional Government, but they did not leave the Soviets themselves. Nevertheless, in November and December 1917, their influence was clearly on the wane. At the First All-Russian Congress of Workers' and Soldiers' Deputies in June 1917, a mere fourteen per cent of the deputies claimed allegiance to the Bolshevik Party. At the Second Congress of Soviets, about sixty per cent did so. At the Third, the Bolsheviks accounted for sixty-six or sixty-seven per cent and, together with the SRs who were at the time included in the CPC, they enjoyed a commanding majority. Of the 360 members elected to the CEC at the Third Congress, 160 were Bolsheviks, 125 left SRs and seven were SR maximalists; only seven right SRs were elected along with the three Communist Anarchists and two Menshevik-defencists.[34] The overall membership of the Bolshevik Party had also grown substantially; in fact it increased twentyfold and more during the course of 1917. However, these figures suggest a political success that was not to endure. Events connected with the costly and humiliating Peace of Brest-Litovsk soon caused most of the petty bourgeoisie and peasantry to desert the Bolshevik Party. Lenin himself referred to this Peace as 'an obscenity' and had to admit that the signing of it, with the consequent acknowledgment of defeat for Russia in the First World War, touched the patriotic feelings of the broad masses of the country's petty bourgeoisie. The Fourth Congress of Soviets, convened for the ratification of the Peace Treaty, appeared to count as a Bolshevik success, since they had seventy per cent of the votes, the others going to left SRs (twenty per cent) and right SRs, Mensheviks, Menshevik-Internationalists and even smaller groups (ten per cent in all). However, the urgency with which the Congress was called meant that many of the outlying provinces, and the Ukraine, went without representation. The left SRs, moreover, objected violently to the Peace of Brest-Litovsk and resigned from the Council of People's Commissars as soon as it was ratified. Many Communists also abstained from voting for it. There were, in fact, 1166 voting delegates, of whom 784 (sixty-seven per cent) voted for Lenin's resolution.[35]

Following the signing of this treaty, dissatisfaction with Soviet government policy continued to spread throughout the peasantry and the petty bourgeoisie. The peasants were incensed by the state monopoly of the market in grain and other foodstuffs, the maintenance of fixed purchasing prices and the ban on free trading. Glaring disagreement arose between the organs of central government and most of the rural Soviets, which rejected the activities of the Food Commissariat, insisted on repeal of the grain monopoly and refused assistance to the grain requisitioners sent out from the cities. On the other hand, the urban population was expressing its dissatisfaction with the worsening economic hardships of unemployment, inflation and food rationing. By Mary 1918, many cities in the industrial zone were faced with actual starvation. All of this led to an increase in anti-Bolshevik propaganda from the SRs and Mensheviks and intensified criticism from the left SRs, whose influence on the mass of the population now began to grow. These groups were in control of many of the Soviets, not only outlying ones or those in odd towns here and there, but also a number of regional Soviets, such as the Executive Committee of the Samara *guberniya* and the city of Balashov in the Saratov *oblast*. Pressure from the mass of the people was so strong that some regional Soviets actually abolished the dictatorship of the People's Commissariat of Supply and declared their own territories free trade areas. It was this popular dissatisfaction in many regions, particularly in the countryside, that made it easy for opponents of the Bolsheviks to organize armed rebellion against them, including new uprisings in the Cossack provinces and in the Czechoslovak corps, and, subsequently, revolts led by the left SRs. Bolshevik-controlled territory was contracting rapidly and by the end of 1918 it amounted to about one-twentieth of the old Tsarist Empire. Even on this territory the Bolsheviks were not always masters of the Soviets, particularly those in rural regions and out-of-the-way places.

The Bolsheviks responded to this threat to their power not only by closing ranks but by tightening up the methods of the dictatorship of the proletariat. The excessive democratism of the Soviets ran counter to this dictatorship, and so, in the summer of 1918, the Bolsheviks took steps to restructure them. On June 14, the CEC voted to expel from its ranks all SRs of the right and centre, and Mensheviks; it also recommended 'that the Soviets of Workers', Soldiers' and Peasants' Deputies should also dismiss the representatives of these factions from their ranks'.[36] This proposal was supported even by the leaders of the left SRs, though within a month the same thing had happened to them. After the critical events of July 6, when the left SR revolt in Moscow ended in defeat, the Fourth All-Russian Congress expelled their leaders from the Soviets. As for the less influential but extremely vigorous Anarchists, their activities had been declared illegal as early as April 1918.

In the countryside, Soviet power had been undermined or completely replaced by committees of the poor which were being set up in villages and settlements on a *volost*-wide basis. The decree concerning these committees was passed on June 11, 1918, though their establishment on a mass scale began in mid-July. By autumn they had spread all over the Russian Federation and numbered about 100,000. They served as organs of local authority, and their leadership was entrusted to local Bolshevik Party organizations or working-class leaders of the grain requisitioners sent out from the cities. An encyclopaedia article on the subject reads, in part, as follows: 'By controlling the activities of the lower Soviets and sometimes taking them over when they were not carrying out their proper duties, the committees of the poor did much to purge the Soviets of class enemies and elements hostile to Soviet power. All these measures effectively undermined the economic basis of kulak power and facilitated the strengthening of the alliance between the working class and the toiling peasantry... The Sixth All-Russian Congress of Soviets, on November 9 1918, resolved to call for new elections to the rural Soviets and entrusted the direct running of them to the committees of the poor. Once this task was completed the committees were reorganized in late 1918 and early 1919 and merged with the Soviets.'[37]

Thus it came about that, by late summer 1918, the Bolsheviks were effectively the only party in the Soviets. They had survived a political crisis and strengthened their authority in central Russia. In the autumn, the Bolshevik-inspired Red Army won a series of notable victories over its opponents. The SR and Menshevik authorities could not hold out against the Bolshevik onslaught, but there were many other counter-revolutionary elements surviving from the vast Tsarist Empire that had been. There were landowners and noblemen who had been robbed of their estates and privileges, capitalists who had lost their factories and businesses, tens of thousands of army officers, ex-gendarmes and once-prosperous Cossacks. The cause of counter-revolution enjoyed widespread support abroad, from the Kaiser's Germany and the countries of the *Entente* to the USA and Japan. These forces had managed to organize themselves by the autumn of 1918, and the petty-bourgeois parties and groups then took a back seat. The volunteer army under Denikin was widening its activities in the Kuban and, on the Don, General Krasnov's government had assumed power. In Siberia, Admiral Kolchak and his supporters dispersed the SR 'Provisional Government' and seized power in the East. Now the Civil War assumed the character of a struggle between the Bolshevik-led Soviet government and the counter-revolutionary force of generals and landowners. This brought about a shift in social strengths throughout the country. The middle peasants may have opposed the Bolshevik policy on food supplies but they certainly did not want the bourgeoisie and landowners to return. In the autumn of 1918, therefore, the middle peasants swung heavily to the Bolsheviks and Soviet power, with the effect of removing all support and authority from the SR and Menshevik parties. The Central Committee of the Menshevik Party announced a cessation of armed opposition to Soviet power in October 1918. Then, on October 30, the CEC revoked its resolution excluding Mensheviks from its ranks. This was followed on February 26, 1919, by a similar revocation of the resolution affecting the right and centre SRs. Even then these parties, once they had resumed their places on the Council, formed only an insignificant minority.

With a view to strengthening the position of the working class and the Bolsheviks within the Soviets, the Bolsheviks repudiated in form and in practice the principle of equal and universal suffrage. The representatives of the former landowning class and the bourgeoisie, former activists in the Tsarist regime, ministers of religion and wealthy peasants who had used hired labour were all disfranchised. Even those who retained the vote were a long way from enjoying equal electoral rights, since the Constitution adopted in 1918 gave a clear advantage to the working-class. For elections to the All-Russian Congress of Soviets, in the cities, one deputy was elected to represent 25,000 voters. (The election of these deputies took place at sessions of the city Soviets which, in the larger cities, were themselves elected by district Soviets, the deputies of these latter bodies being elected at their workplaces.) At the provincial Congresses of Soviets, one deputy was returned to the All-Russian Congress for every 125,000 voters. But not even elections at province or district level were conducted on a basis of equality. At district (*oblast'*) level, the norm was one deputy for every 25,000 voters in the country but one deputy for every 1,000-5,000 voters in the towns. At provincial (*guberniya*) level, the advantage to townspeople was one deputy to 1,000-2,000 voters as compared with the country people's one deputy to 1,000-10,000 inhabitants. This graded electoral system was biased in favour of the workers by a factor of about 5:1 and, as far as the All-Russian Soviet was concerned, nearer 10:1.

By late 1918, the position of the Soviet government had been strengthened partly by a series of victories on the Civil War fronts and also because of the ending of the German occupation of the western regions. Germany had lost the war and accepted a peace treaty with the countries of the *Entente*. In Germany itself a bourgeois-democratic revolution had broken out. The Soviet government took it upon itself to annul the Peace of Brest-Litovsk. Although the victory of the Red Army was by now assured, the Civil War in Russia was to drag on for a further two years, for a number of reasons and with many ups and downs, until the end of 1920. Working outwards from the dependable central regions, the Bolsheviks, by a colossal effort of will, rid the country of the White armies, gradually liberating the vast territories in the south and east, north and west of what had once been the Tsarist Empire. Virtually nowhere in these liberated regions were circumstances propitious for free elections to the Soviets. The Bolshevik organizations were emerging much enfeebled from their underground position. Many of the areas concerned were to remain front-line zones for some time and thus required particularly firm control. In most cases, accordingly, a Revolutionary Committee (*revkom*) rather than a Soviet was set up. These were often staffed not by the local inhabitants but by Communists nominated by the Red Army operating through its political or civil government sections. The same occurred in the other nationalities and the outlying regions, which were as a rule politically backward by comparison with the central districts. Revolutionary Committees were set up in most of the Cossack regions and in the Southern Ukraine when Bolshevik influence was especially thin.

In many instances the *revkom* was appointed for a relatively short period in order to prepare for elections to the Soviet which would then take over power. On the other hand, given the conditions of the Civil War, many of them necessarily continued to exist for some time, from a few months to several years. When there were military activities in the locality, the *revkom* generally occupied itself with military matters but it also had to deal with all sorts of other questions which elsewhere were matters for the Soviet. In the national regions, Revolutionary Committees were often set up to control the whole territory. There was, for instance, a *revkom* for the Tatar district, one for Chuvash, one for Georgia, one for Abkhazia and another for Karelia. For a short time, Revolutionary Committees were set up on a district- or province-wide basis in Russia itself, as in Samara, where the *revkom* was set up on the orders of the officer commanding the Ural-Orenburg front, replacing the existing executive committee with its surviving SR majority. These committees for a time took control of the whole districts of Penza and Yaroslave and even the whole of the Ukraine, Belorussia and Siberia, though it was more common for them to confine their activities to a much smaller territory. On the Don, for instance, in 1920, about 500 of them were operating, a similar number were functioning on the Terek, in the Kuban-Chernomorsk region there were about 700 and a hundred or so controlled the region of Stavropol.[38] In the Cossack regions Revolutionary Committees took control not only of every village but even of the larger farms. There were particularly large numbers of them in the Central Asian region formerly known as Turkestan.

Nowadays Soviet researchers admit that the Revolutionary Committees, appointed as they were rather than elected, were undemocratic organs of government and therefore represented a 'narrowing down' of democracy, but it is claimed that they became an inalienable part of the Soviet state apparatus during the Civil War because the proletariat was so weak and the Bolshevik influence had yet to penetrate properly into large regions of the old Tsarist Empire. An example of this is seen in the comments of N.F. Bugay: 'The influence of Muslim reaction in Central Asia, the Volga region, the North Caucasus and Trans-Caucasia, the weakness in these areas of the proletarian sector and the absence of staff to run the Soviet apparatus, the furious battle against counter-revolution...the pointlessness of returning to the organs of power created during the triumphal procession of Soviet power but now defiled in many places by representatives of the petty-bourgeois parties and nationalistic, kulak and mullah elements also dictated the necessity of setting up Revolutionary Committees. Thus the setting up of Revolutionary Committees was in the interests of asserting and reinforcing the dictatorship of the proletariat in conditions of civil war, military intervention and furious opposition from the exploiting classes which had been overthrown though not yet wiped out.'[39] It is clear that the Revolutionary Committees were the undisguised imposition of power by a revolutionary minority. The idea was to eliminate them as soon as military activities had ceased and the Civil War was over. In January 1920 a resolution of the Soviet of Workers' and Peasants' Defence abolished district and provincial Revolutionary Committees and other 'parallel' organs of power—war commissariats, special executive committees and the like—in the central regions of Russia.[40] After the removal of the White armies from the bulk of the country in the summer of 1920, Lenin asked, in a letter addressed to the People's Commissar for Justice, D. Kursky, whether steps had been taken '1. to establish Soviet power in the liberated regions, 2. to convene Congresses of the Soviets, 3. to expel the landowners and distribute their lands partly among the poor peasants and partly to the Soviets of farm-labourers.'[41] Down in the Crimea, however, and in the Ukraine, the North Caucasus and TransCaucasia, the committees continued to exist in 1921, and in places like Siberia, Stavropol, Central Asia and the Far East they were not abolished until 1925-28.

Towards the end of 1920, the Civil War ended with decisive victory for the Bolsheviks. Throughout the territory of the old Russian Empire, except for Poland, Georgia and Finland, which had become independent, and the Far East, where the battle was not yet won, Soviet power was established. In the summer of that year, with a Bolshevik victory in the Civil War virtually assured, the English philosopher Bertrand Russell, a keen supporter of Fabian Socialism, visited the Soviet Union. His prime intention was to familiarize himself with the workings of the Soviets which, according to Communist claims, were far more democratic than, for example, the British parliamentary system. Russell was bitterly disappointed. Here is part of his account of the visit:

'Before I went to Russia I imagined that I was going to see an interesting experiment in a new form of representative government. I did see an interesting experiment, but not in representative government. Every one who is interested in Bolshevism knows the series of elections, from the village meeting to the All-Russian Soviet, by which the people's commissaries are supposed to derive their power. We were told that, by the recall, the occupational constituencies, and so on, a new and far more perfect machinery had been devised for ascertaining and registering the popular will. One of the things we hoped to study was the question whether the Soviet system is really superior to Parliamentarism in this respect.

'We were not able to make any such study, because the Soviet system is moribund. No conceivable system of free election would give majorities to the Communists, either in town or country. Various methods are therefore adopted for giving the victory to Government candidates. In the first place, the voting is by show of hands, so that all who vote against the Government are marked men. In the second place, no candidate who is not a Communist can have any printing done, the printing works being all in the hands of the State. In the third place, he cannot address any meetings, because the halls all belong to the State. The whole of the press is, of course, official; no independent daily is permitted. In spite of all these obstacles, the Mensheviks have succeeded in winning about 40 seats out of 1,500 on the Moscow Soviet, by being known in certain large factories where the electoral campaign could be conducted by word of mouth...

'But although the Moscow Soviet is nominally sovereign in Moscow, it is really only a body of electors who choose the Executive Committee of forty, out of which, in turn, is chosen the Praesidium, consisting of nine men who have all the power. The Moscow Soviet, as a whole, meets rarely; the Executive Committee is supposed to meet once a week, but did not meet while we were in Moscow. The Praesidium, on the contrary, meets daily. Of course, it is easy for the Government to exercise pressure over the election of the Executive Committee, and again over the election of the Praesidium. It must be remembered that effective protest is impossible, owing to the absolutely complete suppression of free speech and free Press. The result is that the Praesidium of the Moscow Soviet consists only of orthodox Communists...I saw a meeting of the Gubernia Soviet of Saratov. The representation is so arranged that the town workers have an enormous preponderance over the surrounding peasants; but even allowing for this, the proportion of peasants seemed astonishingly small for the centre of a very important agricultural area.'[42]

Russell's visit took place in mid-1920, before the defeat of Wrangel and the Polish-Soviet war, which many people consider to have been the last battles of the Civil War and the *Entente* campaign. It was immediately after these events, when the English philosopher was safely back home, that a new, profound crisis began, the most serious one yet in the all too brief history of the Soviet state. Soviet power itself was under threat.

The very first economic measures adopted in the second half of 1920 in connection with the recovery of the home economy showed clearly that the Bolsheviks were not about to change their economic policy; on the contrary, they saw it as determining the general line of their programme for the building of a socialist society in Russia. This led to an ever-increasing hostility towards the Bolsheviks on the part of the peasants and petty bourgeoisie, and indeed from some of the workers. At the time, the Menshevik and SR (right and centre) Parties were allowed representation on the Soviets along with the left SRs, and they enjoyed the right to elect others and even be elected themselves to the leadership of bodies governing the Soviet state. They had all supported the Bolsheviks during the Civil War period of 1919-20 but they could not possibly support them now in their unchanging economic policy. They were joined in opposition by many ex-Mensheviks and SRs who had transferred allegiance to the Bolsheviks during the war. Within the Bolshevik

Party itself, new factions were formed, demanding a radically new approach to economic policy.

The protests made against the economic policy known as 'War Communism' took several different forms. All over the country there were outbursts of disaffection from the peasants amounting sometimes to out-and-out insurrection. Elsewhere in the provinces, the disaffection rose to such a point that the working masses began to exploit the very convenient form of popular representation provided by the Soviets in order to put pressure on the Bolshevik Party. This was the time when new slogans appeared, such as 'The Soviets without Communists' or 'The Soviets without Bolsheviks', and when it seemed sensible not to reject the Soviets and Soviet power as such but to make use of the electoral system to send new deputies to the Soviets, mainly from Menshevik and SR ranks. In 1921, the Menshevik Party Central Committee required its members to 'become involved actively in elections to Workers' Soviets and in the work of the Soviets themselves'.[43] Fyodor Dan, the leader of the Party, later recalled: 'free elections to the Soviets as a first step towards replacing the dictatorship by democratic rule—that was our everyday political slogan.'[44]

The same policy was adopted by the Socialist Revolutionaries. A right SR resolution adopted on February 15, 1920, on the subject of the election to the Moscow Soviet, states: 'Do participate in the election. Where it is possible to display the Party roll, display prominently a list of those in prison. In other places our candidates to be presented with no party affiliation.'[45] The organization of the left SRs, operating underground because of its weakened condition, also made an attempt to put forward candidates without party allegiance. After the Kronstadt uprising, with its motto 'The Soviets without Communists', the same tactic was adopted not only by the Kadets but also by certain monarchist groups. For instance, a modest little *émigré* journal, the mouthpiece of an organization describing itself as 'The All-Russian Monarchist Council', wrote at the beginning of 1923: 'Our *émigré* community must appreciate that the local Soviets, purged of Communists and scum working against the people, now contain a genuinely creative force capable of reconstructing Russia. This faith in the creativity of the truly Russian, popular and profoundly Christian Soviets must become a property of our *émigré* community. Those who cannot bring themselves to believe in this will sever their ties with the real, living Russia.'[46]

The Bolsheviks were faced with an extremely difficult problem. Their first, mistaken reaction to events in many districts was to impose further limitations on eligibility for the Soviets and to extend infinitely the categories of citizens barred from participation in them as electors or candidates. To take one example, in mid-March 1920, G. Petrovsky, Chairman of the Ukrainian Central Executive Committee, put his signature to a document entitled 'Supplementary Instructions on Elections to the Soviets', which included these directions: 'Categories of people disfranchised shall now include anyone whose activities have discredited him in relation to the revolution, irrespective of whether he actually comes into a category of undisputed disfranchisement. Such people may include working-class elements who have branded themselves by overtly kulak-style activities or by active pronouncements against Soviet power...betrayers of the Ukrainian peasantry, lackeys of the Polish gentry and gangsters of all kinds.'[47] In the Ukraine, where the Civil War had been waged in its most complex and embittered form, limitations such as these could, in many districts, have disfranchised most of the working rural population. And yet, even with the benefit of them, the Bolsheviks were not very successful in elections to the Soviets. For this reason the committees of the poor (or 'committees of independent peasants' as they were called in Ukrainian) were retained there even into 1920. The Chairman of the Ukrainian Council of People's Commissars, Rakovsky, said in a speech to the Fourth All-Ukrainian Congress of Soviets: 'Comrades!... We saw in advance that, in order to bring in new land laws in the countryside, and new laws on grain-sharing, it would be necessary to create a buttress for Soviet power. You will ask me, "Are not the Soviets, the rural and district executive committees, this revolutionary buttress?" Comrades, let's face it, for a long time to come the Soviets in the Ukraine will remain organs of the middle peasantry and the rural poor.'[48] Rakovsky's testimony indicated that not only the Soviets but even the Revolutionary Committees had fallen under 'kulak' influence. Actually, this was soon to apply even to many of the committees of the poor. The Ukrainian and Russian countryside was clearly slipping out of the control of the Bolshevik Party and the central organs of Soviet government.

By the winter of 1920-21, it had become clear that the 'lower orders' did not want to go on living in the old way. But the 'upper echelons' (of the Bolshevik Party, that is) maintained the possibility and capability of taking everyone in a new direction. They made an abrupt U-turn now known as the New Economic Policy (NEP), and this enormous concession to the peasantry soon brought an end to the rural uprisings. There were, however, no political concessions in NEP. Towards one or two non-Bolshevik groups, such as Volte-Face, Lenin considered it possible to adopt a more liberal policy, but as far as the SRs and Mensheviks were concerned, NEP meant not concessions of any kind but a severance of all co-operation and a strengthening of political persecution. Although they were now willing to accept many economic proposals from these parties, at the same time the Bolsheviks tightened the political screws on all their closest political rivals. They were afraid that, under NEP conditions, the SRs and Mensheviks might be able to exploit the Bolsheviks' self-criticism and thus strengthen their own political positions and come to power via the Soviets. It is no easy matter to assess whether they were justified in these forebodings. It seems probable now that neither the Socialist Revolutionaries nor the Mensheviks could ever have gained power, though they might have played a useful role as a constructive opposition. Having survived another crisis, however, Lenin and his fellow-Bolsheviks now feared any kind of opposition, even from within their own Party. And so, in 1921 and 1922, they mounted yet another onslaught against the SRs and the Mensheviks, who were summarily expelled from the Soviets and all other bodies, even those without formal party affiliation. The Bolsheviks were now on course for the total prohibition of legal activity by all other parties, in other words, for one-party dictatorship. All SR and Menshevik activities now counted as counter-revolution. During the first purge of his own Party, Lenin recommended particularly harsh treatment of any ex-Mensheviks and SRs who had transferred allegiance to the Bolsheviks in the period 1917-21. By the end of 1922, the Soviets had lost all claim to be described as multi-party organizations. Within them, the Bolsheviks had now become not the dominant party but the only one.

The Soviets Under a One-Party Dictatorship

The period from 1921 to 1926 saw the abolition of Revolutionary Committees and other temporary bodies and the restoration to power of the Soviets all over Russia. In 1924, the state adopted a new Constitution. The economy had taken an upward turn under NEP and, as a result, political tensions had been dissipated. Many of the limitations on electoral eligibility for the Soviets were abolished and the numbers of the disfranchised were reduced. However, now that they were a one-party system, the Soviets underwent considerable changes in their situation and functions. They were no longer a battle arena for settling inter-party disputes and displaying political platforms. Elections to the Soviets began to lose their political character, since the only party involved in them was the Communist Party. Organizations that had been created directly by the whole work-force and had stood *above* all party differences, representing only various groups of working people, were now in practice reduced to a role that subordinated them to the Communist Party alone. Where earlier the various parties had had to fight it out in the Soviets in order to gain influence and leadership, now these organs were limited to conducting the decisions of the Party leadership to the working masses. Stalin stated baldly that the only controlling force under the dictatorship of the proletariat was the Communist Party, 'the vanguard of the proletariat, its forward troops'. Stalin looked upon the Soviets as 'levers' or 'drive-belts' useful to the Party for directing the country with its basically non-Party population. What was worse, even in this sytem, he assigned the Soviets to a position of secondary importance, after the trade unions. He wrote: 'And what are these "drive-belts" or "levers" under the system of the dictatorship of the proletariat?... They are, in the first place, the workers' trade unions... In the second place, they are the Soviets with their numerous ramifications at the centre of things and in the provinces, in the form of administrative, economic, military, cultural and other organizations of state, plus the innumerable unauthorized mass alliances of workers surrounding these organizations and uniting them with the population. The Soviets are mass organizations of all the workers in town and country. They are not party organizations. The Soviets are a direct expression of the dictatorship of the proletariat. Each and every measure for the reinforcement of the dictatorship of the proletariat and the building of socialism must pass through the Soviets. Through them is realized the leadership of the peasantry by the workers. The Soviets unite millions of toiling people with the vanguard of the proletariat.'[49]

Even in their new form, the Soviets were not always 'on top' functioning as 'drive belts' for the proletarian dictatorship. In the period of Stalinist collectivization and liquidation of the kulaks, and in the difficult early years of the first Five Year Plan, most of the rural Soviets reflected the mood of the rural population in their inability to cope with many of Stalin's demands. This is why they were, in practical terms, replaced by arbitrarily appointed bodies invested with extraordinary powers: the political sections of the machinery and tractor stations. Within a year or two, however, the situation with regard to the rural Soviets had been 'put right'.

There is no need to go into the trivial changes that occurred throughout the 1920s, and in the early 1930s, in the Soviets. We cannot, however, overlook the radical transformations of the forms of Soviet power brought about by the Constitution adopted in 1936. These new forms have remained virtually unchanged until the present day. The first innovation was a complete change in the system of elections to the Soviets. All of them, from the smallest to the largest, were now to be elected not according to workplace but on the basis of territory. Elections, which had been unequal, indirect and organized on a show of hands, would now become equal, direct and based on a secret ballot. All previous limitations of the franchise were abolished except in the case of criminals and lunatics. The system of All-Union Congresses of Soviets, elected irregularly and with a composition that varied, was replaced by the Supreme Soviet of the USSR, to be elected every four (nowadays five) years and consisting of two chambers: the Soviet of Nationalities and the Soviet of the Union. The same system was to apply also to the other Republics in the USSR. The remaining Soviets, in districts, towns and regions, would be elected for shorter periods. The electorate in all constituencies retained the right to recall any deputy. Further details of the Constitution of the USSR and the laws on elections to the various grades of Soviet are irrelevant to our present purpose.

The present-day Supreme Soviet in some respects resembles the parliaments of Western countries. One main distinction has been retained, however. The only party allowed representation in any of our Soviets is the Communist Party or, as it is more customary to say, the bloc of Communist and unaligned members. Moreover, in every constituency—and this is in accordance with the Constitution and electoral law—at all levels only one candidate may be registered for election to the Soviet. Thus there is no choice even between candidates of the same party, or between a Communist and an unaligned candidate. The elections have lost all spirit of competition, and the Soviets still remain not so much independent organs of state as 'drive-belts' or 'levers' for the use of the Party leadership. It is not the Supreme Soviet even, but the Central Committee of the Communist Party that issues the main directives for the Council of Ministers and the more important ministries. All laws are ratified in the first instance by plenary sessions of the Party Central Committee, after which they proceed to the Supreme Soviet. The Praesidium of the Supreme Soviet, which acts as the highest organ of state between sessions of the Supreme Soviet itself, is entirely subordinate to the Central Committee of the Party and its directives. The Supreme Soviet meets only twice a year, usually for not more than two or three days. It hears no speeches *against* the issues raised for discussion; its proceedings are a formality. The USSR provides no right for political minorities to form their own organizations or parties, and thus there is no danger that a person or group of persons might emerge within the Supreme Soviet to act as a legally acceptable opposition to the ruling Party. This single circumstance is what renders the existing Soviet system unacceptable to most Western countries. In the West, freedom is looked upon primarily as freedom for political minorities, for dissidents, for opposition. The Communist parties themselves belong to that opposition. The majority parties in Western countries, those who form the governments, are obviously 'free', which is why the true criterion of freedom in the West remains freedom for minority political opinion and disagreement, the right of free speech for everyone, not excluding dissidents and minorities.

 Democratic freedoms even in Western countries are, of course, circumscribed in many ways. The parliamentary and electoral systems have their own limitations. Under the majority system employed in the USA, United Kingdom, India and elsewhere there are many parties which never have a chance to send a member to parliament because they cannot achieve the greatest share of the votes in any single constituency. The system of proportional representation is therefore considered to be more democratic, since it allows for the seats to be apportioned between the parties, once the votes are in, according to the percentages of votes polled. The voting itself is carried out in very large constituencies presenting lists of candidates from the various parties. But this system too has its limitations. In West Germany, for instance, any party obtaining less than five per cent of the total vote is deprived of representation either in the Federal Parliament or in the parliaments of any of the Länder. This bars the doors against relatively small parties and political groups. Proportional representation operates in Italy, in Belgium (in a modified form) and several other Western countries. For all the shortcomings of the present systems of representation in the West, they not only allow for opposition but take it for granted that opposition will exist, including Communist opposition to a bourgeois government. This makes the parliamentary system preferable to the present system of Soviets in the USSR, as far as the mass of the people in the West are concerned. These people have long forgotten that it is theoretically possible under the Soviet system for there to be opposition and free competition between different parties or that even bourgeois parties, as Lenin himself pointed out, could retain the vote even under the dictatorship of the proletariat. This is part of the history of the Soviets in 1917 but it is not now remembered. People in the West, when they think of the Soviets, link them inextricably with the ones they see nowadays in the USSR.

*Communist Parties Abroad
and the Slogan of the Soviets*

The Soviets played an important role and were used as a practical slogan in the policy documents of all Communist parties in the 1920s. The new slogan proposed in 1923 by the Comintern, 'Workers' and Peasants' Government' was not meant to supersede this emphasis on the Soviets. A resolution passed by the Fifth Congress of the Comintern exlained that 'the formula "Workers' and Peasants' Government", born out of the Russian Revolution, is not and cannot be anything other than a method of agitation and mobilization of the masses for the revolutionary overthrow of the bourgeoisie and the setting up of a Soviet order'[50]. The Comintern Programme adopted in 1928, at the Sixth Congress, included a special section on the Soviets beginning with these words: 'The most expedient form of state power, as has been shown by the experience of the October 1917 Revolution and the Hungarian Revolution, which vastly extended the experience of the Paris Commune of 1871, consists in a new type of state differing in principle from a bourgeois state not only in its class nature but also in its internal structure, namely the type known as the Soviet state. This is the type which, because it grows directly out of the broadest possible mass movement of workers, guarantees the greatest activity of the masses and consequently the greatest certainty of eventual victory.'[51]

As it happened, however, the revolutionary movement was on the wane. Sporadic outbursts of armed rebellion in such places as Bulgaria (1923), Saxony (1923), Estonia (1924) and Vienna (1927) were quickly put down without establishing any durable organs of revolutionary power. The Chinese Revolution of 1925-27 also ended in defeat; but after the revolutionary movement in the larger cities had been quelled and the Canton Commune had collapsed, Communist-controlled Soviets did begin to spring up here and there. The first of these were established by the celebrated P'eng P'ac in the Hai-feng and Lu-feng districts of the Kwangtung province. The 'Hai-Lu-feng Soviet Republic' lasted only three months, but, in the spring of 1928, small 'Soviet Republics' began to arise in many regions of South, Central and North-West China. By the beginning of 1931, there were about ten Soviet regions with several million inhabitants. In November 1931, the capital of the Central Soviet zone, the town of Jui-chin in the province of Kiangsi, acted as host to the First All-China Congress of Soviets. This Congress passed a number of laws, including one on land and labour, considered a draft constitution for the Soviet regions, and elected an overall Provisional Soviet Government whose chairman was Mao Tse Tung. This body was given the Russian-style title of 'Council of People's Commissars' and invested with executive and legislative powers.

The development of Soviet regions in China occurred in a context of furious civil war against the forces of Chiang Kai-shek's Kuomintang government. At the height of this development, the Soviet regions occupied a territory of 550-600,000 square kilometres and served a population of 50-60,000,000. It soon became clear, however, that under the conditions of a war of manoeuvre, with its hit-and-run guerilla activity and dispersal of forces, the main buttress of revolutionary power would have to be the army rather than the Soviet. An attempt by leading Chinese Communists to create a permanent territory of Soviet China in the central zone, defended by orthodox static warfare, came to nothing. The Chinese Red Army could not withstand the Kuomintang 'Sixth Campaign' and was ousted from the central Soviet zone, taking the very difficult escape route to the North-East. Between autumn 1935 and autumn 1936, the surviving sections of the Red Army, nine-tenths of which had been destroyed, rallied in the area conjoining the provinces of Shensi and Kansu, the only surviving Soviet region. At the same time, Japan, having marched in and occupied large sections of Northern China, was now mounting an attack intended to seize the whole of the country. The battle for national liberation became the first priority for the Chinese people. The Kuomintang and the Chinese Communist Party arranged a truce, whereupon the CCP adopted the slogan of the Soviets and began confiscating private lands. The Soviet region of Shensi-Kansu was redesignated a Special Region and the remaining units of the Red Army were called the Eighth Army. The Soviets were reorganized into democratic consultative assemblies involving the co-operation of patriotic members of the bourgeoisie and even the landed class. Victory over Japan soon followed and, although the political situation in China changed again with a renewal of civil war against the Kuomintang, the slogan of the Soviets remained immovable.

It proved equally immovable during the anti-fascist battle for liberation in Western and Central Europe. The war against Hitler's occupying forces took on a national character and involved the participation of all political parties—except the fascists—working together. Naturally, the primary slogan was national liberation and the re-establishment of democracy. This meant a return to existing democratic institutions in the West, but not in all cases to the old order as such. It must be remembered that the victory over fascism was followed by the liquidation of monarchist regimes in Italy,

Romania, Bulgaria and Yugoslavia. Many already existing democratic institutions were reorganized with the aim of broadening the workers' representation. The countries of Eastern and South-Eastern Europe set up new forms of power called 'People's Democracies', very different in character from the revolutionary Soviets that had arisen, for example, in Russia in 1917 and 1918. The liberation of Czechoslovakia was followed by the establishment there of a parliamentary republic, with supreme power invested in the National Assembly, on the basis of universal suffrage and a secret ballot. The Communist Party polled most of the votes in the first election, formed the first 'Constituent National Assembly', won control of the national committees in the provinces and in 1946, provided the first government, led by Klement Gottwald.

The parliamentary system came into its own in the capitalist countries of the West following the Second World War, and the suffrage was extended to include women, young people and other disfranchised groups. In the countries freed from occupation, Communists took an active part in reconstructing the parliamentary system and in many cases their influence began to increase substantially. Demands for the replacement of 'outmoded' parliamentarism by soviets, and of democratic parliamentary republics by republics of soviets, were so obviously at variance with the moods and feelings of the toiling masses that a re-examination of the policy documents of Communist parties was begun even during Stalin's lifetime and with his tacit approval. These changes were often referred to in the political jargon of the day as 'the creative development of Leninism by Stalin'. the most interesting example occurred in Great Britain. In this country, the Communist Party had in 1935 adopted a new programme entitled *For a Soviet Britain,* but the slogan could not be maintained in post-war Britain. It was officially removed in 1951, and the new programme bore the title *The British Road to Socialism.* This programme rejected as 'a fiction by the enemies of socialism' the idea that the aim of the British Communist Party was 'the establishment of soviet power in Britain and the abolition of the parliamentary system'. The programme continued: 'Britain will take its own road to socialism... British Communists maintain that the people of Britain can convert a capitalist democracy into a genuine people's democracy by changing a parliament which has grown up as a result of Britain's historical struggle for democracy into a democratic weapon, the will of the vast majority of her people.'[52]

The demand for the setting up of soviets has by now been excluded from the policy documents of every Communist party in the developed capitalist world. They all emphasize, by contrast, that in the event of their coming to power, Communists will preserve all the main democratic institutions of the country concerned and guarantee the continued existence and voting rights of all parties including those opposed to socialism. The Italian Communist Party, for example, invariably emphasizes its allegiance to the democratic constitution adopted by the country in 1947. One of the resolutions passed by the Eighth Party Congress in 1956 includes the following comment: 'Modern conditions are such that violence ... can be avoided through the active support of democratic institutions by the overwhelming majority of the population... working on the basis of the developing international and domestic situation, the Communist Party reaffirms its position and declares that in Italy the essential conditions exist for the working class, *within the framework of constitutional order,* to organize itself into the ruling class by uniting the great majority of the people around a programme of socialist reform for society and the state.'[53] The Communist Party of Great Britain adopted a programme in 1977 which includes this clear statement: 'All democratic parties, including those opposed to socialism, must be guaranteed political rights and the right to contest general elections. The propagation of racist opinions will, however, be banned... The workers' movement, including the Communist Party, declares that it will accept the will of the electorate and that a left-wing government would, in the case of defeat at the polls, renounce power.'[54] One of the resolutions of the 22nd Congress of the Communist Party of Luxemburg speaks as follows: 'By virtue of the sound democratic and parliamentary traditions of our people, the democratic-parliamentary form of state can become an acceptable basis for the working class to find its way into power and construct socialism. The prerequisites for this bloodless road to socialism are close contact between all levels of the toiling people under the leadership of the working class, the exploitation of all parliamentary and non-parliamentary forms of struggle and the firm determination of the people to destroy in embryo any attempts by the forces of reaction to narrow down democracy or abolish it and even resort to force and sabotage in their resistance to socialist legality. The democratic road to socialism does not, however, exclude the possibility of embittered social and political confrontations with the forces of the old, outlived order. Even under the present regime, democratic institutions, rights and freedoms must be reformed and improved. Parliament must become the genuinely sovereign legislative and executive organ expressing the will of the people.'[55]

It goes without saying that this new political direction is extremely remote from the experience of the Russian Soviets. This in no way indicates that the Bolshevik experiment was wrong. The errors committed by them were many, but the slogan 'All Power to the Soviets' was absolutely relevant to the circumstances of Russia in 1917. It remains equally true, however, that the Soviets arose and developed in our country under certain specific conditions— conditions totally different from those obtaining today in the developed capitalist countries. The experience of the Soviet Union is not to be neglected, but we can see clearly from the example of the Soviets that uncritical acceptance of many of the basic tenets of Leninism and automatic application of them to other times and other conditions do not make sense.

4
Majority and Minority in Revolution

The Central Problem of Democracy

Not every political system, nor every political party, nor every politician, has agonized over problems concerning the role and the will of the majority in political and social life. Aristocracies and authoritarian regimes without number have proclaimed the absolute necessity of preserving the privilege and power of a minority—a hereditary nobility, priesthood, clergy or a particular caste or class of people—to the detriment of the majority of the population, and, in particular, its lower strata, which had no say at all in settling questions of national significance. Even today, many countries with authoritarian regimes and many ideologists and politicians continue the attempt to justify the advantages of authoritarian government over democracy. The twentieth century has not only retained a fair number of overtly aristocratic or authoritarian regimes, it has actually spawned new ones in which elitism in its most refined form combines with egalitarianism at its most primitive.

In her *Five Ideas That Change the World,* Barbara Ward refers to nationalism, industrialism, colonialism, communism and internationalism.[1] It seems strange that she should have omitted democracy, which had a great influence on many of the most significant events of the eighteenth and nineteenth centuries and continues to influence the twentieth. In their delineation of forms of government, students of politics generally examine problems such as the apportionment of legislative and executive power, civil rights, the range of citizens' political and economic opportunities and freedoms, the nature of legislation, the role of electoral organs, the character of the judiciary, and so on. The concept of democracy, or government by the people, however, requires us to evaluate the rights and opportunities enjoyed respectively by the majority and the minority of the people.

At a superficial glance, this does not seem a complex problem. In a democratic order, the majority decides and the minority, while submitting to these decisions, retains the right to freedom of opinion and expression as well as freedom of assembly and organization. A genuine democracy will permit neither the minority nor the majority to tyrannize the rest of the population. In practice, these questions turn out to be infinitely more complicated. Even more complicated are the problems of the majority and the minority in a society faced with the crisis conditions of revolution or civil war. The October Revolution is a good example of this.

Simplified Versions of the October Revolution

In modern Soviet society, it is put about that the October Revolution took place *after* the Bolsheviks had gained overwhelming majority support from the population of Tsarist Russia. Here is one version of the events, by K. Zarodov: 'The October Revolution was the most mass, representative and popular of all the revolutions ever experienced by mankind. Not only did it not infringe the will of the people, on the contrary it reflected this from start to finish... The Party of Lenin first declared its aims in the political struggle, in an open and unambiguous manner, and then proceeded to armed insurrection relying in particular on the will of the electorate which had returned it *with a majority*... Yes, it is true that the Bolsheviks had recourse to suppression by violent means, but this was not violence against the people's will, but violence backed by the people, not going against the *majority* of the workers, peasants and other members of the toiling population but against the *minority* of the overthrown classes opposing the *majority* of the people.'[2]

Most Western commentaries on the October Revolution state the reverse, that this was a revolution or 'plot' engineered by the minority who managed to force their will on a passive or openly hostile majority. An American historian claims, for instance, that 'While the population in general remained passive armed sections of the Bolsheviks swiftly and expeditiously seized the strategic positions, the armouries, centres of communication and the strong points in the capital of Russia.'[3]

A professor of Queens' College, Cambridge, J. Dunn, writes that 'the October Revolution was nothing more than the coup of an insignificant group of intellectuals'.[4] Other writers refer to 'the revolutionary elite of the Russian people'. On occasions the concept of a 'Bolshevik plot' assumes a more refined form, as in the case of another historian, T.H. von Laue: 'Whatever the Bolsheviks did for their own good or the good of Russia they did with the help of the masses or at any rate not in defiance of the masses. At the same time they remained actually outside the masses, the manipulators of the will of the people rather than the agents of it... By using propaganda and a thousand different forms of controlling revolutionary discontent, including irrational means of manipulating the masses, the revolutionaries were to form the "awareness of the masses".'[5]

The truth is that the revolutionary events of 1917 were incomparably more complex than many Soviet and foreign historians and journalists would have us believe. But before turning directly to these events, let us review the course of classical Marxist thinking on the question of majority and minority in revolution.

Marx and Engels on the Majority and the Minority

In regard to the *aims* of a people's or a proletarian revolution, it is customary for the revolutionaries to describe themselves as democrats, since they usually claim to be acting in the name of the majority or, at the very least, in its interests. All true revolutionaries take pains to guarantee their people a better life and a better future. In regard to the *methods and forms* of revolutionary struggle, however, revolutionary groups differ considerably in their approaches to the problems of majority and minority.

It was the opinion of Marx and Engels that only two countries, England and the USA, which had no cumbersome state apparatus and no standing army, presented any possibility of a peaceful course for socialist revolution, with the relatively painless transfer of power to the working-class majority. In the countries of continental Europe, as Engels insisted, such a revolution was impossible without the armed conflict and counter-coercion necessitated by authoritarian government.[6] History had taught Marx and Engels that many significant changes in the lives of different countries had been brought about not by popular movements or wars but by palace coups and plots. A small but active group of revolutionaries could exert tremendous influence on the destiny of a nation in the same way that small but well-equipped armies overran many countries of Africa and Asia in the nineteenth century. But a really decisive social upheaval such as a proletarian revolution could not result from the actions of a few conspirators. For this reason Marx's supporters in the First International spoke out against the methods and tactics of the Blanquists, despite Marx's profound admiration for Blanqui himself.[7] But if Marx and Engels were highly critical of Blanqui and of the Blanquists, whose utterances were out of touch with the moods of the working class and the general political situation in the country, this did not mean that they required revolutionary parties to be patient and abstain from revolution until such time as a commanding majority of national opinion had built up on their side. The Paris Commune was supported by the proletarian masses of Paris, but even the entire population of that city formed only a small minority of the whole country. The correspondence between Marx and Engels in the early 1850s shows that they were hoping for a democratic revolution in the countries of Europe very soon. This would grow rapidly into a proletarian revolution, which would usher in the victory of socialism. What this meant was that a well prepared *proletarian minority,* given conditions of revolutionary crisis, could seize power and bring about the socialist reconstruction of society in the interests of the *majority* of the population. Only a month or two before his death, Engels decided to summarize the evolution of his own and Marx's thinking on revolution, and he wrote that, as of the mid-1850s, 'All revolutions up to the present day have resulted in the displacement of one definite class rule by another; but all ruling classes up to now have been only small minorities in relation to the ruled mass of the people. One ruling minority was thus overthrown; another minority seized the helm of state in its stead and refashioned the state institutions to suit its own interests. This was on every occasion the minority group qualified and called to rule by the given degree of economic development; and just for that reason, and only for that reason, it happened that the ruled majority either participated in the revolution for the benefit of the former or else calmly acquiesced in it. But if we disregard the concrete content in each case, the common form of all these revolutions was that they were minority revolutions. ... All revolutions of modern times, beginning with the great English Revolution of the seventeenth century, showed these features, which appeared inseparable from every revolutionary struggle. They appeared applicable, also, to the struggle of the proletariat for its emancipation; all the more applicable, since precisely in 1848 there were but a very few people who had any idea at all of the direction in which this emancipation was to be sought. The proletarian masses themselves, even in Paris, after the victory, were still absolutely in the dark as to the path to be taken. And yet the movement was there, instinctive, spontaneous, irrepressible. Was not this just the situation in which a revolution had to succeed, led, true, by a minority, but this time not in the interest of the minority, but in the veriest interest of the majority? ... interests which, true, were at that time by no means clear to this great majority, but which soon enough had to become clear to it in the course of giving practical effect to them, by their convincing obviousness. And when, as Marx showed in this third article, in the spring of 1850, the development of the bourgeois republic that arose out of the "social" Revolution of 1848 had even concentrated real power in the hands of the big bourgeoisie—monarchistically inclined as it was into the bargain—and, on the other hand, had grouped all the other social classes, peasantry as well as petty bourgeoisie round the proletariat, so that, during and after the common victory, not they but the proletariat grown wise by experience had to become the decisive factor—was there not every prospect then of turning the revolution of the minority into a revolution of the majority?'[8]

In 1848, however, and in the following decade, hopes for a proletarian revolution came to nothing. History was to show that, as Engels put it, 'we and everyone who thought like us were wrong.' The proletariat was still incapable of bringing about a revolution 'by means of a simple and sudden attack'. Engels therefore welcomed the numerical growth of the proletariat and the growth of the Social Democratic workers' parties, on whom he now called to make intelligent use of the vote, which could be changed from a weapon of electoral deception into one of advantage to them. Every election could be turned by the proletariat and Social Democracy into a trial of strength, and every hard-won electoral office into a means of agitation and the extension of proletarian influence. Engels stopped short of recommending a cessation of all the former 'purely revolutionary methods of fighting', the use of which, however, given the rise of mass regular armies, had become problematic. Spontaneous actions in the streets and traditional barricades were, he considered, doomed to failure now. There was no point in the proletariat's offering itself up as cannon fodder. 'The time of surprise attacks, of revolutions carried through by small conscious minorities at the head of unconscious masses, is past. Where it is a question of a complete transformation of the social organisation, the masses themselves must also be in it, must themselves already have grasped what is at stake, what they are going in for, body and soul. The history of the last fifty years has taught us that.'[9]

In rejecting a course of revolution by an insignificant minority and calling on 'the broad masses of the people, in this case the peasants', to become involved in revolution, Engels was not insisting that 'our foreign comrades' or the German workers' party must always achieve a clear, undisputed majority at the polls as a necessary condition for the launching of a revolution. What he recommended was that a revolution should be launched only with the backing of a *decisive force*. In December 1884, he wrote to the leader of the German Social Democrats, August Bebel: 'Now it cannot be expected that at the moment of crisis we shall already have the majority of the electorate and therefore of the nation behind us. The whole bourgeois class and the remnants of the feudal landowning class, a large section of the petty bourgeoisie and also of the rural population will then mass themselves around the most radical bourgeois party, which will then make the most extreme revolutionary gestures, and I consider it very possible that it will be represented in the provisional government and even temporarily form its majority ... As things are at present, an impulse from outside can scarcely come from anywhere but Russia. If it does not do so, if the impulse arises from Germany, then the revolution can only start from the army. From the military point of view an unarmed nation against an army of today is a vanishing quantity ... In any case our sole adversary on the day of the crisis will be the *whole collective reaction which will group itself around pure democracy*, and this, I think, should not be lost sight of.'[10]

The revolutionary movement in nineteenth-century Russia and the problem of majority and minority

The relationship between majority and minority in revolution was a key issue in the discussions of the nineteenth-century Russian revolutionaries. The position of the Decembrists was quite clear. For all their differences, they had one idea in common: they did not trust the mass of the people, even though their demands, if met, must have improved the situation of the general populace in Russia. According to P.I. Pestel, one of the foremost Decembrist ideologists, revolution could arise only from the actions of a select minority aware of the intolerability of serfdom. The best that could be hoped for would be that the people might give the revolutionaries their sympathetic support—there was no hope of active revolutionary co-operation. Pestel was a convinced advocate of armed revolution mounted by a relatively small circle of revolution-minded officers with some support from trusted soldiers. After the overthrow of Tsarism, this circle would set up the dictatorship of a 'supreme government', which would introduce the necessary reforms and prepare the people for the acceptance of a constitution and the setting up of republican electoral organs. For revolutionary noblemen and for the beginning of the nineteenth century, this was in fact the only possible strategic programme.

Was there any possibility that the Decembrists might have succeeded? I believe this possibility is not one to be rejected out of hand. The history of revolutionary movements has seen more than one successful armed coup carried out by even smaller groups of officers. The overthrow of King Farouk by a group of young officers headed by Gamal Abdel Nasser is an interesting example, since Egypt in the early 1950s was not all that different in principle from the Russia of 1825. During the last thirty or forty years, groups of army officers bent on reform have been the driving force behind many successful democratic revolutions in countries of all kinds. Of course there have been failures too. All in all, there does seem to be some substance in the apparently paradoxical attempt made recently by a Soviet historian and journalist, N. Ya Eydelman, to demonstrate that the Decembrists did have at least a fair chance of success and that their defeat was by no means a foregone conclusion.[11]

However, what might have been possible for revolution-minded officers at the beginning of the nineteenth century in Russia was quite impractical for the declassed intellectuals (known as the *raznochintsy*) who made up the membership of the Narodnaya Volya (The People's Will) towards the end of the century. Among the very different groups within this movement, there were many supporters of the Blanquist approach to revolutionary tactics. Without going into too much detail, it is worth glancing at the differences in opinion between Pyotr Tkachev and Pyotr Lavrov.

It was Tkachev's belief that, although there was more than enough combustible material among the mass of the people, they themselves were not capable of independent or creative revolutionary activity. Revolution could only come about at the instigation of a thinking revolutionary minority which must unite to form a centralized conspiratorial party of the Jacobin type. Only a coup carried out by a party like this would create the conditions for the subsequent revolutionary and destructive activity of the mass of the people, which in turn would provide the necessary backing for the minority to be able to crush ruling-class resistance: 'It would be absurd,' said Tkachev, 'to wait for the majority to recognize the necessity for revolution.'[12] The revolutionary minority would be able to count on the people only in proportion to the latter's success in freeing themselves from 'the fear that oppresses them and their dread of authority', and working under the leadership of the 'revolutionary minority', to eliminate 'the direct enemies of revolution' and destroy 'the fortress protecting them'.[13] At this point, the initiative of the people comes to an end; even after a revolutionary coup, 'in its reforming activities the revolutionary minority must not count on the active support of the people'.[14] In Tkachev's mind, the success of a revolutionary conspiracy mounted by a minority was linked with a conviction that the Russian state was, so to speak, 'hovering', without any roots in the reality of the country's economic situation, simply leaning on the traditions of a bygone age. Once this state had been destroyed, the revolutionary minority would take measures to educate the people and reform their way of life along socialist lines.

The other prominent propagandist of populism, Lavrov, took the opposite view. He was quite certain that the reform of Russian society could only come about for the benefit of the people and 'by means of the people', since only the people as a whole could provide the revolution with the energy and power necessary for its success. The intellectuals could not themselves overcome the autocracy and then proceed to the education of the people; they must go to the people, enlighten them and rouse them to fight for their own liberation. In the journal *Nabat,* published in London in the late 1870s, Lavrov wrote the following criticism of Tkachev's ideas: 'It will be best to eliminate the shortcomings of the old and new societies by using the familiar devices of the old society; to compile a code of socialist law with a corresponding section "on punishment", to appoint from the ranks of the most reliable people (members of the Socialist-Revolutionary alliance, of course) a commission of "social security" for justice and punishment, to organize a corps of communal and territorial police made up of detectives ferreting out crime and keepers of public decency looking after "law and order", to put "notoriously dangerous people" under socialist police surveillance, to build an appropriate number of prisons and probably places of execution and staff these as necessary with socialist gaolers and executioners, and then, in order to guarantee socialist justice, to start up this reconditioned machine in the name of working-class socialism.'[15]

Arguments about the forms and methods of the revolutionary struggle continued in Russia after the founding of the Russian Social Democratic Workers' Party. The Anarchists, Socialist Revolutionaries and Social Democrats alike placed the fundamental interests of the revolution higher than any formal principles of democracy. The future Mensheviks were more outspoken on this subject than the Bolsheviks. It was not Lenin but the future Menshevik Pasadovsky who asked this question of the Second Congress of the RSDWP: 'Do we really have to subordinate our future policy to any particular democratic principles, by according them an absolute value, or should not all democratic principles be subordinated exclusively to the advantages of our party? I strongly support the latter. There is no part of those democratic principles which we should not subordinate to the advantages of our party.'— Exclamation: 'What about the inviolability of the individual?'— 'Yes, even that! As a party of revolution striving towards our ultimate goal of social revolution, we must look upon democratic principles exclusively from the standpoint of the most expedient attainment of that goal, the standpoint of party advantage. If any demand is not to our advantage we shall not introduce it...'[16]

Pasadovsky's statements were too outspoken and, as it happened, incorrect. He was essentially identifying party interests with the interests of a social revolution in which other revolutionary parties could also participate, whereas the establishment of a single front uniting the various parties called for a readiness for compromises and agreements that could work to the disadvantage of an individual party but still correspond to the interests of the revolutionary movement as a whole. Besides, no party was immune from error, not even the RSDWP, as experience would show. Plekhanov, without taking issue directly with Pasadovsky, nevertheless refined the latter's primitive formulation of the relationship between the formal principles of democracy and the interests of the revolution: 'I align myself squarely behind what Comrade Pasadovsky has said. Every particular democratic principle must be scrutinized not on its own in abstract terms but in relation to that principle which might be called the basic principle of democracy, the one that proclaims *Salus populi suprema lex esto*. Translated into the language of revolutionaries, this means that the success of the revolution is the highest law. And if, for the success of the revolution, it became necessary for a time to limit the validity of any particular principle of democracy it would be criminal to shy away from such limitation. It is my own personal opinion that even the principle of universal suffrage must be looked at from the point of view of the basic principle of democracy referred to above. There is a hypothetical possibility that we Social Democrats might oppose universal suffrage. The revolutionary proletariat might limit the electoral rights of the upper classes in the same way that the upper classes used to limit their political rights... We should not depart from this viewpoint even on the question of the continuity of parliaments. If, in a rush of revolutionary enthusiasm, the people elected a very good parliament ... we should have to endeavour to make it a "long parliament", whereas if the elections went wrong we should have to endeavour to dissolve it in a couple of years and if possible in a couple of weeks.'[17]

There can be no doubt that Lenin fully shared Plekhanov's view. On many occasions he emphasized the enormous significance for the proletariat of all the achievements gained by bourgeois or 'formal' democracy, which was a tremendous historical step forward from feudalism and autocracy. Lenin could not say, as Stalin did, that the formal principles of democracy 'are bits of nonsense for us Bolsheviks'. In 1905 he wrote: 'The very situation of the proletariat as a class compels it to be consistently democratic. The bourgeoisie looks over its shoulder dreading democratic progress with its ominous strengthening of the proletariat. The proletariat has nothing to lose but its chains and with the help of democracy it is gaining the whole world.'[18] On the other hand he took care frequently to emphasize the relative insignificance of the formal principles of democracy, their limited historical role, and he cautioned the proletariat against superstitious faith in the democratic state alone. The fight for democracy must be subordinated to the fight for socialism, although on any particular occasion it might be quite hard to differentiate between the two. 'We must manage to combine the fight for democracy with the fight for socialist revolution, always subordinating the former to the latter. That is the whole problem. That is the whole point.[19]

Majority and Minority in 1917

Russia's autocratic monarchy was the rule of a tiny minority. The Tsarist government reflected mainly the interests of the Russian landowners and a small section of the bourgeoisie. It was opposed to any sharing of power even with centrist bourgeois parties like the Kadets or parties of democratic reform. The monarchy was not only supported by the police; it also enjoyed the sympathy of certain sections of the population—some of the Cossacks, the better-off peasants, the merchants, and so on. But even here it was a question only of minority support, as was shown particularly by the elections to the State Duma, the extremely undemocratic electoral system notwithstanding. The Russian autocracy managed to retain power during the revolutionary period of 1905-1907, but in February 1917 things were different. The Tsarist government collapsed and the autocracy was destroyed in a matter of days, as a result of disturbances and uprisings in the imperial capital, Petrograd. A small and localized minority had overthrown a three-hundred-year-old monarchy and wrecked an autocratic regime in a vast country. This could only have happened because the action taken in Petrograd won the rapid and almost universal support of a commanding majority of the population at home and among the fighting masses on all fronts of the war. Lenin's comment was a succinct: 'Petrograd woke Russia up. Petrograd liberated her. The great cause of the Petrograd workers.'[20] Trotsky went into more detail: 'It would be no exaggeration to say that Petrograd achieved the February revolution. The rest of the country adhered to it. There was no struggle anywhere except in Petrograd. There were not to be found anywhere in the country any groups of the population, any parties, institutions, or military units which were ready to put up a fight for the old regime... The revolution was carried out upon the initiative and by the strength of one city, constituting approximately about one-seventy-fifth of the population of the country. You may say, if you will, that this most gigantic democratic act was achieved in a most undemocratic manner ... The fact that a Constituent Assembly was in prospect does not alter the matter, for the dates and methods of convoking this national representation were determined by institutions which issued from the victorious insurrection of Petrograd ... Revolutions have always struck such blows at the judicial fetishism of the popular will, and the blows have been more ruthless the deeper, bolder and more democratic the revolutions ... If the capital plays as dominating a role in a revolution as though it concentrated in itself the will of the nation, that is simply because the capital expresses most clearly and thoroughly the fundamental tendencies of the new society. ... In the initiatory role of the centres there is no violation of democracy, but rather its dynamic realization. However, the rhythm of this dynamic has never in great revolutions coincided with the rhythm of formal representative democracy.'[21] Not every revolution, of course, accords such a decisive role to the capital city. This applies even to Russia. At other times, it was Lenin's view that the provincial centres would play the main part in the developing events. In 1905, by the end of the first year of revolution, the centre had shifted to Moscow where the struggle became broader and deeper than in the capital.

After the February Revolution, all political parties and groups close to the people enjoyed unprecedented freedom of expression. Lenin claimed, not without some justification, that at that time Russia had become the freest country in the world. In these circumstances, he projected a peaceful development of the revolution involving the transfer of power to the Soviets and the growth of a revolutionary majority in them by agitation and propaganda among the workers, soldiers, peasants and Cossacks. 'You cannot jump over the people,' he said; 'only daydreamers and conspirators have ever thought that a minority can impose its will on the majority. That was what the French revolutionary Blanqui used to think—and he was wrong. When the majority of the people—through lack of understanding—does not want to seize power the minority, however revolutionary and intelligent it may be, cannot impose its wishes on the majority of the people.'[22]

By mid-summer 1917, the whole country was politically wide awake. Although the capital continued to dictate affairs, victory there no longer automatically ensured the universal triumph of a new stage of revolution. During the July crisis, the Bolsheviks had sufficient strength in the capital to overthrow the tottering Provisional Government, but Lenin himself forbade all attempts in that direction, even though repression was beginning to rain down on the Bolsheviks, forcing them partly underground. He was right to do so. In August, the shift to the left among the masses continued, the influence of the Party among the workers grew steadily and its membership rose by the end of the month to 240,000—ten times its numbers in February.

In the summer and autumn of 1917, elections and re-elections to every conceivable body and organization were held almost continuously, with little regard for fixed terms of office. This meant an unceasing turnover of the personnel working in Soviets and the army and navy committees, new elections every two or three months to regional and city dumas, and constant replacement of the leaderships of professional and trade organizations. The moods of the popular masses could be followed and analysed very closely. An enormous number of self-governing organs sprang up in the countryside, where the mood could be judged also from the number of rural disturbances. At all events, by mid-September it was quite clear that the Bolsheviks carried with them a large majority of the population not merely in Petrograd and Moscow but also in the main industrial centres and in all the military garrisons in and around the two main cities. Their influence was strong in the Baltic navy and on much of the North-West front. Now came the time for Lenin to cease calling for restraint and instead to press the Bolsheviks into urgent activity to bring down the Provisional Government at the earliest opportunity. The Bolsheviks did not yet enjoy an absolute majority of the whole population—they were still weak in the outlying regions—but they did command a powerful political army capable of both bringing down the government and replacing it in power. The success of at least the first phase of the socialist revolution was now certain, and Lenin accordingly had no hesitation in leading his party into armed insurrection.

Lenin on Majority and Minority in the Socialist Revolution

Lenin's statements about the need to work gradually towards a majority *in the Soviets* should not be taken to mean that he considered it necessary for the Bolsheviks to wait for the formal majority approval of the whole population of Russia before embarking on revolution. He did not see majorities and minorities in purely arithmetical terms, and he actually discounted any possibility of achieving an arithmetical revolutionary majority in a country like Russia where the peasant and petty-bourgeois masses were so scattered, illiterate, downtrodden and doomed to a barbarous way of life that it would be unrealistic to expect their behaviour to reflect at all adequately their own political and economic interests. The rural proletariat and the poorest of the peasants were capable *en masse* of supporting the proletariat as a whole only after the decisive victory of working-class revolution over the landowners and capitalists.

This is not to say that the proletariat had no support at all among the peasants, soldiers and petty bourgeoisie in 1917. Revolution would have been unthinkable without some sort of alliance between them. Nevertheless, there was no arithmetical majority behind the Bolsheviks. In his various analyses of the socio-political conditions of Russia, Lenin indicated frequently that in conditions of revolution it is not enough to claim an arithmetical majority of the population, nor is it possible to do so; in order to gain victory a revolutionary party must simply show itself the stronger at the right time and in the right place. On this basis Lenin's views have sometimes been identified as anti-Marxist and close to those of Tkachev. Nikolay Berdyayev once observed that the latter should be described not only as a predecessor of Lenin, he was actually 'more of a predecessor of Bolshevism than Marx and Engels'.[23] Of course this is wrong. Tkachev operated in quite different social conditions, and he rejected any idea of the existence of a bourgeoisie and a proletariat in Russia. The tiny minority capable in his eyes of carrying out a socialist coup there consisted only of the intelligentsia and particularly the activist youth of the country.[24] This was not Lenin's idea of socialist revolution in Russia. He placed his faith solely in the industrial proletariat. He may have claimed that it was wrong to delay revolution until majority support had been obtained among the peasants and the petty bourgeoisie, but at the same time he accepted that socialist revolution was impossible without a *majority of the proletariat*. In 1917 he said: 'We are not Blanquists; we don't want to operate with a minority of the working class against the majority.'[25] The whole strategy of the Bolsheviks that year boiled down to a struggle to win over a commanding majority of the working class. Lenin was nothing if not a sober-minded politician and he saw clearly that a mere majority of the bourgeois class would get nobody anywhere. It was a question of leading millions of peasants towards organization and political awareness and that could only be done by providing overall leadership from one side or the other, the bourgeois or the proletarian.

In 1918, the Moscow publishing house Zemlya i Volya issued a collection of articles entitled *A Year of Russian Revolution: 1917-18*. Lenin studied it carefully and was particularly interested in an article by N.V. Svyatitsky, 'The Constituent Assembly Election Results', to which he responded with a long article of his own published in *Communist International* in December 1919. Svyatitsky set out the statistics of voting patterns in fifty-four of the seventy-nine constituencies electing the Constituent Assembly, embracing almost all the main provinces of European Russia and Siberia. 36,300,000 votes were cast in these regions, 20,900,000 of which went to the SRs and their allies. The Mensheviks polled 1,700,000 votes and the Constitutional Democrats and allied bourgeois and landowners' parties 4,600,000. The Bolsheviks gained 9,000,000 votes, a quarter of the overall total. Svyatitsky's analysis omitted several well-populated areas like the *oblasts* of the Don, Estlandia (later Estonia) and Bessarabia. No figures were available from Central Asia or the *oblasts* of Orenburg and Yakutsk. It is beyond doubt that the Bolsheviks polled less than twenty-five per cent in all these areas. Lenin made no attempt to query the statistics in this SR publication, though he did subject them to close analysis by towns, provinces and fronts. The results came as no surprise to him. As a good revolutionary, he knew them in advance; his intuitions were merely being given exact numerical confirmation. Thus he wrote: 'How can we explain the miracle of victory for the Bolsheviks, when they won only a quarter of the votes...? The Bolsheviks won primarily becaue they carried with them the vast majority of the proletariat and, moreover, the most politically conscious, energetic and revolutionary section, the true vanguard of this leading class... The town cannot be considered equal to the country. The country cannot equal the town in the historical circumstances of our age. The town inevitably leads the country. The country inevitably follows the town. The only questions are: which of the "urban" classes will lead the country and master this problem, and what forms will this leadership take...? Moving on, the Bolsheviks not only carried with them a majority of the proletariat... They had, if you will forgive the military expression, the "striking force" that mattered in the cities. To have an overwhelming preponderance of power at the right time and in the right place—this "law" of military victory is also the law of political victory, especially in that furiously boiling class warfare known as revolution... In both capitals, in both of the main trade and industrial centres of Russia, the Bolsheviks had an overwhelming, decisive preponderance of power. We were about four times as strong there as the SRs. We were stronger than the SRs and Kadets put together... And although in the army we polled about half of the votes overall, we did have an overwhelming preponderance at the fronts nearest to the cities. If you take the Northern and Western fronts, the Bolsheviks gained more than a million votes compared to the SRs' 420,000. In the army too, therefore, the Bolsheviks had the political "striking force" by 1917, and this guaranteed them an overwhelming preponderance of power at the right time and in the right place... But these conditions could have produced a short-lived and uncertain victory if the Bolsheviks had not been able to attract the majority of the non-proletarian toiling masses, to win them over from the SRs and the other petty-bourgeois parties. ... Given the probability of a swift, decisive strike winning both the capitals, both the centres of the capitalist state machine (in the economic and political senses), notwithstanding furious opposition from the bureaucracy and the "intelligentsia", sabotage and so on, we were able to use the central apparatus of state power and prove to the workers and the non-proletariat alike that the proletariat is their only reliable ally, friend and leader.'[26]

Before October, Lenin called on the Bolsheviks to act without waiting for a formal majority even in the Soviets. The Second Congress of Soviets was scheduled for the end of October and the Bolsheviks could be expected to gain an absolute majority in it. For this reason, some of the Central Committee leaders suggested delaying any armed uprising until the Congress was convened. Lenin was strongly opposed to this. He told the Bolsheviks not to wait for 'to-and-fro voting' at the impending Congress but to seize power straight away, since all the main political and military prerequisites were satisfied. The main issues of a revolution were not to be settled by the casting of votes. To evade revolution by voting meant condemning the working class to inaction. On the brink of revolution, Lenin wrote: 'To wait for a "formal" Bolshevik majority is naive. No revolution waits for one.'[27] This call was answered, and the Bolsheviks began their military operations in Petrograd with the Second All-Russian Congress of Soviets just about to assemble. In the event it was a double success, since the Bolsheviks did obtain a majority at the Congress. If the 'to-and-fro voting' had not gone in their favour, they could not have been prevented from seizing power, though in that case events would have become even more complex and dramatic. Lenin drew a clear overall conclusion concerning the problem of majority and minority in revolution: 'The opportunist gentlemen, including the Kautskyites, "teach" the people to pour scorn on Marx's doctrine: first of all the proletariat must win a majority in a general election and then use this voting majority to acquire state power and only after that, on the basis of "consistent" (some would say "pure") democracy, organize socialism. We speak according to Marx's doctrine and the experience of history: first the proletariat must overthrow the bourgeoisie and win state power, then use this state power, i.e. dictatorship of the proletariat, as a weapon of their own class in order to gain the sympathy of the majority of the workers.'[28]

But how was the proletariat to acquire the sympathy of the *majority* of the workers? In the first place, Lenin considered, the very fact of winning state power and destroying the old machinery of government would win vast numbers of petty-bourgeois supporters to the proletarian side. 'For this mass consists of workers and exploited people who have been deceived all along by the bourgeoisie and who, when they acquire Soviet power, are also acquiring for the first time a weapon of mass struggle usable in their own interests against the bourgeoisie. Second, the proletariat can and must, immediately or at least very soon, win over from the bourgeoisie and petty bourgeois democracy "their own" masses, i.e. the masses who are behind them, win them over by means of the revolutionary satisfaction of their most pressing economic needs at the cost of expropriating the landowners and the bourgeoisie.'[29] The leader of the Menshevik-Internationalists, Martov, criticized Lenin and the Bolsheviks in his book *World Bolshevism*. 'The state during the transitional revolutionary period, which in theory was supposed to stand in opposition to the bourgeois state as an organ "of violence by the majority against the minority", the organ of power of the majority, nevertheless turned out to be the organ of power of the minority.'[30] Lenin's reply was simple. First, he said, the theory by which the first proletarian state must be from its inception 'the organ of power of the majority' was the theory not of Marx and Engels but of Kautsky and company. Second, apart from theory, there was such a thing as the living experience of the Russian revolution, which allowed for the testing and, if necessary, correction of the theory of Marxism. Marxism, after all, was not a dogma but leadership towards action.

However, the position of Lenin and the Bolsheviks, for all its correspondence to actual Russian conditions in 1917, contained one great danger. A strong revolutionary minority, having gained power, cannot for long control the majority on the basis of violence, though Lenin did not rule out the possibility of certain measures of coercion. The proletarian minority must win over and retain the sympathy of the majority of the workers or else forfeit power. To this end the proletarian state must follow the right policies and make as few mistakes as possible. As it happened, the world's first proletarian state took a long time to work out its optimum politico-economic line, and made many mistakes in the very process of satisfying 'the most pressing economic needs' of the petty bourgeoisie—mainly those of the peasantry. Thus the Bolsheviks, having gained majority support after the October Revolution, had lost this support by the late spring of 1918 and were not to regain it before the end of the year. Such vacillations on the part of the petty-bourgeois masses were to be repeated several times, in a series of crises that brought Soviet power again and again to the brink of disaster. Lenin discussed this situation as follows: 'The vacillations of the petty-bourgeois population just where proletarian influence is at its weakest have been demonstrated with particular clarity. First they were behind the Bolsheviks when the Bolsheviks gave them land and demobilized soldiers came back with news of peace. Then they swung against the Bolsheviks when, in the interests of the international development of revolution and its safeguarding in Russia, the Bolsheviks concluded the Peace of Brest-Litovsk, thus "offending" the deepest, that is the patriotic, feelings of the petty bourgeoisie. The dictatorship of the proletariat did not greatly appeal to the peasants where there were grain surpluses and the Bolsheviks said they were going to be strict and forceful in the redistribution of the surpluses at prices fixed by the state. The peasantry in the Urals, Siberia and the Ukraine leaned then towards Kolchak and Denikin. Then, later on, experience of Kolchak's and Denikin's "democracy" ... showed the peasants that phrases about "democracy" and "Constituent Assemblies" were in fact only a cover for the dictatorship of the landowner and capitalist. Hence another turn towards Bolshevism and more and more peasant uprisings occurring at the rear in Kolchak and Denikin territory. The Red troops were welcomed by the peasants as liberators. At the end of the day these vacillations on the part of the peasants as the main representatives of the petty-bourgeois masses were what decided the fate of Soviet and Kolchak-Denikin power. But before "the end of the day" there was a fairly prolonged period of desperate fighting and agonizing torment, which lasted for two years in Russia and no certainty that it will be completely finished, let us say, in another year's time."[31]

Sure enough, soon after this was written the Soviet Union witnessed a renewal of conflict between the Bolsheviks and the peasants when, not in the Kolchak-Denikin rear but in the rear of the Red Army itself, peasant uprising began again. This crisis was staved off by the introduction of NEP, which brought a new stability to the country; but the delicate balance was upset once again by the death of Lenin. There followed the grain-requisitioning crisis of the late 1920s, and then the beginning of the enforced collectivization on a mass scale.

Certain questions spring immediately to mind. Why was it that, not only under Kolchak and Denikin but also under Soviet power, the peasants resorted to insurrection and armed resistance for the expression of their discontent? Why did Soviet power fail during its earliest days to establish effective two-way channels of communication by which the new leaders of the country might have been better and more rapidly informed of the desires and opinions of the majority of the population? Why were the Bolsheviks unable to surround their government immediately with a permanent, solid economic base including the absolute majority of the population? Why could they progress only by surmounting crisis after crisis? Questions like these remain unanswered.

It is worth remembering, as a general observation, that in the very complex circumstances of the revolutionary struggle, Lenin was concerned above all with the question of a *ruling* majority or minority. He did not devote enough thought to the question of the majority or minority groups not in power—the opposition. At the height of the Russian Civil War, Kautsky wrote his book *Dictatorship of the Proletariat*, which was intended mainly as a criticism of the Bolsheviks. Lenin's reply came quickly, in a famous book published in late 1918 and called *The Proletarian Revolution and the Renegade Kautsky*. Other Bolshevik theoreticians joined in the argument. Apparently ignoring the circumstances of the world war which was still raging, Kautsky stressed the importance of maintaining certain elementary democratic freedoms including minority rights: 'From the struggles for political rights modern democracy arises and the proletariat comes to maturity; another factor arises at the same time—*protection of the minority, the opposition* in a state. Democracy implies the rule of the majority but it implies no less the protection of the minority.'[32] Here is Lenin's reply: 'Oh, the wise and most learned Kautsky! ... He prefers to tell the workers fairy stories to the effect that democracy means "protecting the minority". It is incredible, but it is a fact. In the Year of Our Lord 1918, in the fifth year of the world imperialist slaughter and the strangulation of international minorities... in all the "democracies" of the world, the learned gentleman Mr. Kautsky sweetly sings the praises of "protection of the minority". Those who are interested may read this on page fifteen of Kautsky's pamplet.'[33] Bukharin's attitude to Kautsky was not dissimilar: 'One glance at this splendid reasoning is enough to show that Kautsky does not understand the first thing about current events. Can we be expected to advise the Russian proletariat to protect the rights of the "minority", i.e. the rights of counter-revolution which good, kind Kautsky describes nicely as "the opposition"? To protect the rights of the Czechoslovaks, Tsarist police agents, generals, speculators, priests, all those people who are coming after the proletariat with bombs and revolvers—this would be to act like a fool or a political charlatan. But this is what must be done, according to your dim petty bourgeois who is trying to reconcile the classes and cannot see that the heavyweight bourgeoisie, supported by him, will first settle things with the proletariat and then eat him up too.'[34]

Kautsky's mistake had been to formulate his question in terms too abstract for the current situation. Lenin and Bukharin, however, were equally wrong to draw absolute conclusions from the experience of Russia, to attempt to solve a serious problem of general theory with reference only to 'the Year of Our Lord 1918'. Concern for the protection of minorities is not an example of 'political charlatanism'. The Bolsheviks themselves, in 1917, eager to protect the rights of their own party to engage in political activity and eager to defend internationalists in the other countries at war, had demanded nothing other than 'the protection of minority rights'. It is obvious that 'minorities' and 'majorities' have to be considered in very varied sets of political inter-relationships, and that there can be no absolute formula applicable to all situations. The majority (of a people, nation, class or party) must respect the rights of the minority, or minorities, but only on the understanding that the latter respect majority rights and accept majority decisions. If the minority rises against the will of the majority by the use of armed strength or other violent means, including slander, provocation and terror, it would be odd if we were to condemn the use of reciprocal violence. Bukharin and Lenin went too far, in 1918, in identifying the activities of minority anti-Bolshevik groups with the activities of 'generals and Tsarist police agents', the Czechoslovak insurgents and, in fact, all those people who were 'coming after the proletariat with bombs and revolvers'. Had not Bukharin himself headed the minority 'left-wing Communist' faction in 1918, and did he not stand out against the majority of the Party in the defence of his own minority views on the Peace of Brest-Litovsk and a number of economic questions? Even then, the Bukharin faction yielded to the decisions of the majority, which persuaded Lenin to confine the conflict between them to the realm of ideology rather than resort to political violence.

As a general rule the problem of majority-minority relations is complicated by the multiplicity of special circumstances arising at a time of violent revolution. Such revolutions tend to occur in countries without adequate democratic institutions allowing the majority of the population to express its will and insisting on the acceptance of that will by the minority. These comments are, incidentally, not intended to disparage Lenin's strategy in the run-up to October and the conduct of the Revolution. Conditions in 1917 really were such that there was no possibility of asking the nation for a mandate *first* and then taking over, only to transfer power immediately to another party as soon as the majority of the population lost confidence in Bolshevik rule. The situation was such that many of the country's problems could only have been solved by violent means. The Bolsheviks may be criticized for their failure, even under Lenin, always to make proper use of the enormous power that had fallen to them, though the first experience of such a difficult operation could scarcely have been expected to proceed without any serious mistakes being made. What was lacking was honest and fair scrutiny of these mistakes in order to avoid their repetition.

The October Revolution and National-Democratic Revolutions in the Developing Countries

The attitude adopted by Lenin and the Bolsheviks towards the problem of majority and minority in revolution was determined ultimately by political conditions in Tsarist Russia. The strategic plan for socialist revolution developed by Lenin worked out successfully in practice precisely because it corresponded both to contemporary Russian conditions and to the international situation in 1917-20. This also enabled the Bolsheviks to retain power despite their many mistakes and the recurrent crises. The October triumph made a tremendous impression on socialist and other radical movements all over the world and led to the formation of a new, 'Communist', International. Naturally enough, the experience of the Revolution followed by the Civil War was, to begin with, the main source of experience for the other young Communist parties. Lenin stood beside the cradle of the Comintern not only handing on Bolshevik experience to 'the new arrivals' but also warning them against mistakes and distractions.

The Comintern went on to discuss the problem of majorities and minorities at several of their congresses. The Third Congress in 1921 set the Communist parties the task of winning over a majority of the working class to Communist influence and drawing its more decisive sections into the struggle. The Fourth Congress in 1922 confirmed the need to 'gain control of a majority of the working class in America and Europe' and accepted the task of creating Communist parties in the colonial and semi-colonial countries as 'parties representing the general interests of the proletariat'. The following resolution was passed in 1924. 'The Fifth World Congress of the Communist International ... takes notice that, on the one hand, incorrect rightist tendencies are demanding the winning of a statistical majority of the toiling masses and proposing that there can be no question of any serious revolutionary battles until the Communists win over virtually ninety-nine per cent of the workers. On the other hand, the Fifth World Congress rejects the error of the "ultra-leftists" who have still failed to comprehend the meaning of the slogan "to the masses", which has world-wide historical significance, and who continually repeat that Communist parties are parties of the proletarian "terrorist minority" which, without mass appeal, can nevertheless lead the masses into battle at any moment.'[35]

This conclusion was based primarily on the experience of the Russian Bolshevik Party, which must be taken into account even today when the proper tactics and strategy of Communist parties are under consideration. In the 1920s, however, not only the young Communist parties but also Lenin himself tended to exaggerate the universal relevance of this experience. It was Lenin who was responsible for the formula 'Bolshevism serves as a model of tactics for everyone', which is still repeated nowadays, although it is becoming more and more usual to hear the more reliable formula that 'no two revolutions are the same'. It is true, for instance, that in the Russian Revolutions of 1906s-1907 and 1917 the centre and the driving force of the revolutionary movement were in the town. However, a strategy based on the assertion that 'the town cannot be considered equal to the country ... the town inevitably leads the country' or a strategy of gaining 'a decisive preponderance of power at the right time and in the right place' would be inapplicable to a number of large-scale revolutions headed by Communist parties. We should remember: Lenin himself said that the countries of the East, with their overwhelmingly rural populations, would show the world more specific methods of fighting for freedom than Russia had done. This came true in the case of China where the beginning of the revolution was welcomed by Lenin, though its actual circumstances were so specific that it was difficult for the leaders to make any real use of the Bolsheviks' strategy and tactics. The Chinese Communists themselves long held the opinion that, in their country, revolution would be achieved in the cities, with peasant support, and they also attempted to raise a political army of revolution capable of seizing power in the country, or at least in its vital centres, by armed insurrection. As it turned out, all the urban insurrections in China ended in defeat. Legal conditions there did not permit the raising of a political army of popular-democratic revolution, and everything else—the vastness of the country, decentralized power, the backwardness and unevenness of development in the provinces, bad roads and communications—militated strongly against centralized work of an illegal nature. In these conditions, the wait for a 'preponderance of power in the vital regions of the country' might have gone on for another century. China did not possess a single vital politico-economic centre such as Paris in France, London in England, Rome in Italy or Petrograd in Russia. What major cities there were—Shanghai, Canton, Nanking, Peking—held small but very active sections of the revolutionary proletariat, but they were also centres of imperialist influence, housing various military groups. Their vulnerability to counter-revolutionary forces made it likely that any victory of the working class in the cities would be uncertain and short-lived. Things were different in the country, where there were hundreds of millions of the poorest peasants with a propensity going back thousands of years for rocking the ancient empire with peasant wars. In 1906 Lenin wrote: 'Preaching the seizure of land, we call the peasants to insurrection. Would we be right to do so ... without counting on insurrection by the workers in the towns in support of the peasant toilers?'[36]

But in China these Bolshevik tactics and strategy were inappropriate. The revolution began to prosper only after it had been defeated in most of the major cities and when the centre of the revolutionary struggle had shifted to the outlying rural regions. The main development of the Chinese Revolution in the 1930s and 1940s came not through strikes and insurrection in the cities but through uprisings in the remote rural areas, which gradually merged into a real war between the peasants and a Chinese counter-revolution assisted by international intervention, and the latter forces were based at first in the towns. In the long run, it was not the town that liberated the country, but the country that emancipated the town from feudal reaction and imperialism. The Bolsheviks had no independent Party cells in the countryside in 1917, but in China the reverse was the case, the rural Communists having no rivals like the SRs to contend with. Indeed, at the time of the formation of the Chinese People's Republic, ninety-five per cent of the Chinese Communist Party consisted of peasants or soldiers with a peasant background.

The departure of the Chinese Revolution from some of the principles of Leninism and Bolshevism concerning majority-minority relationships in revolution and the respective roles of town and country was amply justified by local circumstances. In China, revolution could only have begun as a movement initiated by a tiny minority of people, and it continued as such for some time, although claiming to represent the interests and aspirations of an overwhelming majority. This is no justification of the many errors committed by the CCP leadership, but most of these errors—and crimes, even—were committed, in any case, after the Revolution

The Bolshevik experience of majorities and minorities in revolution was also inapplicable to Vietnam, Yugoslavia (during the wartime anti-fascist revolution) and Cuba, when, in particular, the revolutionary struggle was defeated in the towns only to triumph later on in the rural regions despite the fact that, in the first months of the revolution, insurgent groups in the countryside had amounted to no more than a few dozen men. However, attempts to transfer the experience of the Cuban Revolution to other countries of Latin America and the Third World have not proved successful. It is quite possible that in some of the proletarian revolutions yet to come in Third World countries, success will come from the application of Bolshevik strategy and tactics in relation to revolutionary majorities and minorities and town versus country.

The October Revolution and the Present Situation in the Developed Capitalist Countries

We do not propose in this work to analyse the situation existing in the countries of Western Europe in the period 1918-23. Restricting ourselves to present-day circumstances in the countries of developed capitalism, we can see that in most cases the Communist parties believe not in the strategy of gaining a 'decisive majority in the decisive centres' but in the attainment of a parliamentary, or 'statistical', majority earned through all forms of political activity but finally determined by the ballot box. At present, in Western Europe, a large majority of the people belong to the working class and allied groups of working people. Democratic traditions and democratic institutions abound and enjoy universal respect. The Communist parties operate legally and are aware that even those people who always vote Communist, and who might therefore be described as their political army, believe for the most part in a peaceful, parliamentary transfer of power to their own party. These parties have been in existence for sixty-odd years, but even in the most successful cases, they command no more than fifteen to twenty-five per cent of the vote; only in Italy does the Communist vote rise to about a third of the electorate. This is, of course, more than the Bolsheviks had in the Constituent Assembly elections, but it is still quite insufficient for the Communists to come to power and carry through the socialist reforms whose preconditions have been maturing for so long in the West. All the indications are that this can be achieved not through fierce political conflict with the other, more moderate left-wing parties (as in the case of the Bolsheviks in 1917) but only through a solid alliance of the left, which must exist both before and after the assumption of power by the left-wing bloc. This, of course, does not preclude inter-party argument and discussion, as long as these are not allowed to undermine the alliance as a whole.

Despite the defeat of fascism and the parties of the extreme right, the imperialist forces in Western countries remain very strong. For this reason, the triumph of the socialist revolution in those countries must be looked upon not as a single operation but as a prolonged process of structural reform, at each stage of which the left-wing alliance must command a large majority, thus neutralizing many of the centre parties. (The left-wing alliance will also require the support of large sections of the armed forces.) Western Communists must therefore think of themselves as revolutionaries and as reformers at one and the same time, and they must take into account not only the experience of the Bolsheviks, but also that of the whole socialist movement in Western Europe, which is rejected all too unceremoniously by CPSU theoreticians. The French Communist leader Marchais has spoken as follows about conditions in France: 'In the battle for socialism, nothing, absolutely nothing, in a country like ours and at a time like this, can take the place of the will of the majority of the people democratically expressed in the battle of the ballot box. Whatever the different roads to socialism in our country, which cannot be foreseen in detail, we must be certain that at every stage the political majority coincides with an arithmetical one.'[37] This position was set out in greater detail at the end of 1975 in a joint declaration by the French and Italian parties: 'Italian and French Communists believe that the movement towards socialism, and the construction of a socialist society envisaged as a future development in their countries, must be realized within the framework of a continuous democratization of our economic, social and political life. Socialism will comprise the highest stage of democracy and freedom—democracy "taken to its extreme".

'On this basis, all freedoms resulting from the great bourgeois-democratic revolutions and the great popular struggles of our age, headed by the working masses, must be guaranteed and consolidated. Under this heading we include freedom of thought and expression, publication, assembly and association, demonstration and movement within the country and abroad, the inviolability of private life, religious freedom, and the full expression of philosophical, cultural and artistic tendencies and opinions. French and Italian Communists stand for a multiplicity of political parties, including the right to existence and activity of opposition parties, and for *the free formation and possible democratic succession of majorities and minorities*, for the secular character and democratic functioning of the state and for the independence of the judiciary. They stand also for free activity and independence of the trade unions. They place particular importance on the development of democracy at work, the kind of democracy guaranteeing the genuine participation of workers in management and the wide extension of workers' rights in decision-making. The democratic centralization of the state must increase the importance of local and regional collectives, which must enjoy wide-ranging autonomy in the execution of their power.

'The socialist method of social reform presupposes control by society of the chief means of production and exchange, their progressive socialization, and the implementation of a democratic plan at national level. The sector of small-scale or medium property-owning, small-scale or medium industrial and commercial enterprise will be assigned a positive role in the building of socialism. Such a programme of reform can result only from great conflict and powerful pressure exerted by the masses uniting around a working-class *majority* of the population. It requires the existence of democratic institutions fully representative of popular sovereignty, guaranteeing an extension of the power of a people and the implementation of equal and universal suffrage on a proportional basis. Within this framework, both parties, which have always respected the ballot box and will continue to do so, envisage the workers coming to power and running the state. The Italian and French Communist Parties acknowledge the value of the principles behind all these conditions of democratic life. The present attitude of these Parties is not a tactical move, it results from a bipartisan analysis of the peculiar material and historical circumstances of the two countries and their thinking about shared international experience.'[38]

The perspective outlined in this declaration remains the same today; indeed, it has been made more specific on a number of counts, not least on the crucial issue with which this chapter has concerned itself: the role of the majority in a period of revolutionary reform.

5
Socialism in One Country

It is commonly claimed, even in the works of many Western Sovietologists, that the theory of 'socialism in one country' was the brainchild of Stalin. This is quite untrue. Stalin was an active contributor to the argument on this subject that was current in the 1920s, and we shall have more to say about this shortly.

But the basic theory belongs to Lenin. What is more, it should logically be treated as nothing less than one of the basic tenets of Leninism. Here we must agree with K. Zarodov. 'The conclusion concerning the victory of socialist revolution first of all in a few countries or even in a single one is in the nature of a basic principle, as may be seen when one examines the notable contribution that Lenin made to the development of the Marxist theory of revolution, although historically speaking it represents a consequence rather than a prerequisite of the prolonged scientific research conducted by Lenin himself in the area of revolutionary theory, research distinguished by a whole series of other major discoveries. This deserves particular emphasis, firstly, because we sometimes come across fruitless attempts to reduce the development of Lenin's theory of revolution to this conclusion alone, and, secondly, because there are authors who simplify matters by ignoring or breaking the obvious theoretical threads connecting the conclusion concerning the possibility of the victory of Socialist revolution in one country with other ideas promulgated by Lenin earlier or later than this.'[1]

Marx and Engels on Socialism in One Country

This question was considered by Marx and Engels almost as soon as they became socialists. In the 'Principles of Communism' Engels wrote: 'Will it be possible for this revolution to take place in one country alone? ...No. Large-scale industry, already by creating the world market, has so linked up the peoples of the earth, and especially the civilized peoples, that each people is dependent on what happens to another. Further, in all civilized countries large-scale industry has so levelled social development that ...the bourgeoisie and the proletariat have become the two decisive classes of society and the struggle between them the main struggle of the day. The communist revolution will therefore be no merely national one; it will be a revolution taking place simultaneously in all civilized countries, that is, at least in England, America, France and Germany.'[2]

It is clear that Engels bases his thesis of simultaneous Communist revolution in several leading countries not first and foremost on the danger of intervention by neighbouring countries but on their economic interdependence and the equalization of their social development. He knew, of course, that these countries had taken different paths of capitalist industrial development, but he believed that this would be reflected in the differing rates of socio-economic reform resulting from their revolutions, which would nonetheless be simultaneous. Marx was in complete agreement. In *The Class Struggles in France,* he stated that the revolution must 'leave its natural soil immediately and ...conquer *the European* terrain, on which alone the social revolution of the nineteenth century can be carried out.'[3]

Observation of revolutionary outbreaks in the middle of the century, and the refinement by Marx and Engels of their economic, political and philosophical concepts, brought about several changes in their theory of socialist revolution. There were to be no more statements in quite such categorical terms about the simultaneous occurrence of communist revolution throughout Europe. On the contrary Marx and Engels began to speak of proletarian revolution beginning inside one country—though subsequently, of course, it would spread like fire to other countries. They also extended the list of countries that, according to their conception, could become the detonator of European revolution. Poland, Italy, Hungary and Spain were added; and then, in the late 1870s and early 1880s, having earlier considered Russia the most conservative force in Europe, they decided that this country might also provide the spark that would ignite the fire of European revolution. Nevertheless, neither changed his basic opinion that the European socialist revolution would be a practically simultaneous event realized by the proletariat in the major capitalist countries. Shortly before his death, Engels wrote to Paul Lafargue: 'Industrial development in France lags behind that of England; at the moment it even lags behind that of Germany, which has taken giant strides forward since 1860. The workers' movement in France does not compare with the workers' movement in Germany. But neither the French, nor the Germans, nor the English, none of them individually will enjoy the glory of destroying capitalism; if France, perhaps, gives the signal then Germany, as the country most deeply affected by socialism and where the theory has penetrated the masses most profoundly, will settle the issue, but even then neither of them will be able to guarantee total victory while England remains in the grip of the bourgeoisie. The liberation of the proletariat can only be an international matter. If you try to make it a matter for the French alone you will make it impossible.'[4]

Trotsky's Views

The views of Marx and Engels on the necessary conditions for the victory of socialism in Europe came under fire from other socialists even in the nineteenth century. In fact, even in pre-Marxian utopian socialism there was an overriding belief that an equitable communist society could be built first of all in a single country or even on an island like the mythical utopia itself. During the lifetime of Marx and Engels, various countries—mainly the USA—saw attempts at creating independent socialist enterprises and agricultural communities. These have continued into the twentieth century, as we have seen in the famous kibbutzim in Palestine and the co-operative movements in West Germany, England and elsewhere. However, the Marxist parties and movements changed Engels's thesis concerning the impossibility of revolution in a single country into a dogma. This dogma was shared by the Russian Marxists. Perhaps the most detailed exposition of the idea was Leon Trotsky's, in his book on the 1905 Revolution, written in prison at the beginning of 1906 and published almost immediately. He wrote 'But how far can the socialist policy of the working class be applied in the economic conditions of Russia? We can say one thing with certainty—that it will come up against political obstacles much sooner than it will stumble over the technical backwardness of the country. *Without the direct State support of the European proletariat the working class of Russia cannot remain in power and convert its temporary domination into a lasting socialist dictatorship.* Of this there cannot for one moment be any doubt. But on the other hand there cannot be any doubt that a socialist revolution in the West will enable us directly to convert the temporary domination of the working class into a socialist dictatorship.'[5] Trotsky went on to explain his point of view as follows: 'Should the Russian proletariat find itself in power, if only as the result of a temporary conjuncture of circumstances in our bourgeois revolution, it will encounter the organized hostility of world reaction, and on the other hand will find a readiness on the part of the world proletariat to give organized support. Left to its own resources, the working class of Russia will inevitably be crushed by the counter-revolution the moment the peasantry turns its back on it. It will have no alternative but to link the fate of its political rule, and, hence, the fate of the whole Russian revolution, with the fate of the socialist revolution in Europe. That colossal state-political power given it by a temporary conjuncture of circumstances in the Russian bourgeois revolution it will cast into the scales of the class struggle of the entire capitalist world. With state power in its hands, with counter-revolution behind it and European reaction in front of it, it will send forth to its comrades the world over the old rallying cry, which this time will be a call for the last attack: *Workers of all countries, unite!*'[6]

Lenin Advances a New Idea

The first person to challenge the now entrenched Marxist view was Lenin. He did not respond in any way to Trotsky's book, but decided to approach the problem from a different direction. If Trotsky drew his conclusion from the belief that the course of the Russian Revolution would inevitably bring the Russian proletariat into hostile confrontation with the peasantry, Lenin came to quite different conclusions by considering the prospects for proletarian revolution on a world scale in the conditions of imperialism. Study of imperialism, as the latest and highest stage in the development of capitalism, led Lenin to the view that the inequalities in the development of capitalist countries were growing, and that this trend would entail to the possibility, perhaps the inevitability, of socialist revolution achieving victory not universally but first of all in a single country or group of countries.

Socialists and pacifists all over Europe began using the catchphrase 'The United States of Europe' before the First World War. During the war, it was reiterated and defended first by Kautsky and then by Trotsky. The Bolsheviks supported it for a while, referring encouragingly to the 'Republican United States of Europe', which meant the overthrow of the monarchies in Germany, Russia and Austria. After much discussion at conferences of the Party's foreign sections and in the editorial office of the newspaper *Sotsial-Demokrat* (The Social Democrat) the Bolsheviks adopted Lenin's proposal to discard the phrase since, as Lenin explained, it might give rise to 'a false interpretation of the impossibility of the victory of socialism in one country and the relationship between that one country and the others'. He went on in greater detail: 'Inequality in economic and political development is an absolute law of capitalism. From this it follows that the victory of socialism is possible at first only in a few countries, perhaps only in one individual capitalist country. The victorious proletariat of that country, having expropriated the capitalists and organized socialist production for themselves, would then rise against the rest of the capitalist world, attract the oppressed classes of other countries and call them to insurrection against the capitalists and, when necessary, use military force against the exploiting classes and their states.'[7]

Trotsky took issue with Lenin in his Paris newspaper, *Nashe Slovo* (Our Word): ' "Inequality in economic and political development is an absolute law of Capitalism." From this *The Social Democrat* concludes that the victory of socialism is possible in one country and therefore there is no need to underwrite the dictatorship of the proletariat in each individual state by the creation of a United States of Europe. That capitalist development is unequal is a perfectly irrefutable proposition. But this inequality itself is extremely unequal. The levels of capitalism in England, Austria, Germany and France are not identical. But compared with Africa and Asia all these countries represent capitalist "Europe", which is ripe for socialist revolution. That no country must "wait for the others" in its struggle is an elementary idea that it is both useful and essential to repeat, so that the concept of parallel international action does not turn into the concept of an international waiting game. Without waiting for anyone else, we are beginning and continuing the struggle on national soil with every confidence that this initiative will give an impetus to the struggle in other countries; but if this did not happen it would be useless to imagine—as history and theory clearly demonstrate—that, for example, revolutionary Russia could stand up against a conservative Europe, or socialist Germany could remain in isolation within the capitalist world.'[8]

Lenin no doubt knew of Trotsky's objections. Nevertheless, the next year (1916), he published an article on the military programme of the proletarian revolution in which he used virtually the same expressions to repeat his conclusion concerning not only the possibility of the victory of socialist revolution but the victory of socialism itself, the expropriation of the capitalists and the organization of socialist production.[9] Moreover, he refrained from any attempt at nominating any particular capitalist country as standing nearest to socialist revolution, and even extended his theory to relatively small, neutral countries like Switzerland. In December 1916, he wrote: '... it is obviously right for us to say that either the Swiss people are going to starve, and starve more hideously with each passing week, and daily run the risk of being drawn into the imperialist war, i.e. being killed off in the interests of the capitalists, or else they will follow the advice of the best sections of their proletariat, gather their strength and bring about a socialist revolution ... And yet the Great Powers will never countenance a socialist Switzerland—the first signs of socialist revolution in Switzerland will be squashed by the colossal advantage of strength enjoyed by these powers! This would doubtless be the case if, first, the earliest signs of revolution in Switzerland were conceivable without arousing a movement of class solidarity in the border countries, and, second, if the Great Powers were not involved in the deadlock of a "war of attrition" that has already led to the attrition of the tolerance of the most tolerant nations.'[10]

Lenin by no means excluded autocratic Russia from his analysis. While acknowledging that a bourgeois-democratic revolution, or 'the liberation of bourgeois Russia from feudal imperialism (i.e. Tsarism)' came first on the agenda here, he had stated as early as

November 1915 that the Russian proletariat would use the overthrow of Tsarism 'not in order to help the prosperous peasants in their struggle against the rural workers, but for the achievement of the socialist revolution.'[11] In 1915 and 1916, of course, Lenin could not have foreseen that the first country in which the strain of the imperialist war would lead to revolution would be Russia herself. However, when he came to analyse the circumstances of 1917, he considered it no chance event that Russia had proved to be the weakest link in the imperialist chain, snapping the chain itself by demonstrating the possibility of democratic and even socialist revolution. Lenin's call for a transition from the victorious bourgeois-democratic revolution to the socialist revolution itself came under fire from all sides, not only from the Mensheviks but even from certain Bolsheviks. His opponents declared that Russia was not yet ripe for socialist revolution and that socialism could not possibly be built in so backward a country. Lenin rejected such arguments. Russia, he reasoned, for all its backwardness, was still a capitalist country; it had not only a satisfactory minimum of the basic objective prerequisites for socialist revolution but, in addition, certain vital subjective prerequisites, such as a revolutionary proletariat headed by a revolutionary party that could count on considerable support from the peasants and soldiers, who hated the war and longed for land and peace. The Russian proletariat had no right to pass up this historic opportunity to launch a new age of world-wide proletarian revolution and set an example of escape from the imperialist slaughter. Lenin's view prevailed in the Bolshevik Party and won over most of the proletariat of Russia, leading, thereby, to the victory of the socialist revolution in October 1917.

Lenin and Trotsky: the Civil War Years

The victory was achieved rather easily and within a few months Soviet power had spread almost throughout the territory of the fallen Empire. The triumphal procession of the Soviets, however, was far from a guarantee of internal solidity or international security. The phrase 'a weak link in the imperialist system' was not just a well chosen metaphor. Russia was for the time being the weakest of all the major European powers in economic and military terms. Although the Soviet Government, unlike its recently overthrown predecessor, the Provisional Government, could not be accused of uncertainty and vacillation, its overall position was in many respects more difficult. The peasants had taken over the land, but they were dissatisfied with the increasing severity of the state monopoly controlling the grain trade and other foodstuffs, and the squeeze on trade in general. Industrial output continued to fall, transport was disrupted and the value of money was plunging. The vast army was collapsing and dispersing, its supplies uncertain; soldiers in their hundreds of thousands were deserting the trenches and returning home. Once the largest component of the old state apparatus, the army could no longer fight, as became abundantly clear when the German divisions attacked in February 1918. When Lenin faced the difficult task of insisting on ratification of the humiliating Peace of Brest-Litovsk, he knew only too well that Soviet Russia was in no condition to wage any sort of 'revolutionary war' against the Kaiser's Germany, which was what the left-wing Communists and left SRs wanted. It was, moreover, in no condition to 'rise against the rest of the capitalist world, attract the oppressed classes of other countries...and when necessary use military force against the exploiting classes and their states', as he had proposed only three years before.

Lenin now took a sober view of matters, and his comments on the prospects of Socialism in Russia were not by any means identical with the theoretical principles he had outlined in 1915-16, with regard to the possible victory of socialism in a single country. He felt certain that the world-wide proletarian revolution that had begun in Russia would spread and develop rapidly, and certain too that the ever-increasing fury of the imperialist war would necessarily lead to the victory of socialist revolution in one, or perhaps in several, of the capitalist countries. However, Russia could assist these revolutions only by example and propaganda. The main task of the Bolsheviks, as Lenin saw it, was to reinforce the proletarian dictatorship in their own country and to hold out by any means available until the socialist revolution was achieved in other capitalist countries. The spread of the Civil War in Russia made matters even more complicated. Exploiting the relative weakness of the proletarian state and its mistakes in economic policy, and assisted by generous contributions from most of the capitalist powers, the Russian counter-revolution managed to inflict a series of heavy defeats on the young

Soviet state, and to re-establish control over nine-tenths of the territory of the old Empire. The Bolsheviks' situation in 1918 and 1919 was so critical that, in many of his statements, Lenin actually said that the Russian Revolution *could not possibly achieve victory* without support from a European socialist revolution. This was said at the time by many other Bolshevik leaders, including Trotsky, as they made their speeches and wrote their articles, promoting the theme of world revolution virtually to first place. Here is Lenin addressing the Seventh Congress of the Russian Communist Party (Bolsheviks) in March 1918: 'History has placed us now in an unusually difficult position; we are having to endure a series of agonizing defeats in our unprecedentedly difficult organizational work. Of course, if we view this on a world-wide historical scale, there can be no doubting the truth that if it were not for the revolutionary movement in other countries our cause would be a hopeless one.'[12] A year later, in March 1919, addressing the Petrograd Soviet, he said: 'Only by assessing the role of the Soviets on a world scale shall we be able to work out the details of our internal life properly and regulate them in good time. *The work of construction depends entirely on the speed with which revolution achieves victory in the most important countries of Europe. Only after such victory shall we be able seriously to undertake the work of construction.*'[13] Here he is again, eighteen months later, addressing a meeting of the Moscow Soviet on the occasion of the third anniversary of the October Revolution: 'We have always stressed that we take an international view and that *a cause like socialist revolution cannot be achieved in a single country...*'[14]

Trotsky was saying much the same thing during those years. At a workers' meeting on April 14, 1918, he made this prediction: 'If the existing governments remain in power in the other countries, that's the end of our Russian Revolution. The Peace of Brest-Litovsk will be followed perhaps by a Peace of Petrograd or a Peace of Irkutsk that will be three times as bad or ten times as bad. The Russian Revolution and European imperialism cannot co-exist for long. We exist now only because the German bourgeoisie is waging a bloody war against the English and French bourgeoisies. Japan is fighting America, so her hands are tied. That is why we are holding out. As soon as these predators conclude a peace treaty they will all turn against us and then Germany together with England and America will tear the body of Russia to pieces. There can be no doubt about this; the Peace of Brest-Litovsk will not survive. A much more severe, arduous and merciless peace treaty will be prescribed for us. This will happen if European and American capital stays in the saddle, that is, as long as the working class does not dislodge it. That will be the end of us, and, of course, the labouring Russian people will pay for everything, with their blood and their toil, they will pay in decades, generation after generation.'[15]

Despite the obvious similarities between Lenin and Trotsky here, there was, in fact, a clear difference between them. As far as Lenin was concerned, calls to 'hold out' until the victory of European revolution became inevitable were a consequence of the particular circumstances obtaining in Russia in the period 1918-20, whereas for Trotsky this was a matter of absolute principle—he could not conceive of the victory of socialism in a country like Russia without direct support and assistance from revolution abroad. Trotsky's comments on the relationship between the Russian Revolution and world-wide revolution did not contradict his earlier or subsequent statements. Lenin's current pronouncements on these issues, however, did differ substantially from what he had said in 1915-16 and what he would go on to say in 1921-22. It is known that Lenin himself was not particularly embarrassed by inconsistencies of this kind; he was prepared to remove obsolete slogans and admit both his own mistakes and those of his Party as a whole. This is why it is a mistake to appraise Lenin's views, or, more generally, Leninism itself, on the strength of quotations alone; the development of his views, that is the totality of his statements on any given issue, must always be taken fully into account.

Later on, in an address to the Third Congress of the Communist International after the Bolshevik victory in the Civil War, Lenin openly admitted to certain substantial changes in his ideas on Russian and world revolution. 'Before the Revolution, and even after it, we used to think that, either immediately or at least very soon, revolution would break out in the more developed capitalist countries—and that if it did not we were lost. Despite this awareness we did all we could under all circumstances and at any cost to maintain the Soviet system, since we knew we were working not just for ourselves but for the cause of international revolution. We knew this and we expressed the view many times before the October

Revolution, as we did also immediately after it and during the signing of the Peace of Brest-Litovsk. And that was, in general terms, the right thing to do.'[16] However, circumstances were not to work out as Lenin and the Bolsheviks had predicted in October 1917 and during the furious battle against counter-revolution. The war ended in victory for the countries of the *Entente* and defeat for Germany. Bourgeois-democratic revolutions did indeed occur in certain countries, but the sporadic outbreaks of socialist revolution in Hungary for example were soon put down. Capitalism held out in every single country of Europe except Russia. On the other hand, the Bolsheviks emerged victorious from the Civil War and the battle against attempted intervention by the imperialists. Poland's *Entente*-inspired attack also ended in defeat. The desire for peace among the workers, peasants and soldiers in Western Europe was so strong that 'conservative Europe' had to shelve its plans for any further intervention. It was clear that Soviet Russia had gained a breathing space, though no one could say how long it would last. On the other hand, the economy of Soviet Russia was in ruins and there was no point in hoping for direct economic assistance from the proletariat in the developed countries of Europe. Industrial output was more than ninety per cent down from the 1913 level. The policy of 'War Communism' was all but exhausted, and there was increasing opposition to it among the peasants and petty bourgeoisie; this in turn was reflected in the sullen mood of demobilized Red Army men and of those in the newly created 'armies of labour'. Attempts to stiffen state regulation of the economy still further and to increase the requisitioning of farm produce caused a number of peasants' and soldiers' uprisings. The worst of these, in Tambovsk and Kronstadt, together with new insurrections in the Cossack regions, were put down only at great cost and with loss of life. Soviet Russia was going through a terrible crisis and seemed doomed to inevitable destruction, unless the revolution succeeded world-wide.

Lenin never wavered in his profound certainty that a world-wide proletarian revolution would come about, but he could not soberly sit back and consign the fate of Soviet Russia to the unpredictable zigzag of the world revolutionary movement. The search for a solution led to the NEP, his most vital contribution to the theory and practice of the socialist movement.

The New Economic Policy

The New Economy Policy was not something that could be introduced in its entirety in a month or even a year. Neither was its full significance clear even to Lenin himself. At first considered by many Bolshevik leaders a necessary evil and a temporary expedient or tactical manoeuvre, the NEP was so successful in securing a rapid return to stability and an improvement in the country's economic and political position that Lenin soon realized that it was something more than this. He became convinced that this was nothing less than the optimum policy available to Russia, given its economic backwardness and its workers' government. It not only guaranteed a breathing space for Soviet Russia, now abandoned as a lonely island of socialism in a hostile capitalist sea; not only was it calculated to enable them to 'hold out' pending the arrival of the 'main forces' of world revolution; not only did it permit the restoration of the shattered industrial base and ruined agriculture: NEP made possible, albeit at a slow pace, just what the Bolsheviks had dreamed of, the construction of a socialist society. It was, in other words, a serious long-term policy, and Lenin set out to formulate its underlying theoretical principles in an appropriately serious way. He reasoned that although the USSR would long remain a country of predominantly bourgeois production, nevertheless a socialist sector had now been created, represented by state institutions like the railways, the banks, the merchant navy and the inland waterways. The socialist sector also held the land and mineral resources of a huge country, as well as a monopoly of foreign trade. With these vital economic advantages behind it, the Soviet state could, in the interests of the country as a whole, make use of certain capitalist enterprises and concessions; this would be called state capitalism. Working through international trade, the Soviet state could also embrace many of the technological achievements of the capitalist countries and put them to the service of socialism. Lenin was particularly keen on cooperative ventures of all kinds in town and country. If the New Economic Policy were properly implemented, there was no real danger in the resuscitation and development of some capitalist features, for NEP guaranteed the advantageous development of the socialist economy, and it was in any case a programme for the construction not of a capitalist society (such as the Volte-Face group were counting on) but emphatically a socialist one. In a note 'On Cooperation', Lenin wrote: 'As a matter of fact, the power of state over all large-scale means of production, the power of state in the hands of the proletariat, the alliance of this proletariat with the many millions of small-time and very small-time peasants, the assured leadership of the peasantry by the proletariat, etc.; is not this all that is necessary in order to develop the cooperatives—the very cooperatives that we formerly treated as huckstering...—is not this all that is necessary in order to develop them into a complete socialist society? This is not quite the construction of socialist society, but it is necessary and sufficient for it.'[17] He concluded: 'Our opponents have told us more than once that we are undertaking the rash task of implanting socialism in an insufficiently cultivated country. But they were misled by the fact that we did not start from the end that was assumed in theory (the theory of all sorts of pedants), and that in our country the political and social revolution preceded the cultural revolution, the cultural revolution that now confronts us. This cultural revolution would be sufficient to transform us into a completely socialist country.'[18]

In his last articles and notes (and sometimes in conversation, especially with Bukharin) Lenin managed to work out the main lines of an elegant theory of socialist construction in a country like Russia. It is clear that he was counting on the objective and subjective factors of the domestic economy and the political development of Russia itself; his new programme for socialist construction was compiled with full account taken of the possibility that world-wide proletarian revolution might be long delayed. Without looking over his shoulder at Western Europe, but instead making a sober assessment of real conditions in the Russia of 1922, Lenin said that 'NEP continues to be the main, regular and exclusive slogan of the present day', and predicted with confidence that 'from NEP Russia, socialist Russia shall emerge'.[19]

Trotsky Maintains His Position

We have already taken note of Trotsky's views as he expressed them in 1906 and 1915. He was convinced that the revolutionary movement could develop successfully and come to victory only in its pan-European form; if it remained constricted by nationalism, it was doomed to certain failure. In particular, he was sure that the revolution could not triumph in Russia or England without victorious revolution in Germany, and vice versa. These opinions had not changed essentially by 1922-24, as was emphasized by the republication of certain pertinent articles from 1915, in the third volume of Trotsky's collected works and also in a collection entitled simply *1905*.

In 1922, as Lenin began the detailed formulation of his plan for the transition from 'NEP Russia' to 'socialist Russia', Trotsky claimed that 'the contradiction between a workers' government and an overwhelming majority of peasants in a backward country could be resolved only on an international scale, in the arena of a world proletarian revolution'.[20] The 'Afterword' to his earlier *Programme for Peace*, written the same year, reiterated this conviction.[21] And even after Lenin's writings of 1922, which left no room for doubt about his new approach to the prospects of the Revolution in Russia, Trotsky issued another collection of articles in which the following statements appeared: 'We are suffering from a decline in productivity as a result of the imperialist war, the Civil War and the blockade. The only thing that can help us is an injection of large-scale technological ancillary aids, exemplary skilled workers, steam-engines and so on—and certainly not constant unsuccessful insurrections in the odd state here and there. That Soviet Russia can hold out and develop only if accompanied by world-wide revolution, this is something you can read about very precisely, comrades, in everything we have ever written... The New Economic Policy is calculated to suit certain specific conditions in space and time: it is a manoeuvre adopted by a Soviet state still inhabiting a capitalist environment and counting all the time on the revolutionary development of Europe... The New Economic Policy is only a tool to regulate the tempo of this development.'[22]

No one disputed these assertions at the time. The last writings of Lenin had not yet been properly assessed, and, in Western Europe, the revolutionary crisis of the period 1918-23 had not yet run its course. Everyone remembered many statements made by Lenin during the Civil War that seemed to accord with the views now being expressed by Trotsky. It is also the case that even Stalin, not to mention Zinoviev and Kamenev, was at that time voicing very similar ideas. In April 1924, for instance, in his guest lectures at

Sverdlovsk University, he had this to say about the possibility of the victory of socialism in one country: 'The overthrow of bourgeois power in one country and its replacement by proletarian power do not guarantee the complete victory of socialism. The main task of socialism—the organization of socialist production—still lies ahead. Can this task be completed, can the ultimate victory of socialism be achieved in one country without the joint efforts of the proletariats in several leading countries? For the overthrow of the bourgeoisie the efforts of one country will suffice—the history of our revolution tells us so. For the ultimate victory of socialism, for the organization of socialist production, the efforts of one country, particularly a peasant country like Russia, are insufficient; for this, the efforts of the proletariats in several leading countries are essential.'[23]

One can only suppose that it was Bukharin who pointed out to Stalin the contradiction between this formulation and the opinions expressed so clearly by Lenin in his last articles, and even in earlier articles going back to 1915 and 1916. At all events, the whole of this paragraph was omitted from the second edition of the published text. What is more, Stalin, with his customary inability ever to admit a mistake, announced in a later article that this particular formulation had been 'directed against statements made by critics of Lenin, against Trotskyists who asserted that the dictatorship of the proletariat in one country without victory in other countries could never "hold out against conservative Europe". In so far—and only in so far—as this formulation then (April 1924) appeared to be an adequate one, no doubt it served some purpose'.[24] It is worth emphasizing the obvious point that Stalin's formulation differed very little from the propositions advanced by Trotsky. At the very end of 1924, Stalin issued a collection of his own articles and statements of the year 1917, and, in his preface, he advanced for the first time what was for him a new formula concerning the possible construction of socialism in the USSR. In the same breath, he turned for the first time to make a strong criticism of Trotsky's views on the same subject. Trotsky never bothered to respond.

The first flashes of controversy on this issue came soon afterwards. The external stimulus to discussion was the fact that the capitalist world had just emerged from a period of 'wars and revolutions' and was entering a period of 'temporary stabilization'. The USSR, by contrast, was at the end of a period of reconstruction, and consideration of the path to socialism was now particularly relevant. The internal impetus for renewed inner-Party debate was the sharpening conflict between Stalin on the one hand and Zinoviev and Kamenev on the other. Debate and discussion ranged freely over many questions during 1925: the nature of state industry, the significance of NEP, attitudes to the peasantry, the Party regime, relations with Trotsky, and so on. The question of the prospects for the construction of Socialism in the USSR was inevitably raised. Very cautiously at first, not in print but at a meeting of the Politburo, Zinoviev and Kamenev began to criticize what Stalin had said on this topic, and accused him in particular of underestimating the chances of world-wide revolution and adopting too narrow and national an attitude. The majority of the Politburo were against them. That, however, was not the end of the matter. Politburo meetings were usually unrecorded, and arguments there did not usually spill over into the Party; but on this occasion Stalin decided to publicize the comments made by Zinoviev and Kamenev. The Leningrad press, reflecting the fact that the Party organization of that city was run by supporters of Zinoviev, had for some time been directing oblique criticism at the Stalinist majority in the Politburo. Disguised criticism of the Bolshevik Party was also evident in the resolutions of the 22nd Leningrad Provincial Party Conferene. At this stage, the Moscow Committee of the Communist Party wrote to its Leningrad equivalent. The letter, obviously written on Stalin's initiative, was a long one. Here is an extract from it: 'Recently in the Politburo, Comrades Kamenev and Zinoviev have been defending the view that, because of our economic backwardness, we cannot cope with our domestic difficulties unless we are rescued by international revolution. Together with a majority of the Central Committee, we are of the opinion that we can construct socialism, we are doing so and shall do so, in spite of our technological backwardness—in defiance of it. We believe, naturally, that this construction will proceed much more slowly than in conditions of world-wide victory, but nevertheless we are moving forward and shall continue to do so. We put it to you that the views expressed by Comrades Kamenev and Zinoviev mean that they have no confidence in the inner strengths of our working class and the peasant masses behind them. We put it to you that this is a departure from Lenin's principles.'[25] The question of the prospects for socialist construction in the USSR was put to the Fourteenth Party Conference in April 1925, which approved a set of theses 'Concerning the Tasks of the Comintern and the Russian Communist Party (Bolsheviks)'. Part of it went as follows:

'Speaking in general terms, the victory of socialism (not in the sense of ultimate victory) is possible in one country... On the other hand, the co-existence of two diametrically opposed social systems raises the constant threat of a capitalist blockade, other forms of economic pressure, armed intervention and restoration. The sole guarantee of the ultimate victory of socialism, i.e. guarantee against restoration, is therefore victorious socialist revolution in a series of countries. In no way does it follow from this that there is no possibility of constructing a complete socialist society in a country as backward as Russia without "assistance at state level" (Trotsky's words) from countries of more advanced technological development... A country with a dictatorship of the proletariat, a world base for international revolution, must look upon itself as a colossally powerful lever and support of revolution; on the other hand, the ruling proletarian party there must work as hard as possible to construct socialism, in the certain knowledge that this construction can be and probably will be victorious if only the country can be defended against all attempts at restoration. In other words, the correct policy for the Russian Communist Party in relation to the peasants within the country and in the realm of international relations must be to overcome all the difficulties arising from the decelerating pace of worldwide revolution.'[26]

Neither Zinoviev nor Kamenev spoke out against the thesis of the possible ultimate victory of socialism in the USSR; in fact they voted along with the other delegates in favour of this resolution. Clearly they had no desire to turn this issue into a subject of contention within the Party. Stalin, however, used the conference decisions to renew his attack on Trotsky—which was also directed obliquely at Zinoviev and Kamenev. We can see from his report 'Summing Up the Achievement of the Fourteenth Party Conference' that he had taken good care to scrutinize all the main pronouncements made by Lenin on the subject, which put him in an invulnerable position, at least as far as Party dogma was concerned.

But the question was not just one of accurate quotation. An overwhelming majority of Party activists at that time supported the idea that the victory of socialism in the USSR was a real possibility. Without going deeply into theoretical niceties, these people naturally wanted their hard work to lead this poor and backward country to prosperity and plenty, and in the shortest possible time. Stalin organized these desires to maximum effect, criticizing every hint of vagueness in Zinoviev's formulations. Now it was that, first by suggestion and then more and more overtly, a long-running argument began between the Leningrad and Moscow press on the widest possible range of problems arising in the construction of Socialism. The publication of Zinoviev's *Leninism* in 1925 brought renewed attacks upon the author. This book quotes a good deal from Lenin, and particularly his comments on the possibility of building socialism in a single country (or perhaps in one or two countries). It is also very critical of Trotsky. However, in his own commentary, Zinoviev was guilty of a number of rather vague formulations concerning the distinction between socialism and communism, and the construction of socialism in the USSR. He seemed to suggest that it would be possible to start the construction of socialism, but not to finish it, in a single country, particularly one as backward as the USSR. All these ideas, however, were of a preliminary and unsystematized nature. Forthright and decisive comment emerged from the 'new' or 'Leningrad' opposition only at the Fourteenth All-Russian Party Conference of December 18-31, 1925.

When he addressed this conference, Stalin made no mention of 'Socialism in one country', considering the question settled. Neither did the opposition raise it as an issue. Other problems occupied the attention of the gathering. Zinoviev, however, as seconder of the opposition, had the right of winding up the debate and, when doing so, in the heat of discussion, he mentioned the problem of the construction of socialism. He began by referring to Stalin's *Foundations of Leninism,* which mirrored, in fact, the assertions of his own *Leninism*. He continued: 'Just look at what was said, for instance, by Comrade Yakovlev at the last provincial Party Conference in Kursk. "Can we in one country," he asks, "surrounded on all sides by capitalist enemies, can we, under these circumstances, in one country, complete the building of socialism?" He replies, "On the basis of all that has been said, we can say with every justification that not only have we started the construction of socialism, despite the fact that so far we are the only Soviet country, Soviet state, in the world—we shall finish it too." (*Kurskaya Pravda*, no. 279, December 8, 1925). Is that a Leninist way of putting the question? Is there not a whiff of narrow-minded nationalism in this?'[27] Stalin waited until after the conference was over and then rounded on Zinoviev and Kamenev. In January 1926, he wrote a long pamphlet entitled 'A Contribution to Questions of Leninism' which was almost entirely devoted to a rejection of the ideas of Zinoviev and Kamenev, including the former's contradictory statements about the construction of socialism in the USSR.

Something must be said about Bukharin's position. In many modern publications, one reads that Bukharin shared what is referred to as 'Trotsky's and Zinoviev's lack of faith in the possibility of constructing socialism in the USSR'. F. Vaganov, for instance, claims that 'the Trotskyists under the banner of the "left-wing" revolutionary faction may have stated their denial of the possibility of constructing socialism in our country quite openly, but the right-wingers, without putting it into words, also in fact wrote this off as a possibility'.[28] This is excessive. In reality, it was Bukharin who from 1924 to 1928 acted as the main theoretician of our party and supervised the preparation of its main policy documents and resolutions. It is not surprising that both the 'new' opposition and the 'united' opposition formed in 1926 frequently directed their critical fire as much at him as at Stalin. In point of fact, all the main statements made by Bukharin on the important questions—the victory of socialism in the USSR, the role of NEP, the nature of state enterprises, the role of co-operatives—were in theoretical terms more precise, more carefully considered and more neatly formulated than anything said by Stalin. When the Fourteenth Party Conference was over, to be followed in Leningrad by the 23rd Extraordinary Provincial Conference of the All-Russian Communist Party, Bukharin was deliberately entrusted with the task of reporting to this follow-up conference on behalf of the Party Central Committee and speaking on the results and lessons of the previous one, particularly in relation to the defeat of the Leningrad opposition. Here is part of what he said: 'When we accuse our comrades of an incorrect formulation of the question of the construction of socialism in our country, what are we actually accusing them of, and what do we think it so necessary to fight against? We think it is necessary to fight decisively against one principle which was proposed by comrade Kamenev and comrade Zinoviev at a meeting of the Politburo—the principle that we shall perish because of our technological backwardness unless economic help manages to reach us in time from a victorious West European proletariat. We are accused on this account of narrow-minded nationalism but that reproach could only be well-founded if we were to say that we shall stick it out alone under all circumstances. That would be wrong, and that would be narrow-minded nationalism... We are defending a truly Leninist standpoint when we assert that, despite our technological backwardness, our large numbers of peasants, despite the fact that our technology and economy are lagging far behind, nevertheless we can, step by step, construct socialism and we shall finish the construction of it unless armed interference from the capitalist power prevents us from doing so... Can we be defeated by armed strength? We say: yes, we can. Can we therefore in all reality turn away from the course of international revolution. No, we cannot. International revolution is the sole guarantee against our being strangled by the capitalist powers. Can we then conclude that our technological and economic backwardness will ruin us? We say this is a different question and anyone who says that is sowing the seeds of disbelief in the inner strength of our working class and the possibility of its controlling the peasantry, and that person stands in outright opposition to Lenin.'[29]

Aspects of the Party Controversy in 1926-27

Trotsky kept quiet throughout the battle against the Leningrad opposition. The defeat of Zinoviev and Kamenev was soon followed by another stage in the battle against so-called 'leftist' opposition, which lasted for more than a year, from mid-summer 1926 to the autumn of 1927. During this period, Trotsky, Zinoviev and Kamenev shelved their recent differences, bitter though they had been, and came together to lead a new 'united' faction. The theoretical platform of this new opposition group embraced virtually all the main themes of both the Trotskyist opposition of 1923-24 and the Leningrad opposition of 1925. The main problem over which they took issue with the policy of Stalin and Bukharin concerned attitudes to the capitalist elements in town and country. The opposition demanded an escalation of the battle against kulaks and NEP men and more severe taxes on their economic activity. They also insisted on stepping up the rate of industrialization. Thus the course adopted by the opposition did not run counter to the general party line on the construction of socialism. They were merely calling for the use of methods that did not square with the main principles of NEP. They were also insisting unrealistically on an acceleration that was beyond the country's means. Not one of the opposition leaders ever suggested that socialism should not or *could* not be constructed in the USSR. They were not, however, prepared—Trotsky in particular was not prepared—to admit any errors or go back on their stated principles in the matter, and all three of them tried to avoid being drawn into discussions about it.

For the Fifteenth All-Russian Party Congress the united opposition prepared a platform containing no assertions of the impossibility of constructing socialism in the USSR. On the contrary, it claimed that the Stalin-Bukharin line was an obstacle to the speedy construction of socialism, in that it allowed the unjustifiably rapid growth in town and country of capitalist elements that were a menace to socialism. The platform also included a great number of critical comments and suggestions concerning the situation of the working class, the trade unions, the strengthening of the class struggle in the country, the collective farms and state farms, the housing question, unemployment, the financial policy of the Soviet state, the fight against bureaucracy, the five-year plan, and so on. Very many of these suggestions and observations were fair and reasonable. But Stalin had no desire to confront the opposition on their own platform. He turned things around so that the main thesis and subject for discussion became the question of the possibility of the ultimate victory of socialism. He made two speeches directed against the 'united' opposition, 'On the Social-Democratic Tendency in our Party' (at the Fifteenth Congress, on November 1, 1926) and 'More on the Social-Democratic Tendency in our Party' (at the seventh augmented plenary session of the Executive Committee of the Comintern on December 7, 1926). Much of his time was spent 'demonstrating' the disbelief of the opposition leaders in the ultimate victory of Socialism in the USSR and quoting extensively from Trotsky's writings of the 1905-15 period and later. It has to be admitted that in this respect Stalin achieved his aim, since his reasoning on this issue was closer than Trotsky's to the Leninist line and also more comprehensible and acceptable to the majority of Party activists.

Following the defeat of the united opposition, controversy over this question ceased. It did not arise during the period of 'rightist' opposition, nor when Stalin, after the defeat of this faction and after collectivization had been pushed through, proposed the slogan of an all-out frontal attack by socialism. Many of the erstwhile leaders of the left and right oppositions simply capitulated before Stalin, and failed to speak out against the Party leadership between 1930 and 1933, when our party and people endured one of the most arduous periods in their history, comparable only to the Civil War years. Despite hidden grumblings of discontent from a large and growing number of Party activists discontented with Stalin's leadership, the Seventeenth Congress went down officially as a 'Congress of Victors'. In actual fact, by 1934, the Party and the Soviet people really had achieved great successes in the construction of socialism, though retrospective historical analysis shows quite clearly that if this 'third "Stalinist" revolution from above' could have been avoided, even greater successes would have been attainable, and without the sacrifice of so many millions of lives. Stalin had nothing to say about the enormous cost of the successes he enumerated, and touched only in passing on the question of socialism in one country. 'Experience has shown in our country', he said, 'that the victory of socialism in one individual country is perfectly possible. What can anyone say against that fact?'[30]

Of all the opposition leaders, only Trotsky, the exile who had put together a vocal but largely ineffective group of *émigré* supporters and was to organize the Fourth International, continued to criticize the theory of socialism in one country. In his book *Permanent Revolution* (1930) he wrote: 'The theory of socialism in one country, which rose on the yeast of the reaction against October, is the only theory that consistently and to the very end opposes the theory of the permanent revolution. The attempt of the epigones, under the lash of our criticism, to confine the application of the theory of socialism in one country exclusively to Russia, because of its specific characteristics (its vastness and its natural resources), does not improve matters but only makes them worse. The break with the internationalist position always and invariably leads to national *messianism*, that is, to attributing special superiorities and qualities to one's own country, which allegedly permit it to play a rôle to which other countries cannot attain. The world division of labour, the dependence of Soviet industry upon foreign technology, the dependence of the productive forces of the advanced countries of Europe upon Asiatic raw materials, etc., etc., make the construction of an independent socialist society in any single country in the world impossible.'[31] This was subsequently taken over as a principled position of the Fourth International found by Trotsky and his followers in 1938.[32]

Trotsky's claims were disproved by the experience of the next ten to fifteen years. But this should not be taken to indicate that Stalin's interpretation of the theory of the construction of socialism in a single country was one-hundred-per-cent accurate. On the contrary, subsequent eperience showed up many errors in Stalin's version of socialist construction in general and of socialism in one country in particular. Some of these errors are worth looking into.

Nationalism and Great Power Chauvinism

It is important to remember, first and foremost, that Stalin never showed any particular concern for the problems of international Communism. He played almost no part in the work of the first congresses of the Comintern, and what interest he had in the organization had dissolved into apathy by the mid-1920s. He did no work for the journal *Communist International* and his name did not appear in the long list of politicians assisting it. His descriptions of the October Revolution as a first step towards world-wide revolution read more like a dutiful nod in the direction of official Leninist doctrine than sincere conviction on his part. A contemporary researcher working on Stalinism is right when he states: 'Lenin's feeling for the organic wholeness of world-wide revolution, his sense of participation in it and of direct responsibility not just for revolution in Russia but for revolution everywhere, was alien to Stalin; for him it was something introduced from outside, insubstantial and unreliable. He lived in a different psychological atmosphere well away from the sudden upheavals and problems of world-wide revolution. Such revolution was for him nothing more than westernizing bookishness, theorizing by literary men who had grown up miles away from Russia in emigration, and also an agitational device for cheering up the largely unconscious, gullible popular masses in Russia, who were finishing their Russian revolution.'[33]

In their understanding of the relationship between the October Revolution and revolution on a world scale, Trotsky and Stalin departed from Lenin, as it were, in opposite directions. The national destiny of Russia was for Trotsky an empty noise; Russia was 'merely' a platform for world-wide revolution, and Trotsky himself stressed the word 'merely'. Stalin's view was quite the reverse. In a policy document entitled 'The Political Strategy and Tactics of the Russian Communists', he wrote: 'The achievement of the overthrow of the bourgeoisie in one country led therefore to a new task, carrying the fight on to an international scale, the fight by the proletarian state against hostile capitalist states, and the Russian proletariat, which until now had been just one of the units of the international proletariat, henceforward became the vanguard of the international proletariat. In this way, the goal of developing revolution in the West *in order to make it easier for herself, Russia, to complete her own revolution* has turned from a wish into a practical daily task.'[34] It is curious to note that this document, although written by July 1921, remained unpublished until 1947 when it came to light in the fifth volume of Stalin's collected works.

Stalin had practically no part to play in the Sixth and Seventh Congresses of the Comintern, despite the fact that they were settling questions of the greatest importance to the international workers' movement. His *Short Course* does not even give them a mention, though the Seventh Congress in particular, by adopting a resolution in favour of united people's fronts and a changed attitude towards Social Democracy, brought about a strategic change in the whole Communist movement. Such examples of Stalin's leanings towards a nationalist form of Bolshevism could be multiplied without any difficulty, and show how right Lenin was to warn the Party of Stalin's proneness to 'Great-Russian nationalist distortions'.[35]

Although Stalin constantly denied that the governmental interests of the USSR could ever be at variance with those of the world Communist movement, this possibility could not be ruled out in practice. This was shown, not for the first time or the last, by the signing of a non-aggression treaty between the USSR and Germany in 1939. The justification and significance of that treaty are subjects for endless discussion, but what is beyond doubt is the falseness of the directives sent by Stalin to the Comintern, which proposed turning anti-fascist propaganda upside-down and indicting England and France as the guilty parties, the warmongers all too ready to start a second world war. Stalin also badly underestimated the importance of supporting Republican Spain in the period between 1936 and 1939, and the anti-fascist effort of 1939-41. We can say without fear of contradiction that on all these occasions, when the national interests of the Soviet Union were for a time at variance with those of the international workers' and Communist movements, Stalin invariably set an absolute priority on national interests, wildly distorted though his idea of the latter may have been.

Socialism and Pseudo-Socialism in the Soviet Union

In the 1930s and 1940s, as his conception of the practical construction of socialism in the USSR evolved, Stalin was guilty of wild distortion and profound errors. For the moment, we may set aside this man's innumerable crimes against humanity, the illegal repression and murder on a mass scale, the elimination of millions of innocents and genocide directed against whole peoples. This is a subject to itself. On this occasion, we are referring only to a number of serious mistakes in his very understanding of socialism. When, in the 1920s, he spoke of the construction of socialism in one country, he had in mind first and foremost the economic aspects of this construction, the quantitative pre-eminence of socialist over capitalist enterprise. Thus he announced the decisive victory of socialism in the USSR in the mid-1930s, even though in terms of productivity and economic efficiency his state enterprises, not to mention the collective and state farms, were a long way behind the level of achievement of analogous institutions in the USA and Western Europe. But he was wrong, in any case, to suggest that socialism as a form of society is a matter of economics alone. Naturally, Stalin was familiar with Marx's warning that a revolution in property-owning must be accompanied by a corresponding revolution in the complex superstructure of society, but it was his belief that problems of 'the superstructure' were much easier to solve than those of the 'base'. At the Seventeenth Party Congress, he put this into words as follows: 'We have already laid the foundations of a socialist society in the USSR and all that remains is for us to top them with a superstructure—and there is no doubt that this is an easier matter than laying the foundations of a socialist society'.[36]

As it turned out in reality, the problems of the superstructure were the most difficult of all. The first and most important objective in our situation should have been the formation of a genuinely democratic socialist state. Both Marx and Engels believed that fully developed socialism would lead to the gradual withering away of the state; Lenin wrote on this subject in his *The State and Revolution*. But in a socialist country surrounded on all sides by capitalist powers the most important thing was not to encourage the state to wither away but to build up its socialist strength. It was necessary to construct a socialist state, which Bukharin was right to call 'State Socialism', the term he saw as most appropriate for this form of Soviet society.[37] However, what was in question was not merely a secure state but a democratic one guaranteeing maximum freedom for all its citizens. It is hardly necessary to record that Stalin did not succeed in doing this, that, on the contrary, he virtually eliminated democracy from our society and our Party by setting up a huge, clumsy, authoritarian, bureaucratic apparatus of governmental power that was anything but a socialist 'superstructure' built on a socialist 'base'. Even worse, within that apparatus, the repressive organs eventually acquired a greater weight and influence than the organs of the Communist Party itself.

It is also true that many other areas of the superstructure contained too many pseudo-socialist constructions. We are thinking here of the rules of justice much publicized by Vyshinsky, the realms of culture and philosophy and the whole of Soviet ideology, which became more and more centred around a religious cult of Stalin's own personality rather than the tenets and principles of scientific socialism.

In the thirties and forties, along with the expansion of socialism and socialist attitudes, there occurred an even faster expansion of pseudo-socialism. This was noticeable most of all in the Soviet countryside. In 1922, Lenin had considered the cooperative system to be a constituent part of socialist organization, since it reconciled the personal interests of the peasants with the collective interests of the cooperative itself and society at large. But did Stalin's collective farms bear any resemblance to socialist enterprises? Did the collective-farm workers, toiling in society's fields, on society's farmland, receive material compensation 'according to their labour'? Did not millions of them work virtually unpaid, making ends meet by doing what they could with their private plots? This sort of labour brings to mind the system of corvée (*barshchina*), which the peasants were forced to endure in the nineteenth century, and the taxes they paid under the new system bring to mind the quit-rent (*obrok*) extorted by the Tsarist state. In this manner, monstrous semi-feudal arrangements, the binding of the peasant to his collective farm by means of a system of passports and passes, arose under Stalin in the guise of socialism.

It is almost superfluous to state that the huge system of industrial enterprises and construction projects based on the organization known as 'the Gulag' had nothing to do with any principle of socialist economy. The labour demanded from millions of prisoners locked up in Stalin's concentration camps was nothing less than a revival of slavery. One hastens to add that the abolition of this system of concentration camps following the Twentieth Party Congress, the overt criticism of the cult of Stalin, the restoration of an interest for the farm-worker as a return for his work in a collective enterprise, the cessation of mass terror throughout the country and the limitations placed on the use of extraordinary powers and on the influence of the repressive organs, the correction of many Stalinist distortions in national policy, in the realms of culture and ideology, as well as a certain broadening of political democracy in Party and civil affairs—all of this work, which has proceeded steadily over the last twenty-six years, coinciding with a rapid growth in the development of industry, housing construction, science and agriculture, points to a restoration of socialism in our country.

It is a mistake to believe that the situation in the USSR today remains essentially what it was twenty-six or twenty-seven years ago. On the other hand, it would be equally wrong to believe that the work of establishing a fully developed socialist society has been completed. It would be premature to describe Soviet socialism, in its economic and political aspects, as 'developed' or 'fully matured'. We should speak more properly of socialism as it currently exists, still in a developing state and still facing many difficulties that will have to be surmounted.

The Unsolved Problem

To judge by the Soviet press, the problem of constructing socialism in a single country has been solved long ago and can have no further relevance today for the European Communist parties or indeed those in any other capitalist country. It is true that in the country of the Soviets a relatively well-developed socialist society has been constructed. Socialism has also achieved victory in many other countries of Europe and Asia, and even in Cuba. All these countries have come together to form a socialist camp united in politics and economics (in the form of Comecon) and to some extent militarily (though the Warsaw Pact). For this reason, the victory of socialist revolution in any of the countries of Europe could no longer be considered a victory 'in a single country' since any working-class victory there would receive political, economic and if necessary military assistance from the whole socialist camp. A hundred years ago, Marx and Engels envisaged the formation in Western Europe and the USA of a strong socialist camp, which would be joined gradually by the more backward countries in the Eastern and Southern regions of our planet. In the event, history has worked itself out in more tortuous ways. The socialist camp has been formed, but in the East rather than the West and we now wait for the countries of the West to join it. From the standpoint of human history, however, viewed at a point of transition between different socio-economic systems, the specific forms may have varied but the essence of the transition remains unaltered. That is how matters stand, if we are to judge the processes of history according to contemporary Soviet writing. Without doubt there is a grain of truth in all of this, but the actual situation is much more complicated.

In the first place, the existing forms of socialism simply do not appeal to the Communists of Western Europe, let alone other socialists. To use their terminology, these 'models' are not appropriate for them. Western European socialism is not favourably impressed by the existence in the USSR of a rather draconian one-party system, and the exclusion of any form of political pluralism. Not only have all other political parties 'outlived their use', as

Soviet writers put it, but they are banned by law. Thus the USSR is disqualified by one of the fundamental principles of democracy, the possibility for political minorities to formulate and defend their own points of view. The USSR also curtails proper freedom of the press, freedom of speech, freedom of assembly and demonstration. Democratically-run trade unions are forbidden. General elections long ago became an empty formality with no choice between candidates. According to the Soviet 'model', the state, far from becoming simplified and 'withering away', has become inordinately complicated and now penetrates into every nook and cranny of social life. There is no means of controlling the activities of the highest organs of state government, and, at many vital points in the state apparatus, bureaucracy and irresponsibility persist. The Party organization is top-heavy, its apparatus consisting of Party functionaries. Constructed strictly on the hierarchical principle, this apparatus is scarcely controlled by the membership; it has in practice turned into a vital structural element of the state machinery. The security organs play an exaggerated role in the internal affairs of Soviet society. Literature, the theatre, the cinema and all other branches of culture are subject to strict control. A vigilant censorship still functions and prevents the publication of much valuable scientific and artistic material. The vast mechanism of Soviet management is grossly inefficient, with personal and private initiative largely discouraged. Centralized planning applies not only to large-scale enterprises but even to the small ones. The economy of the country suffers from unwieldy, bureaucratic leadership and lacks all flexibility. All of this results in low productivity, substantial wastage and low-quality goods and services. These industrial shortcomings exist to a great degree also in our agriculture, because of which a country with tremendous agricultural advantages is forced to import food in millions of tonnes. There is, of course, another side to this picture. One can point to a number of considerable achievements in many areas of the economy, and the social and cultural life of the country. There is no noticeable unemployment, no inflation and no bitter social conflict to speak of. Medical treatment is free, as is universal secondary education. The housing problem is being resolved fairly quickly. The production of consumer goods is constantly increasing, as is the whole range of goods and services available to Soviet citizens. These lists of advantages and disadvantages could be extended indefinitely, but it is true to say that the achievements of 'real socialism' are not sufficient, in the eyes of Western socialists and Communists, to make up for its lack of democracy.

The socialist camp includes not only the Soviet Union and its close allies but also China. It is deeply divided and on the verge of military confrontation. Simultaneously, the Soviet bloc is engaged in fierce political and military rivalry with the USA and its allied powers. Détente has mitigated, but not removed, the dangers of this situation. It comes as no surprise that, despite its support for the workers' and socialist movement in Western Europe, the Soviet Union tends to look upon events in terms of global policy, which by no means always corresponds to the national interests of European countries eager to preserve their independence. This same eagerness for independence on the part of the European countries leads them into trouble in another way, however. We have seen that Trotsky often referred to the impossibility of the victory of socialism in a single country on the grounds that all the capitalist countries are strongly interdependent economically and financially, that they depend too much on the world markets and so on. Practice has shown that many of Trotsky's misgivings were unjustified. By introducing a foreign trade monopoly, the Soviet Union succeeded in bolstering its economy against negative influences from outside and creating the conditions necessary for the rapid development of its own industry. It then managed to overcome the boycott mounted by the capitalist countries and gradually to harmonize two-way trade relations that stimulated rather than slowed down its own development. However, the degree of integration of the capitalist countries is incomparably greater now than in 1917. Multinational corporations, usually American in origin, play an increasingly significant role in the economies of the capitalist world. The processes of integration are accelerating not in the East but in Western Europe, where they have more than twenty years' experience of the so-called Common Market, where a single financial system is being worked out, a European parliament has been established and there is talk of setting up an effective supra-national parliament. In these circumstances, the victory of socialism in any one country would create all kinds of economic and political difficulties. Thus, despite the existence of a large and powerful Soviet camp, the West continues to ask each of its countries—is the victory of socialist revolution possible in any single capitalist country?

The Response of the Western Communist Parties

A number of western theorists, particularly of the social-democratic persuasion, and many Soviet dissidents think the answers to these problems are very simple. They claim that the society and government existing today in the Soviet Union are not socialist and that not one of the countries describing itself today as socialist is anything of the kind. No country can call itself by that name if its productivity is below that of the developed capitalist countries, or if it fails to guarantee fundamental democratic freedoms and uses state bureaucracy to dominate and control the whole of society. In this respect there is not a single socialist state anywhere in the world; the self-styled socialist countries are state capitalist regimes in which power belongs to a kind of 'new class', a new privileged caste ruling over the country's workforce. This point of view is shared by many Trotskyists who, unlike Trotsky himself, deny that the Soviet state is in any way proletarian; it has degenerated just as Trotsky predicted it would. Socialism, therefore, has yet to see the light of day. They go on to argue that the victory of socialism is still impossible in a single country—it must occur on a world scale.[38]

Not everyone thinks along these lines. Some Western theorists and sovietologists, and even some Soviet dissidents (such as I. Shafarevich and A.A. Zinoviev) think the very opposite. They believe that the socialism existing today in the USSR and elsewhere is indeed true socialism of the kind dreamt of by Marx, Engels and Lenin, and that there can be no other form. 'Socialism with a human face' they consider a utopian concept. Socialism and democracy cannot be joined; they are opposite and mutually exclusive. 'Democratic socialism' is a contradiction in terms, an absurd pipe-dream. These people claim that all the fine talk of European Communist leaders about respecting democracy and democratic traditions is simply a tactical manoeuvre calculated to delude the electorate. In the event of their coming to power, the Western Communists would establish in their own countries a regime every bit as authoritarian as that of the USSR, and would try to eliminate their former allies in the 'leftist bloc', politically and even physically.

Both of these extremes are wrong. The difficulties we face must not be underestimated, but there is no cause for despair. The social systems that have come into being in the Soviet Union and Eastern Europe are a long way from completion but they are basically socialist systems, even if they still embody many of the features and characteristics of earlier social formations (the 'birthmarks' of capitalism and, further East, feudalism). These immature socialist organisms are gradually developing, and, in order to bring about a transition to the stage of mature, highly developed socialism, no revolution will be necessary, though many serious structural reforms and socio-political changes will be required. The socialist countries in the East need to develop the potential invested in them, and they need considerable technological, economic and cultural assistance from the developed West. They are receiving this assistance on a limited scale, though it would be greatly preferable if they could receive it from a socialist West.

At the same time, then, the socialist countries in the East can and must lend assistance to socialist revolutions and programmes of socialist reform in Western countries, where a transition to socialism is the only reasonable alternative to the growing decline of capitalism. The deficiences and wrongdoings of socialism in the Eastern countries have been very great, but the West need not go over the whole difficult terrain traversed by the socialist process in Eastern Europe. Western Communist parties must work out their own paths to socialism, and indeed are doing so at this moment. We have already considered some aspects of the approach by Western Communist parties to the problems of socialist revolution. One further and vital aspect is the renunciation of revolution conceived as a rapidly executed act of violence intended to alter the socio-economic character of Western society suddenly and decisively. Nowadays the Communist parties of Western countries are preoccupied with new conceptions of the transfer of power into working-class hands, according to which it will occur gradually, accompanied not by mayhem and destruction but by a steady restructuring of the bourgeois state apparatus. A member of the political committee of the Communist Party of Great Britain wrote as follows, in explanation of a draft new programme:

'Another aspect of our programme ... concerns the revolutionary process. We do not envisage the achieving of socialism through insurrection and civil war. Such a prospect bears no relation to the reality of political life in Britain. We see our forward movement as a process of democratic struggle which includes destroying the power of the capitalist class in all spheres of life, political, economic and cultural and attracting people over to a socialist policy, a process not to be achieved overnight. The duration and future characteristics of this process will be determined by the outcome of the struggle at various stages... The left-wing government whose establishment we regard as one of the important stages would be radically different from previous Labour governments. Instead of attempting to solve the crisis by transferring the burden of it to the workers it would alter class alignments to the disadvantage of large-scale capitalists and their allies. It would not be a socialist government carrying out a socialist revolution, but with the support of a mass struggle outside parliament and stimulating this, it would begin to introduce massive democratic reforms in Britain... In view of the complexity of the problems of abolishing the power of the capitalist class this process might possibly take up the terms of more than one left-wing parliament, with the composition of these governments changing to the benefit of the left; the Communist Party will win representation in parliament and government; new forms of alliance between Labour Party members and Communists will spring up.

'While rejecting civil war as a strategy we do not consider that the advancement towards socialism will be smooth, harmonious and continuous. Our approach is quite different from the recipes of the "gradualists" who rely on the almost imperceptible conversion of capitalism into socialism without any serious inhibitions being imposed on the ruling large-scale capitalist monopolies and the capitalist state. On the contrary, there will be a hard struggle and serious clashes. "Gradualism" leaves the basic elements of capitalism untouched. Our policy envisages an attack on the power of the capitalists. Its effectiveness and strength are not diminished by the fact that it will probably be a fairly long drawn-out process during which the key positions of capitalist power will be taken one by one by the workers. The successive stages in the process would represent a period of revolutionary transition to socialism which would finally result in the transfer of power to the working class and its allies.

'The Communists have no illusions about the resistance which the British ruling class will show to left-wing governments, including furious propaganda campaigns, economic sabotage and attempts to create the conditions for a military coup. The programme emphasizes that in the event of an attempted coup a left-wing government would be obliged to take any necessary measures, including the use of force. A coup is neither inevitable nor impossible. An attempted coup, and its outcome, depend on the disposition of political forces, including the composition of the armed forces and their positions...'[39]

The Communist Parties of Italy, Spain, France and a number of other countries take roughly the same attitude. The gradual nature of the transition does not, of course, entail that the process will occur at exactly the same rate in all the countries of Europe. The formation of a left-wing government in one Western country does not therefore depend on the necessary appearance of similar left-wing administrations in the other countries of Europe. But the Communists claim that victory for them in any one country will certainly not entail severance of relations with the rest of the Western world and its interlocking system of economic, political and cultural agreements. No one can guess what the details of such a configuration might be, but it cannot be ruled out as a possibility. Would an Italy that voted in a government of 'historical compromise' have to leave the Common Market—or NATO? Collaboration with the West as well as the East would enable a Western country with a Communist administration to exercise a beneficial influence on the development of democratic tendencies in the Eastern bloc and the development of socialist tendencies in the West. Such a country, far from being a bone of contention, could well be a force for purposeful development and détente. It is foreseeable that socialism will triumph in some Western countries in the course of the next ten or fifteen years. This will not solve all the world's problems, but perhaps it will simplify some of them and bring their solution a little closer.

II

6
Communists and Social Democrats in the West

One of the most serious problems facing the workers' movement in the countries of mature capitalism concerns the relationship between the Communist parties and the parties of the Socialist International. Both currents claim to represent the working class and all toiling people. They criticize the shortcomings of contemporary capitalist society and state that the ultimate aim of all their activity is to construct a new, more equitable and more democratic socialist society. However, until very recently there have been substantial differences between them over what constitutes an 'equitable and socialist society' and over the various possible methods of achieving it. They have naturally adopted different attitudes to the experience of the Soviet Union and the other socialist countries, and have thus attacked capitalism from different angles.

Both groups accept that they derive ideologically and historically from the working-class movement in the latter half of the nineteenth century, which resulted in alliances of workers' parties like those of the First and Second Internationals. In almost all the capitalist countries, Communist parties sprang up after the First World War on the basis of left-wing factions in Social Democratic parties. Even in Russia, the birthplace of Leninism, the Bolshevik Party existed for some considerable time as the formal left wing of the Social Democratic Party. These historic ties have led to anything but friendly relations between Communists and Socialists. In Russia, relations between the Bolsheviks and Mensheviks were marked by extreme hostility. The October Revolution was directed not only against the power of the bourgeoisie but also against the Mensheviks and Socialist Revolutionaries who were part of the power bloc. This enmity spilled over into the years that followed, interrupted only by brief truces and short periods of cooperation. On numerous occasions, the Bolsheviks arrested SRs, Mensheviks and Anarchists, and even had them executed, considering them their worst enemies; and many a Bolshevik was felled by a Menshevik, SR or Anarchist bullet during the Civil War. Nevertheless, when Moscow was threatened by Denikin and his White armies, the Mensheviks and SRs, freed from imprisonment, sped to the front to fight for Soviet power. At the same time, Makhno's Anarchist peasant units were battling against certain regiments of Denikin's army in the Southern Ukraine. Once the general danger was averted, however, the hostility between the Communists and socialists of other persuasions flared up with renewed vigour.

The same sort of picture emerged in Europe after the First World War. The November Revolution of 1918 abolished the monarchist regime in Germany and this was replaced by the right-wing Social Democratic government of Friedrich Ebert and Philipp Scheidemann in coalition with some of the bourgeois parties. Then, in January 1919, the working class was provoked into premature armed insurrection in Berlin, and it was a Social Democrat and trade union leader, Gustav Noske, who headed the repressive organs, which put down the uprising with great ruthlessness. 'Someone has to become a bloodstained dog', Noske announced before the conflict began, 'and I am not afraid of the responsibility.'[1] It should be recalled in this connection that, in order to suppress premature armed insurrection by the workers and soldiers in Petrograd in early July 1917, a force made up of certain Cossack regiments and divisions was recalled from the front and placed under the command of G.P. Mazurenko, a member of the Central Executive Committee of the SRs. Fortunately, after the Smolny defeat, Lenin went quickly to ground and thus avoided the fate that overtook Rosa Luxemburg and Karl Liebknecht eighteen months later. It was not the workers, soldiers and sailors who died that July, but the dead Cossacks of the forces of order who were given a solemn funeral, and, on that occasion, the SR leader V. Chernov and the Menshevik leader M. Skobelev laid wreaths from the Petrograd Soviet Executive Committee bearing the inscription 'To the defenders of the revolution, victims who fell in the course of their revolutionary duty'.[2] Within a matter of six weeks, however, when General Kornilov rose against the Provisional Government and the

Soviets and began to march on Petrograd, Bolsheviks, Mensheviks and SRs joined together to put down this rebellion, and their co-operative venture was crowned with instant success. In Germany, soon after the murder of Luxemburg and Liebknecht, the monarchist generals carried out an attempted counter-revolutionary coup aimed at bringing down the Social Democratic coalition. The Communists, Social Democrats and unaligned workers immediately came together to create a force that took only five days to put down the 'Kapp putsch' and demolish the reactionary Kapp government in Berlin. There are many such examples.

In 1919, the armed forces of the Ebert-Scheidemann-Noske government in Berlin destroyed the Bavarian Soviet Republic, which had been welcomed enthusiastically in Munich by all Communists and left-wing Social Democrats. That same spring, the leaders of the Hungarian Social Democratic Party who had taken over full power in the country not only released the imprisoned leaders of the recently formed Communist Party but actually invited them and other left-wing socialists to form a Revolutionary Government with a Social Democrat, Garbai, as Chairman and a Communist, Bela Kun, as People's Commissar for Foreign Affairs and political leader of the Hungarian Soviet Republic. This Republic lasted for 133 days before military defeat at the hands of the *Entente*-supported armies of Romania and Czechoslovakia, along with pressure from the Social Democratic right, brought down the government and put an end to Soviet power in Hungary.

These examples of united activity on the part of Communists and Social-Democrats have been the exception rather than the rule. In the 1920s, the rule was mutual hostility, which led straight to the victory of Fascism in Italy, and, later, to the rise of Hitler in Germany. In the German elections of 1932, the Nazis polled 11,700,000 votes whereas the Social Democrats and Communists together polled 13,200,000. The two latter groups, however, continued to fight it out, giving Hitler his chance to rise to the head of the government. The appalling dangers of fascism, which pursued the most ruthless repression of the workers' organizations, soon induced a more sober attitude. In France, the formation of a People's Front prevented the victory of fascism. Then, during the Second World War, the alliance between the USSR and the Western democracies brought about the rout of fascism, helped on by united fronts formed to resist the 'New Order' in practically all the occupied countries. After the war, the anti-Hitler coalition soon fell apart, the anti-fascist united front was dispersed and the Cold War began. Communists had been expelled from their Western governmental placements by the beginning of 1948, and, reciprocally, all independent socialists and other non-Communist anti-fascist groups had been removed from the governments of Eastern Europe. The old ideological and political enmity between the Communists and the Social Democrats had flared up all over again.

There is no point now in trying to sort out the rights and wrongs of this struggle. Both sides have had much to complain about, but time marches on and most of the grievances have slipped away into the past. In the last thirty years, Communism and socialism have endured much and their image has changed both in the world at large and within individual countries, East and West. The images of contemporary socialism and capitalism have also changed. Some of the more influential Western Communist parties have turned to more liberal programmes and methods and no longer reject out of hand what used to be called 'revisionism', 'opportunism' or 'reformism'. At the same time, many socialist parties have taken a more radical turn, refusing any longer to buttress capitalist society and taking up the cause and the slogans of real socialist development. More significantly, world political and economic development has in recent decades given rise to a whole series of problems that may be ignored only at the risk of destruction for the whole of mankind, and whose solution is impossible without the joint efforts of different political movements, not least Social Democrats and Communists. Every international Communist party conference today resounds not only with criticism of the Social Democracy but also with calls for unity between the two movements. International Socialist gatherings do not rule out such a dialogue, but it remains true that examples of cooperation are rare and results so far are not inspiring.

Prejudice, a mutual sense of alienation and distrust, often only too justified, are still too strong for any such unity to be established quickly and without major difficulties. Differences of ideology and political practice are still unbridgeable. The Communist movement all over the world has yet to rid itself of many evils that inspire real and justified misgivings in any who sincerely believe in a fair and democratic society. Social Democracy itself still permits its own characteristic evils and lists towards its right wing. Other forces are raising their heads nowadays, however, which are hostile to Socialists and Communists alike and are not prepared to discriminate between the various versions of democratic Communism and pluralist Socialism. This raises the question of a renewal of the Communist-Socialist united front, which in turn calls for a re-examination of certain Leninist principles that are clearly irrelevant to today's world. It calls equally for a re-examination of many principles dear to conservative Social Democracy. In order to explain this idea more fully, it will be useful to consider certain details from the history of the working-class movement in the nineteenth and twentieth centuries.

Marxism and Nineteenth-century Socialist Movements

The Communist League established by Marx and Engels in 1847 and sustained for five years, was the first international Communist organization in history, but it was by no means the only European organization aiming for the liberation of working people. In France, at about the same time, Auguste Blanqui was setting up his Central Republican Society, and earlier still he had formed a secret Society of the Seasons. In Spain a Union of Classes brought together workers in several different professions, Germany saw the creation of a Workers' Brotherhood and Workers' Union, and the left-wing Chartists in England formed groups called Brother Democrats and, later on, the Workers' Parliament. Besides this assortment of legal associations and secret societies, there also existed in Europe a number of other diverse tendencies and doctrines working under the broad banner of socialism: petty-bourgeois socialism, utopian socialism and communism, in their various manifestations, were among the foremost. One popular figure was the anarchist theoretician Joseph Proudhon, who, on the one hand, proposed the abolition of the state and yet, on the other, claimed to be working out an approach to 'socialism from the standpoint of bourgeois interests.' Another thinker who corresponded with Marx and Engels was the young Ferdinand Lassalle, who had produced his own version of petty-bourgeois socialism over the previous decade or so and had founded the Universal German Workingmen's Association. Marx had also, in 1844, come to know the young Russian revolutionary socialist Mikhail Bakunin, though the latter was to become more closely attached to Proudhon.

Marx and Engels were sharply critical of all these institutions and associations—and many other doctrines and tendencies besides, although they all claimed allegiance to the socialist banner. Here is Marx, for instance, in the *Communist Manifesto,* taking issue with the first major writings of Proudhon, which satisfied the desire of a large section of the bourgeoisie to 'cure social diseases in order to consolidate the existence of bourgeois society':[3] 'The Socialistic bourgeois want all the advantages of modern social conditions without the struggles and dangers necessarily resulting therefrom. They desire the existing state of society minus its revolutionary and disintegrating elements. They wish for a bourgeoisie without a proletariat. The bourgeoisie naturally conceives the world in which it is supreme to be the best; and bourgeois Socialism develops this comfortable conception into various more or less complete systems. In requiring the proletariat to carry out such a system, and thereby to march straightway into the social New Jerusalem, it requires in reality, that the proletariat should remain within the bounds of existing society, but should cast away all its hateful ideas concerning the bourgeoisie. A second and more practical, but less systematic, form of this Socialism sought to depreciate every revolutionary movement in the eyes of the working class, by showing that no mere political reform, but only a change in the material conditions of existence, in economical relations, could be of any advantage to them. By changes in the material conditions of existence, this form of Socialism, however, by no means understands abolition of the bourgeois relations of production, an abolition that can be effected only by a revolution, but administrative reforms, based on the continued existence of these relations; reforms, therefore, that in no respect affect the relations between capital and labour, but, at the best, lessen the cost, and simplify the administrative work, of bourgeois government.'[4]

Critical and utopian socialism was attacked no less severely by Marx and Engels. This movement did reflect the demands of the proletariat, but an *immature* proletariat, one incapable of altering its position in society. 'The first direct attempts of the proletariat to attain its own ends, made in times of universal excitement, when feudal society was being overthrown, these attempts necessarily failed, owing to the then undeveloped state of the proletariat, as well as to the absence of the economic conditions for its emancipation, conditions that had yet to be produced, and could be produced by the impending bourgeois epoch alone. The revolutionary literature that accompanied these first movements of the proletariat had necessarily a reactionary character. It inculcated universal asceticism and social levelling in its crudest form.' It is true, Marx and Engels go on to say, that the creators of these critical and utopian systems do have plans to defend the interests of the working class as the class that suffers most. But the proletariat exists for them only in that capacity. 'Hence, they habitually appeal to society at large, without distinction of class; nay, by preference, to the ruling class. For how can people, when once they understand their system, fail to see in it the best possible plan of the best possible state of society? Hence, they reject all political, and especially all revolutionary, action; they wish to attain their ends by peaceful means, and endeavour, by small experiments, necessarily doomed to failure, and by the force of example, to pave the way for the new social Gospel. ... But these Socialist and Communist publications contain also a critical element. They attack every principle of existing society. Hence they are full of the most valuable materials for the enlightenment of the working class.'[5]

During the decline of revolutionary movement in Western Europe and following the disbanding of the Communist League, Marx and Engels concentrated most of their attention on the theoretical elaboration of their philosophical, economic and historical doctrine, which was already being described as 'Marxism'. This doctrine drew its ideas from three sources: the classical inheritance of philosophical, economic and political thought, the study of surrounding contemporary reality, and debate with numerous socialist, pseudo-socialist and even bourgeois theories and teachings. The two thinkers took issue with the ideas of Proudhon, Lassalle, Bakunin and Blanqui, with Russian Populism and English trade unionism, with Dühring in Germany and with the French Possibilists. However, theoretical disagreement never prevented Marx and Engels from seeking political association with their ideological adversaries whenever they considered this to be in the interests of the working class. Their basic principles on this question, from which they never departed, were declared in the *Communist Manifesto:* 'The Communists fight for the attainment of the immediate aims, for the enforcement of the momentary interests of the working class; but in the movement of the present, they also represent and take care of the future of that movement. In France the Communists ally themselves with the Social-Democrats, against the conservative and radical bourgeoisie, reserving, however, the right to take up a critical position in regard to phrases and illusions traditionally handed down from the great Revolution. In Switzerland they support the Radicals, without losing sight of the fact that this party consists of antagonistic elements, partly of Democratic Socialists, in the French sense, partly of radical bourgeois. ... In Germany they fight with the bourgeoisie whenever it acts in a revolutionary way, against the absolute monarchy, the feudal squirearchy, and the petty bourgeoisie.

'But they never cease, for a single instant, to instil into the working class the clearest possible recognition of the hostile antagonism between bourgeoisie and proletariat ... In short, the Communists everywhere support every revolutionary movement against the existing social and political order of things. In all these movements they bring to the front, as the leading question in each, the property question, no matter what its degree of development at the time. Finally, they labour everywhere for the union and agreement of the democratic parties of all countries.'[6]

After the revolutionary defeats of 1848-49, the democratic and socialist movements went into decline, making impossible any further international alliances of working-class parties. It was only in the 1860s that the situation began to change. One of the stimuli behind the new upsurge of democratic and working-class sympathy in Europe was the uprising of the Polish national liberation movement at the beginning of 1863, which was brutally suppressed by the Russian autocracy. In order to express solidarity with the Polish people and discuss the possibility of uniting the forces of the European working classes, a meeting was called for September 1864 in London, to be attended by representatives of the working-class movement from England, France, Germany, Italy, Poland and Ireland. Not only did Karl Marx attend this meeting; he actually sat on a special committee set up to look into the question of uniting the workers of different countries. Many suggestions were made for the rules and declared principles of the new international workers' association, but the ones accepted were those of Marx, who soon became to all intents and purposes the director of this association, soon to be called the International, in all its political and administrative affairs. At the first congress of the International, held in Geneva in 1866, there were sixty-six delegates representing twenty-five sections and eleven different societies in Britain, France, Switzerland and Germany.[7] Later, the International would be joined by organizations in Belgium, Italy, Spain and the United States and individual representatives from Russia, Denmark, Australia and one or two other countries.

Marx may have been the founder and leader of the First International, but it would be wrong to suppose that Marxism therefore became the ideological basis of the organization. At first Marx had rather a small number of consistent supporters. Many followers of Proudhon, Blanqui, Bakunin and Lassalle were also in the International. The workmen's organizations in England were represented by several trade unions who gave political support to the Liberal Party. From Italy came Mazzini's supporters and there were also some disciples of Robert Owen. Marx fully appreciated what a motley group of organizations and individuals it was that composed the First International. This was, however, the only way of beginning the unification of the working class and Marx took full account of the situation when composing documents like the 'Constituent Manifesto' and the 'Rule Book' of the International. He explained the problem to Engels who was at that time living in Manchester:'At the meeting of the general committee my address, etc., was agreed to with great enthusiasm (unanimously) ... It was very difficult to frame the thing so that our view should appear in a form acceptable from the present standpoint of the workers' movement ... It will take time before the reawakened movement allows the old boldness of speech. It will be necessary to be bold in matter, mild in manner.'[8]

Marx and Engels and their small band of supporters worked hard to advertise their views both within the International and in the workers' movement outside. Marxism still did not become the predominating doctrine of the International. At the Lausanne Congress of 1867, attended by seventy delegates, and the Brussels Congress of 1868, attended by more than a hundred, the majority leaned towards one or another of the various Proudhonist factions.

Blanquists and Proudhonists predominated in the leadership of the Paris Commune in 1871. As the influence of Marxism grew, so did internal ideological and organizational wrangling. Particular damage was done to the unity of the International by Bakunin's followers, who set up a secret international organization, but despite opposition from this quarter, the Hague Congress passed a very important resolution proposed by Marx. This referred to the necessity of creating in every country an independent political party opposed to the parties of the property-owning classes. Political persecution and internal dissension soon led to the decision to transfer the General Secretariat of the International to the United States. Although the International was to continue in formal existence for several more years, in practice its real activity ceased after the Hague Congress. In July 1876, a conference in Philadelphia accepted a resolution to dismiss the General Council and wind up the affairs of the organization.

The winding up of the First International was no defeat for Marxism. The organization had been responsible for setting up in many European countries institutions and groups that became centres for the unification of the workers' movement and the nuclei of new working-class parties. In 1869, for instance, at a congress held in Eisenach, Bebel and Liebknecht founded the Social Democratic Party, which adopted a predominantly Marxist programme and expressed solidarity with the First International. In 1875, this party joined with Lassalle's Universal German Workingmen's Association on the basis of a compromise policy to form the Socialist Workers' Party. The Marxist majority in the leadership was maintained, and in 1890 the Party changed its name back to the Social Democratic Party of Germany. In 1876, a Socialist Workers' Party based on several independent socialist groups was founded in the USA, and the socialist movement in that country was generally much influenced by a close follower and friend of Karl Marx, F.A. Sorge. The Workers' Party of France was created in 1880 under the leadership of Guesde and Lafargue, and one of its main self-appointed tasks was to disseminate Marxism throughout the country. The more liberal, reformist groups of French 'municipal' socialists, or 'possibilists', soon left the Workers' Party to form their own political movement. The Blanquists did the same. In 1883, Plekhanov formed the first Russian Marxist group, the Emancipation of

Labour, and other, smaller political organizations following a Marxist line were set up in England, Austria-Hungary, Italy, Belgium and elsewhere. In September 1874, Engels wrote to F.A. Sorge: 'With your resignation the *old* International is entirely wound up and at an end. And that is well. It belonged to the period of the Second Empire, during which the oppression reigning throughout Europe entailed unity and abstention from all internal polemics upon the workers' movement, then just reawakening ... Actually in 1864 the theoretical character of the movement was still very confused everywhere in Europe, that is, among the masses ... For ten years the International dominated one side of European history—the side on which the future lies—and can look back upon its work with pride. But in its old form it has outlived itself ... I think that the next International—after Marx's writings have had some years of influence—will be directly Communist and will openly proclaim our principles.'[9]

This prediction was borne out fifteen years afterwards when, in the late 1880s, the idea of a new International began to be mooted. Preparatory work lasting several years was initiated, to the accompaniment of great controversy arising between the Marxists, headed by Engels, and the other tendencies of the working-class movement. At long last, in Paris in 1889, on the hundredth anniversary of the storming of the Bastille, an international socialist congress was convened to mark the inception of the Second International. There were about four hundred delegates at the opening ceremony, bearing about 383 mandates from some three hundred workers' and socialist organizations. The delegates to the conference represented about one million socialist-voting workers. By that time, Marxism had come to dominate the working-class movement and for this reason the Marxist delegates were in the majority. Several other ideological tendencies were also represented, however—there were Anarchists, Blanquists, Russian Populists, Possibilists and 'independent' socialists. Although the meetings of the Congress were characterized by controversy and stormy debate, the main documents of the Paris Congress all had a basis in Marxism. Engels was no less satisfied by the results of the next conference held in Brussels in 1891. In September of that year he wrote once again to Sorge: 'The Congress eventually turned out to be a brilliant success for us. The Broussistes never turned up at all and the

Hyndman supporters had to pocket their opposition. Best of all, we showed the Anarchists the door ... An immeasurably broader International, declaring itself Marxist, is starting just where the old International left off.'[10]

Two years later, in 1893, Engels was invited to the next Congress and, in fact, made the final speech in English, French and German. He was then seventy-three years old and was given a stormy ovation. 'The unexpectedly marvellous welcome you have accorded me, and which has moved me deeply, I accept not for myself personally but only as the colleague of a great man whose portrait hangs there above us. Exactly fifty years have passed since Marx and I entered the working-class movement by publishing our first socialist articles. Since that time socialism has developed from a few small sects into a mighty party that sets the whole official world atremble. Marx is dead, but if he still lived there would not be a single man in Europe or American who could look back on his life's work with such pride.'[11]

The successes recorded by Marxism at the very end of the nineteenth century and the beginning of the twentieth were truly remarkable. The overwhelming majority of the leaders and theoreticians of the workers' movement came to regard themselves as Marxists. Their names are still widely known today—one thinks of Liebknecht, Plekhanov, Bebel, Mehring, Lafargue, Guesde, Zetkin, Luxemburg, Kautsky, Adler, Labriola and others. There were, of course, some workers' leaders who were not Marxists; these included, for instance, the independent socialist Jean Jaurès and the future president of France, Alexandre Millerand. Another non-Marxist was Eduard Bernstein, a follower of Dühring in his youth, who in the late 1890s wrote *The Problems of Socialism and the Tasks of Social Democracy,* in which he described most of Marx's basic principles as obsolete. The founder of the English Social Democratic Federation, Henry Hyndman did claim to be a Marxist, and knew Marx personally, though in his mind some Marxist principles were confused with non-Marxist ones. The Second International was supported also by many trade union leaders, Fabians, French anarcho-syndicalists and Russian Socialist Revolutionaries. Despite the ban on Anarchists in the International, many famous representatives of that movement took part in the first congresses as members of national workingmen's organizations from Spain, Italy and other countries. But it was Marxism that dominated the working-class movement in these years, gaining ground all the time, and when a workers' party was founded in Russia in 1903, it declared Marxism to be its guide to action. The Stuttgart Congress of the Second International was attended by Lenin, at the head of a Bolshevik delegation.

The rise of Marxism within the workers' movement was accompanied by rapid development of the movement itself, on a scale that may be judged from the following figures: in 1907, an electoral army of some 7,415,000 voters backed the socialist deputies in the parliaments of the world; by 1910 this number had risen to 8,600,000, and trade union membership rose over the same period from 4,080,000 to 6,122,000.[12]

The last major undertaking of the Second International was the Extraordinary Congress held in Basle in 1912, which approved a manifesto calling upon all workers and all socialists to unite in resisting the threat of world war. The Congress welcomed 555 delegates from twenty-three countries, though not all the parties of the International attended. The International Socialist Bureau, which coordinated the activities of the parties between congresses, represented forty-one socialist parties in twenty-seven countries, and 3,787,000 members in all. Affiliated trade unionists numbered up to eleven million more.[13]

The successes achieved by Marxism in Europe and America, however, turned out to be less secure than they appeared at first sight. Many of the working-class politicians had joined the movement only in a formal sense, their ideas and policies belonging elsewhere. Even the Marxist movement itself suffered serious splits. The controversial issues dividing Marxist from Marxist within the Second International and in the various socialist parties became exacerbated and led to factional hostility. In Russia there occurred a division between Bolsheviks and Mensheviks. There were some self-styled Marxists and extreme left-wing groups that Marx would probably have disowned as belonging more properly to immature, narrowly sectarian, ascetic or barrack-room forms of socialism. There were also right-wing groups that he would have dismissed as examples of bourgeois or petty-bourgeois socialism, but they too called themselves Marxists. Nationalism, indeed chauvinism, was penetrating deep into the socialist movement, against the essential principles of the International and of Marxism. The International collapsed in 1914, overwhelmed by the world war, in which the great majority of the German and Austrian Social Democrats stood by their governments, while almost all the English, French and Russian Socialists (excluding the Bolsheviks) rallied to the *Entente* governments now arranged against them.

Marx and Engels made much of Germany's special revolutionary calling, which touched the German working class and, subsequently, German Social Democracy. As early as the *Communist Manifesto* they had claimed that 'Communists turn their attention chiefly to Germany'.[14] It was a matter for pride that the German Social Democrats became the largest and most mature working-class party anywhere in the later nineteenth century. In 1884 Engels wrote to Bebel: 'About our proletarian masses I have never been deceived. This secure progress of their movement, confident of victory and for that very reason cheerful and humorous, is a model which cannot be surpassed. No European proletariat would have stood the test of the Socialist Law so brilliantly and have responded after six years of suppression with such a proof of increased strength and consolidated organization; no nation would have achieved this organization in the way it has been achieved without any conspiratorial humbug ... Our great advantage is that with us the industrial revolution is only just in full swing, while in France and England, so far as the main point is concerned, it is closed ... (We) achieved an industrial revolution which is more deep and thorough and spatially more extended and comprehensive than that of the other countries, and this with a perfectly fresh and intact proletariat, undemoralized by defeats and finally—thanks to Marx—with an insight into the causes of economic and political development and into the conditions of the impending revolution such as none of our predecessors possessed. But for that very reason it is our *duty* to be victorious.'[15]

Engels had a remarkable gift for prophecy. Not only did he predict the coming of the Second International—he foresaw the future war and its results with striking accuracy. He also predicted the possible salvation of capitalism not through the most reactionary parties of capitalist society but through one of the most democratic. In the same letter, he continued: 'As to pure democracy and its role in the future I do not share your opinion. Obviously it plays a far more subordinate part in Germany than in other countries with an older industrial development. But that does not prevent the possibility, when the moment of revolution comes, of its acquiring a temporary importance as the most radical *bourgeois* party ... and as the final sheet-anchor of the whole bourgeois and even feudal regime. At such a moment the whole reactionary mass falls in behind it and strengthens it; everything which used to be reactionary behaves as democratic. Thus between March and September 1848 the whole feudal-bureaucratic mass strengthened the liberals in order to hold down the revolutionary masses, and, once this was accomplished, ... naturally, to kick out the liberals as well ... This has happened in every revolution: the tamest party still capable of government comes to power with the others just because it is only in this party that the defeated see their last possibility of salvation.'[16] This was a surprisingly exact prediction of what occurred during the revolutionary crisis that followed the War. But how further surprised Engels might hve been if he could have known that, in Germany itself in 1918, it would turn out to be the Social Democratic Party that acted as the 'sheet-anchor' of the German bourgeoisie and Junker class, and which was entrusted with the formation of a government in the Weimar Republic, having shown itself to be 'the tamest party still capable of government'. The same thing had happened in Russia in 1917, with the Mensheviks and SRs; and elsewhere in Europe, right-wing Social Democrats and some of the centre parties acted out the part played by the Liberals in 1848. Engels would have been still more surprised to learn that, in the first quarter of the twentieth century, Marxism acquired its most committed followers and successors in Russia, and that, of all countries, Russia—justifiably regarded by them in the nineteenth century as the great bastion of European reaction—would experience the first victory of socialist revolution.

Lenin's Struggle Against Social Democracy

Lenin spent all his life in a continual struggle not only against the bourgeoisie and the autocracy, imperialism and absolutism, but also against his opponents in the revolutionary-democratic camp, against the parties, factions and individual politicians in the socialist and workers' movement whom he considered inconsistent, 'opportunist', 'over-accommodating' or 'revisionist'. Such controversy was normal enough for any revolutionary or any revolutionary-democratic movement, especially one *in statu nascendi,* since it is from argument that truth tends to emerge. The doctrine known as 'Leninism', like 'Marxism' before it, drew on three sources: the classical inheritance of revolutionary thought both in Russia (where Lenin considered Chernyshevsky's ideas to be of paramount importance) and in the West (where he turned, of course, to Marx and Engels); his own environment, in the form of the contemporary political and economic situation of Russia and world capitalism in general; and polemical discussion with opponents in and outside the Social Democratic Party and, later on, the Communist Party. Let us consider one or two of the characteristics that marked Lenin's distinctive approach to this ideological and political struggle.

Lenin's political and revolutionary activity began in the 1890s, when the workers' movement was just beginning in his country, and Marxism was unknown to most people and unpopular with the revolutionary intelligentsia. Plekhanov's Emancipation of Labour group did much to propagate and popularize Marxism in Russia, but the linkage of Marxism with the workers' movement was beyond his powers. This was the task attempted by the group organized by Lenin and called The League of Struggle for the Emancipation of the Working Class. In the process of defending Marxism and, along with his sympathizers, preparing the soil for the creation of an independent workers' party, Lenin took issue with Populism, with Economism and so-called Legal Marxism. The wide dissemination of Marxist ideas throughout Russia, achieved largely by the newspaper *Iskra,* to which Lenin devoted so much effort and attention, prepared the way for the formation of the first Russian working-class party, the Russian Social Democratic Workers' Party. The party split into two factions at its inception, or at least at its Second Congress, the Bolsheviks led by Lenin, and the Mensheviks headed by several prominent figures, Plekhanov, Martov and Dan in particular. The differences between them were at first organizational, but they were to grow throughout the revolutionary period of 1905-1907, eventually touching on the basic strategy and tactics of revolution. Nevertheless, both factions, Bolshevik and Menshevik, continued in all sincerity to regard themselves as Marxists and it was to Marx and Engels that they turned for justification of their arguments.

The details of this struggle need not concern us here. Nor is it worthwhile to attempt to decide which faction adhered more closely to Marx and Engels in the interpretation of their ideas. It would not be difficult to argue that the Mensheviks stood nearer than the Bolsheviks to 'orthodox' Marxism, since Lenin introduced a number of quite new principles that were at variance with nineteenth-century Marxist dogma, though it is equally arguable that these were truer to the spirit, if not the letter, of Marxism. We have already taken note of the suggestion made by Marx and Engels that the Communists were 'fighting alongside the bourgeoisie against the absolute monarchy', though only 'to the extent that the bourgeoisie has any revolutionary leanings'. The Russian bourgeoisie could scarcely have been called a revolutionary class, but on many issues it was certainly opposed to the Tsarist autocracy. When the first Russian Revolution began, the Mensheviks were among the most active participants. They assumed that it was not merely possible but essential to come to an agreement or, better still, to form an alliance with the liberal bourgeoisie, particularly since some of the more extreme methods employed by the Bolsheviks seemed calculated to frighten the bourgeoisie away from revolution and send them straight into the camp of reaction. Not so Lenin: he insisted that, although the Russian Revolution was really a bourgeois-democratic affair, it must be led and dominated not by the liberal bourgeoisie but by the proletariat. At the time the Bolsheviks were not interested in uniting with the liberal bourgeoisie; as far as they were concerned, the sooner the Russian bourgeoisie left the Revolution the better. This could only make it easier for the proletariat to lead the great mass of the peasantry and the petty bourgeoisie and would permit them not only to put through a number of radical bourgeois-democratic reforms but to go on from that point and, depending on their organizational awareness and readiness, proceed to a new, socialist revolution. In defence of this attitude, Lenin frequently referred to Marx and Engels and their ideas on continuous or 'permanent' revolution.

The differences between the Bolsheviks and their opponents in the revolutionary camp in those years did not lead to a break. Mensheviks and Bolsheviks worked hand-in-hand arranging strikes, demonstrations and, in one or two towns, in armed working-class insurrection. Numbers of Bundist socialists, members of European workingmen's organizations, assisted with the work of agitation and propaganda among the sailors in the Black Sea Fleet, and the Anarchist and Anarchist-Communist parties also made an influential contribution to this effort. The armed uprising of workers in Moscow in 1905 was led jointly by the Bolsheviks and the Socialist-Revolutionaries, who fought side by side on the streets of Krasnaya Presnya. The following year saw the 'unifying' Fourth Conference of the Social Democratic Party, attended by both Bolsheviks and Mensheviks, in Stockholm. The Fifth Conference, held in London, was also attended by both factions. Even after the Bolsheviks became an independent political party, they continued to accept alliances with the Mensheviks (with the Plekhanov faction in 1912, for example) and to negotiate with representatives of anti-Tsarist bourgeois parties during the war.

All political parties attempt in the natural course of events to widen the sphere of their own political influence. The Bolsheviks, considering themselves to be the most consistent and revolutionary working-class party, made every effort to extend their influence to *the whole* of working-class Russia, in other words to elbow out of the workers' movement all the Mensheviks and members of other social-democratic parties whom Lenin regarded as channels of bourgeois and petty-bourgeois influence among the proletariat. Political conditions in Russia at the beginning of the twentieth century were quite different from those in the Kaiser's Germany where the trade unions and the Social Democratic Party had operated legally and freely for some time and exercised some considerable influence in the Reichstag. The Russian proletariat lagged far behind its German counterpart in organization and education; it was a generation or two younger than the German proletariat and several generations younger than the English. But despite its 'youth' and correspondingly closer ties with the countryside and the peasantry, the Russian proletariat had a more pronounced tendency towards action and revolution at that time. This was a result not so much of Bolshevik propaganda as of the overall objective situation. The Russian working class had suffered brutal exploitation not only at the hands of the bourgeoisie of the country but also under the autocratic land-owning police state in general. It was also subjugated by the bourgeoisie of Western Europe, which had enmeshed Russia in a complex system of financial dependence and directly owned a large proportion of the industry, banks, transport and mines in many of the country's major cities. The very situation of the Russian proletariat made it hospitable to Bolshevik propaganda, which accounted, naturally enough, for the growth in Bolshevik influence at working-class level.

There would be little sense in reproaching Lenin for his desire to consolidate and extend the Bolshevik contribution to events in the Russian political arena. We cannot, however, pass over one in particular of his polemical devices—one that had nothing to do with Bolshevik principles or tactics, since it amounted to a personal skill, the individual quality of a politician and revolutionary much emulated by other Bolshevik leaders. This was the abruptness and coarseness that characterized his attitude towards anyone who took issue with him, a fault frequently censured by the ideological enemies of Bolshevism. For instance, he attempted to present the Mensheviks and other opponents not simply as people with mistaken ideas, given to over-dogmatic thinking, but who nevertheless had the interests of the working class at heart; he referred to them in his speeches and articles as deliberate frauds and betrayers of the working class and socialism itself. When he did so, he was relying less on cogency of argument than on force of expression and out-and-out denigration. This form of discussion was not, and is not, to his credit. On most occasions he was essentially in the right and could have achieved almost certain victory through straightforward political argument expressed in 'parliamentary language' devoid of all vulgarity. Then, perhaps, he might well have won over to his side not only the Bolsheviks in the working-class masses but also some of the very Menshevik opponents with whom he was crossing swords. But no, Lenin was normally sharp-tongued and crude when rounding on his opponents and he sometimes even attempted to justify his own crudity. Early in 1907, for example, the Social Democratic Party Central Committee set up a special court to scrutinize the most flagrant accusations made by Lenin in one of his pamphlets against the Mensheviks and the extremely disloyal attitude adopted by him towards the Mensheviks during the election to the Second State Duma. The Party was already split down the middle but formal unity had been preserved and both the factions were represented at the Fourth and Fifth Party Congresses. Lenin decided to remit a special report to the Fifth Congress by way of self-justification. Here is part of what he wrote:

'A split means the severance of all organizational contact, transferring the conflict of views from the ground of influence within the organization to the ground of influence from without, from the ground of persuasion of one's comrades to the ground of destroying their organization, to the ground of arousing the masses of the workers, and the people in general, against the splinter group. Things that are impermissible among members of a united party become permissible and obligatory between the sections of a split party. You cannot write about party comrades in terms that systematically sow hatred, revulsion, scorn etc. among the workers for those who think differently. Such terms can and must be reserved for the splinter organization.

'Why "must"? Because a split obliges us to wrest the masses away from the splinter group. People say to me, "You have introduced discord into the ranks of the proletariat." I reply, "I have consciously and deliberately introduced discord into the ranks of that section of the Petersburg proletariat which followed the Menshevik splinter group on the eve of the election and I shall always act like this when there is a split."

'My caustic, offensive comments about the Mensheviks ... were intended to rattle the ranks of the proletariat which trusted them and followed them. That was my aim. That was my duty ... For after the split it was necessary to destroy the Menshevik ranks that were leading the proletarian ranks after the Kadets, to bring disarray into those ranks, and to arouse in the masses hatred, revulsion and scorn for those people who had ceased to be members of a united party, who had turned into political enemies ... In relation to political enemies like these I have waged—and if the split should recur or grow wider I shall continue to wage—a war of destruction ... Anyone who tried to use measures appropriate for conflict within the party in conflict brought about by a split ... would have to be considered either childishly naive or else a hypocrite ... From the psychological point of view, it is quite clear that the severance of all organizational contact between comrades denotes the highest degree of mutual animosity and enmity, developing into hatred...

'Are there any limitations to conflict permissible on the ground created by a split? In Party terms there are not, and cannot be, any such limits, for a split means an end to the Party's existence ... Any limitations to conflict on the ground created by a split are not Party ones, but political ones in general, or we might even say more properly, general, civil limitations, the limitations imposed by the criminal law and no other kind.'[17]

Lenin was profoundly mistaken in this defence of his own treatment of dissident opinion and in forming his own quite independent Party faction. In the first place, the Mensheviks, and many other members of socialist and democratic parties who came in for similarly rough critical treatment by the Bolsheviks, simply did not become, even after the split, the political enemies of the Bolsheviks *in all respects*. In many respects they remained political allies, for at that time the outcome of the democratic revolution of 1905-1907 was uncertain. The Mensheviks were acting not out of calculated malice but according to firm political beliefs which merited as much respect as those of any other dissident group and of the Bolsheviks themselves. In the second place, this polemical method 'embarrassed' and alienated not just the Mensheviks but also some of the Petersburg workers who continued to trust the Menshevik leaders and follow them. In the third place, here we see Lenin throwing away any possibility of out-arguing the Mensheviks, including some of their leaders, and winning them over to his own side, thus reducing the magnitude and the danger of the split and increasing the number of his own followers. Circumstances within the Party at that time by no means justified 'a war of destruction' against the Mensheviks. In any case, that kind of warfare can only ever be justified on the real-life battlefield—not in a political argument between competing groups and factions of fellow-socialists. The mere fact that, as things turned out, Lenin's crude political warfare against the Mensheviks did achieve 'useful' results for the Bolsheviks, extending their influence in St Petersburg and reducing that of their rivals, is no justification of his polemical method. By using other methods, of a more nuanced kind, Lenin might well have achieved even better results.

After the collapse of the autocracy in 1917, the question of an alliance or general cooperation between the Bolsheviks and the other socialist parties in Russia seldom arose. A spontaneous form of alliance sprang up whenever a wave of bourgeois-landowner counter-revolution swept the country, as, for instance, in the days of the attempted coup by Kornilov. In 1917, not only the right-wing monarchist parties but even the Kadets saw their influence drain swiftly away. The Provisional Government 'moved leftwards' with each successive attempt at reorganization, and, by mid-July 1917, the Russian bourgeoisie was clinging to power only through the presence of Menshevik and SR leaders in key government positions. The Mensheviks and SRs proved to be 'the most accommodating of the parties still capable of forming a government' and they assumed 'the role of sheet-anchor for the whole bourgeois economy'. It was natural for the Bolsheviks to concentrate the fire of their criticism on the parties of accommodation, which were carrying out in Russia the very work that, in 1918 and 1919 in Germany, would fall to the right-wing Social Democrats. The subjective reasons for such a policy may vary a good deal from leader to leader of the Social Democratic movement. Some may believe in all sincerity that the premature assumption of power by the working class might bring it more harm than good. Others shift consciously to bourgeois positions but continue to camouflage their policy with socialist phrases. Thus, the behaviour of Social Democratic parties at any given moment should never be taken as a prediction of their future behaviour. In any case, not every revolutionary situation allows the bourgeois or feudal-monarchist parties the opportunity of turning to the more moderate and accommodating left-wing parties for help. Nevertheless, later systematizers of Leninism have converted what was a tactical political ploy by Lenin and the Bolsheviks during a revolutionary crisis in Russia into virtually a fundamental principle of Leninist tactics and a basic rule in the very strategy of Leninism. Here it is appropriate to turn not to Lenin's works but to those of Stalin, which were read by young Communists in the mid-1920s as sources of instruction on the strategy and tactics of Leninism. In 1924 Stalin wrote: 'What does the basic strategic rule of Leninism consist in? It consists in acknowledging that: 1. the most dangerous social buttress of the enemies of revolution during a period when the revolution is coming to a head are the parties of accommodation; 2. the overthrow of the enemy (Tsarism or the bourgeoisie) cannot be achieved without the isolation of these parties; 3. the main effort, in a period of preparing for revolution, must therefore be directed towards the isolation of these parties and the alienation from them of the broad working masses.

'In the period of conflict with Tsarism,' Stalin continued, 'the period of preparation for bourgeois-democratic revolution (1905-1916) the most dangerous social buttress of Tsarism was the liberal monarchist party, the party of the Kadets. Why was this? Because it was a party of accommodation, of conciliation, between Tsarism and the majority of the people, i.e. the peasantry in general. Naturally the Party directed its main thrust at that time against the Kadets for, without the isolation of the Kadets, we could not have counted on the peasantry breaking from Tsarism and without ensuring this break we could not have counted on the victory of the revolution. At the time, many people failed to understand this nicety of Bolshevik strategy and the Bolsheviks were accused of excessive "Kadetophobia", of allowing the Kadet conflict to "obscure" the conflict with the main enemy—Tsarism. But these accusations ... revealed a complete lack of understanding of Bolshevik strategy, which required the isolation of the party of accommodation in order to facilitate and advance victory over the main enemy... In the period of preparation for October the centre of gravity of the combatant forces shifted. The Tsar went. The Kadet party changed from a power of accommodation into a ruling power, the dominant power of imperialism. Now the battle was not between Tsarism and the people but between the bourgeoisie and the proletariat. In this period the most dangerous social buttress of imperialism consisted of the petty-bourgeois democratic parties of the Mensheviks and SRs. Why was that? Because these were then the parties of accommodation, the parties of conciliation between imperialism and the toiling masses. Naturally the main thrust of the Bolsheviks was directed at that time against these parties, for without the isolation of these parties we could not have counted on the toiling masses breaking from imperialism and without ensuring this break we could not have counted on the victory of the Soviet Revolution. At the time many people failed to understand this nicety of Soviet tactics and they accused the Bolsheviks of "excessive hatred" towards the SRs and Mensheviks and of "forgetting all about" the main aim. But the whole period of preparation for October is eloquent proof that only by employing this tactic were the Bolsheviks able to secure the victory for the October Revolution.'[18]

This extract illustrates Stalin's correct assessment of the niceties of Bolshevik strategy and tactics in relation to the accommodationist parties, the 'intermediate' forces in a revolutionary situation. But he does not make the necessary qualification that the strategy and tatics of the Bolsheviks were largely determined by *those specific Russian conditions* and not by any general laws of revolutionary struggle. As it was, at the beginning of the twentieth century, Tsarism became demoralized and lost the confidence of the majority of the population. The monarchy was in a state of acute crisis and, to make matters worse, the weak-willed and indecisive Nicholas II did not have a single intelligent and strong-willed politician in his camp. In other words, the main enemy of revolution—the autocracy—was in a feeble state and incapable of hanging on to power by its own strength alone. In these conditions, the main buttress of Tsarism turned out to be not a mighty monarchist party and army but the bourgeois Kadets.

A similar situation arose in 1917. The bourgeois party then in power was in a feeble state, economically and politically. A large proportion of the country's industry and finance belonged not to the Russian but to the English, French and Belgian bourgeoisies. The Russian bourgeoisie had no experience of power and the influence of the Kadets among revolution-minded people was weak and declining. It was incapable of retaining power through the bourgeois parties alone. Under these conditions the SR and Menshevik parties, by no means averse to accommodation, really were in a position to perform an invaluable service for the bourgeoisie. Another such situation arose a year or two later in Germany. This kind of situation, in point of fact, is far from exceptional—though it must certainly not be seen as an obligatory rule applicable to each and every revolution. Stalin, however, insisted on the observance of what he described as a 'basic strategic rule of Leninism', even when the political situation in Europe was totally different. In the mid-1930s, for instance, the European bourgeoisie clearly staked everything not on the accommodationist Social Democratic parties but on the National Socialist Party of Germany and the other fascist parties which were emerging all over Europe in one guise or another and, in some countries, coming to power. The Comintern drew its own conclusions from these events and called on all Communists to fight for the creation of a united front of all workers' and socialist parties. At that very moment, Stalin's *Short Course* was published in Russia. Here is an extract from its concluding section:

'The history of the Party teaches us further that without the destruction of the petty bourgeois parties which are active in the ranks of our working class, pushing the backward sections of the working class into the arms of the bourgeoisie and thus undermining the unity of the working class—the victory of proletarian revolution is impossible. The history of our Party is the history of the struggle against and the destruction of the petty-bourgeois parties: the SRs, Mensheviks, Anarchists and Nationalists. Without overcoming parties like these and driving them out of the ranks of the working class that working class could not possibly have achieved unity and without the unity of the working class the victory of proletarian revolution could not possibly have been ensured. Without the destruction of these parties which stood at first for the preservation of capitalism and then, following the October Revolution for the restoration of capitalism it would not have been possible to preserve the dictatorship of the proletariat, to defeat foreign intervention and to build socialism.

It is no coincidence that all the petty bourgeois parties which once called themselves "revolutionary" or "Socialist" in order to deceive the people—the SRs, Mensheviks, Anarchists and Nationalists—became counter-revolutionary parties even before the October Socialist Revolution took place and then afterwards turned into agents of bourgeois intelligence, a gang of spies, saboteurs, diversionists, murderers and traitors to their homeland.

"The unity of the proletariat," says Lenin, "in an age of social revolution can only be achieved by an extreme revolutionary party of Marxism, only through ruthless conflict with all other parties."[19]

There would have been little point in calling on the Social Democratic parties of Europe to form a united front in opposition to imperialism and fascism while insisting that the most vital aim of the Communists was ruthless conflict culminating in the total destruction of those very parties by the working class. There would have been little point in asking for the trust of the Social Democrats as partners in an alliance or united front, while simultaneously branding them as future 'spies, saboteurs, diversionists, murderers and traitors to their homeland'. Lenin's views on European Social

Democracy may have been open to question, but Stalin reduced them to the absurd.

Communists and Socialists in the Civil War

In order to appreciate the full complexity of the relationship between the Bolsheviks and the other Russian socialist parties it is not enough to consider their rivalry in 1917 or the short-lived alliance against Kornilov. We must also turn briefly to the period from 1918 to 1920.

For a whole year following the October victory, the hostility between the Bolsheviks and the other Soviet parties steadily increased. If the right SRs and Mensheviks showed direct opposition to the Bolsheviks immediately after the setting up of the Council of People's Commissars, then the subsequent measures taken by the Soviet government—the dissolution of the Constituent Assembly, the acceptance of the Peace of Brest-Litovsk, the tightening of the grain monopoly, the creation of grain requisitioning units and committees of the poor, and a total embargo on free trade—led to a rift between the Bolsheviks and the great mass of the middle peasantry and the urban petty bourgeoisie. The Bolsheviks also broke with the left SRs, Menshevik-Internationalists and Anarchists, and with all the other minority socialist parties and factions. In 1918, the opposition of all these disaffected groups spilled over into civil war. The 'Red Terror' announced in the autumn of that year was directed not only against the bourgeoisie and its parties but also against the petty bourgeoisie and its political leaders.

Within a matter of weeks, however, the situation changed. The world war came to an end, allowing the countries of the *Entente* to step up intervention and aid to the counter-revolutionaries. Extreme right-wing forces began to prevail in all the anti-Soviet groupings, which were taken over by the generals, the landowners and the bourgeoisie, and came together to form a powerful bloc made up of former monarchist parties, Kadets and the upper strata of the Cossacks. This move reinforced counter-revolution in the purely military sense but weakened it politically, since a large proportion of the peasantry refused to support Kolchak and Denikin and went back to the Bolsheviks instead. The Bolsheviks may have taken grain surpluses away from the peasants, but they did not threaten to rob them of their newly acquired land, and to give it back to the landowners along with governmental power. This shift in class alignments led to a change in the positions of the SR and Menshevik parties. On November 20, 1918, Lenin wrote: '... the facts are causing the petty-bourgeois democrats of Russia, despite their hatred of Bolshevism nurtured on the history of our Party in-fighting, to turn aside from their hostility to Bolshevism first to neutrality, then to support for it. The objective circumstances that alienated such patriotic democrats so sharply from us have now passed away. Objective circumstances have arisen, on a world scale, that are causing them to turn again in our direction... One of the most urgent tasks at the present time is to take account of and make use of this swing ... from hostility to Bolshevism first to neutrality, then to support for it.'[20]

In November and December 1918, both the Mensheviks and many of the SR groups made declarations calling off the struggle against Soviet power. For its part, the Soviet government called off the 'Red Terror' and began the work of reorganizing the committees of the poor and re-establishing Soviets in the countryside. A number of SR and Menshevik newspapers were given permission to resume publication. With the petty-bourgeois parties in mind, Lenin spoke as follows to a meeting of party workers in Moscow on november 27, 1918: 'It would be a serious mistake for anyone to bring forward automatically the slogans of our revolutionary struggle in the period when there was no possibility of conciliation between us, when the petty bourgeoisie was against us, when our unshakable resolve demanded that our only conciliation should be terror. Today that would not be unshakable resolve, it would be plain stupidity and an inadequate understanding of Marxist tactics.'[21] In mid-December, he said: 'Now that the German revolution has begun, the Mensheviks and SRs have begun to swing round. The best of them had striven before towards socialism but they thought the Bolsheviks were chasing after ghosts and fairy tales. Now they have realized that what the Bolsheviks anticipated was not the product of a wild imagination but reality itself, that this world-wide revolution is now under way and is growing all over the world, and the best of the Mensheviks and SRs are beginning to repent of their mistakes ... But when there are people who see where they went wrong, we must accept them and be charitable towards them.'[22] And then, in the spring of 1919, he declared: 'The Soviet Republic is entering the most trying period of its existence... The months to come will be months of crisis ... Only the greatest effort of will can save us. Victory, however, is quite possible. This meeting ... declares to all Mensheviks and SRs who are truly willing to assist us in our arduous struggle that the workers' and peasants' power will extend complete freedom to them and guarantee them the full rights of citizens of the Soviet Republic. This meeting further declares that the task of Soviet Power now consists in ruthlessly combating those Mensheviks and SRs who ... actually hinder our struggle and are allies of our sworn enemies.'[23]

In this period, the Bolsheviks also made concessions to the Anarchists led by Makhno, who had put together substantial military units from the peasantry in the Southern Ukraine and were fighting the White Guards. At the end of April, for instance, a special train brought the Commander of the Ukrainian Front, Antonov-Ovseenko, into the 'capital' of Makhno's outlaw territory. He took stock of the local situation and telegraphed Moscow as follows: 'Spent full day with Makhno. Makhno, his brigade and whole area in a strong military force. No conspiracy. Makhno himself would not allow it. Region can easily be organized, excellent material, but this must be left to you, not Southern Front. With proper work will become impregnable fortress. Punitive measures—madness. Immediately stop press campaign beginning to persecute Makhno men.'[24] At the beginning of May 1919, L.B. Kamenev, a close friend of Lenin, chairman of the Moscow Soviet and a member of the Party Central Committee, arrived to inspect Makhno's troops in Gulyay Pole. By no means everything in Makhno's sphere of operation met with his approval—it was a rallying point for many of the leaders of the Anarchist movement from Moscow. Nevertheless, in an 'Open Letter to the Commander of the Third Brigade, Comrade Makhno', Kamenev wrote: 'After visiting personally the region of Gulyay Pole and speaking to Comrade Makhno and his colleagues, I consider it my duty to announce publicly that all rumours concerning separatist or anti-Soviet plans in the insurgent brigade of Comrade Makhno are entirely without foundation. In the person of Makhno, I have seen an honest and courageous warrior who, under arduous conditions, deprived of essential supplies, is gathering forces and battling manfully against the White Guards and foreign aggressors.

For their bravery, for their front-line fighting, I salute them... Let the insurgents headed by Comrade Makhno show these people, the leaders of Anarchism from Moscow and Petrograd, their proper place. Let it be stated clearly that Comrade Makhno's Third Brigade is no haven for political adventurists. That will put an end to all misunderstandings between the central authority and local forces: then, with an all-out thrust and a united front, we shall unseat Kolchak and Denikin, clean up the Donets basin and the Sea of Azov, and open up a road to the Caucasus. Let it be known to our insurgent comrades that all fronts are of equal concern to Moscow and Kiev and that the central authority knows what the shortages are—armaments—and will make every effort to supply everything possible. Once more—gettings to the Third Brigade! Greetings to those who fight for the reinforcement and extension of Soviet power!—Authorized Representative of the Extraordinary Defence Committee, L.B. Kamenev.'[25]

Lenin was finding it difficult to comprehend the exact situation in the Anarchist camp. Since he was receiving contradictory reports and telegrams about the Ukrainian situation, he reserved judgment in his own statements. Knowing enough to reject the demands from some Ukrainian workers and workers on the Southern Front (the likes of Sokolnikov) for the 'liquidation' of the Third Brigade, he sent the following telegram to Kamenev: 'For time being, until Rostov taken, must be diplomatic with Makhno troops. Have personally dispatched Antonov there and given Antonov personal responsibility for Makhno troops.'[26] These hopes for the speedy capture of Rostov came to nothing. In the summer and autumn of 1919, Denikin's armies launched a successful attack on the Southern Front, seized the whole of the Don region, much of the Ukraine, and the central section of the province of Russia, so that Moscow itself came under threat. In those months of crisis, it was not only the Bolsheviks who did battle against Denikin but the Mensheviks and SRs as well. The actual contribution made by these parties to the defeat of Denikin cannot be assessed, because neither of them created their own individual military formations. The effect of Makhno's Anarchist Brigade is clearer: by waging unremitting war on the pick of Denikin's regiments in the rear of his front, it rendered enormous assistance to the Red Army. At the very height of the battle for the distant approaches to Moscow, Denikin was obliged to recall significant detachments from the front to the Ukraine in order to defend his headquarters and communications.

At long last, in late autumn 1919, the crisis was weathered, Denikin's troops suffered a crushing defeat and retreated south at full speed to the Sea of Azov and the city of Rostov. Yudenich's armies were routed near Petrograd and Kolchak's decimated army was on its last legs. Lenin was now very optimistic that the Bolsheviks would be able to maintain the military and political alliance with the peasant and petty-bourgeois masses and the Menshevik and SR parties. On December 6, 1919, addressing a meeting of the Seventh All-Russian Congress of Soviets, he said: 'Comrades, I have been observing the development and the activities of the Mensheviks perhaps more, and more closely—though it gives me no pleasure to say so—than anyone else. And on the basis of fifteen years of observation I must say ... that the whole development of the Mensheviks, especially at that great moment that began the history of Russian revolution, demonstrates the greatest degree of vacillation among them, which, in the last analysis, boils down to the fact that they depart from the bourgeoisie and its prejudices only with the greatest of difficulty and reluctance. They keep getting stuck but they are beginning to move—very slowly, but they are beginning to move—towards the dictatorship of the proletariat, and a year from now they will have taken several more steps—I am certain of that.'[27]

Lenin's prophetic powers let him down at this point. A year later, in December 1920, Bolsheviks and Mensheviks were once again in opposing camps and at each other's throats. It was the Mensheviks' turn to bring the workers out on strike in several cities in protest against the retention of the policy of 'War Communism'. Meanwhile, the SRs were rousing many peasant communities to insurrection in protest against the system of requisitioning farm produce, the cutting edge of which was now hurting the middle peasants, the kulaks having been almost entirely expropriated during the Civil War. Down in the Southern Ukraine, fierce exchanges between sections of the Red Army and Makhno's units were the order of the day, despite the many occasions in the recent past when these forces had fought together to ensure the defeat of the common enemy, Denikin.

In one respect, Lenin was quite right in 1919: the Mensheviks and

SRs were finding it very difficult indeed to renounce their earlier alliance with the Kadet bourgeoisie. But neither the Mensheviks nor the SRs nor the Anarchists could bring themselves to join the Bolsheviks in quelling the peasant and Cossack uprisings or the insurrection of the sailors and soldiers in the Kronstadt garrison. In that situation, it was inevitable for them to come down on the side of the disaffected, rebellious sections of the masses. This was no fault of the Mensheviks and SRs. It was simply a tragedy for the whole country, and Lenin, when he proposed the radical change represented by introduction of NEP, openly accepted, on behalf of his party, a large part of the responsibility for this tragedy.

Once NEP was introduced, the political crisis in the country began gradually to resolve itself. The peasant and Cossack uprisings were put down and, although their leaders were severely punished, most of the participants were amnestied. The Russian Federation Council of People's Commissars ordered the release of peasants and workers imprisoned in jails and labour camps for 'speculation'. However, the restoration of the alliance of workers and peasants, which Lenin had considered the Bolsheviks' first priority during that period, was not accompanied by a restoration of political rights to the SRs, Mensheviks and Anarchists. On the contrary, punitive measures restricting the activities of these parties were greatly strengthened. So frightened were the Bolshevik leaders following the crisis of 1920-21 that, for the time being, they forbade the setting up of any alternative groupings or factions—even within their own party. They were even more wary of opposition outside the Party, which might express itself within the framework of the Soviets. Here, there was formal provision for SR and Menshevik activity, but, in practice and under various pretexts, this was forbidden, so that the two parties were forced to operate semi-illegally by sending forward their own delegates ostensibly as unaffiliated members. The Bolsheviks did not want to countenance any legal opposition that might put at risk the power won with such difficulty and at such a cost in lives.

No law was actually passed in 1921 or 1922 proscribing alternative parties, but in August 1922 the Twelfth All-Russian Conference of the Communist Party passed a special resolution dealing with 'anti-Soviet parties and tendencies'. This required the Bolsheviks to put an end to Menshevik and SR activities in the trade unions and the cooperatives, in secondary schools, in higher and auxiliary educational institutions, in the youth movement and the publishing world. At the same time, the Cheka was instructed to crack down on all forms of illegal activity by these parties. This was the transformation of Soviet Russia into a one-party state.

The Socialist and Communist Internationals Between the Wars

It is no part of our purpose to attempt a world-wide historical survey of the Communist movement and Social Democracy during the 1920s and 1930s. However, we must not overlook certain crucial events in the relationship between the Socialist and Communist Internationals in the period between the wars.

After the First World War, the Social Democratic parties tried to renew not only the old contacts but the mutual cooperation that had once existed. In February 1919, the leaders of many groups of right-wing and centrist Social Democracy arranged a conference in Berne at which the creation of a 'Berne International' was announced. No representatives of the extreme left-wing or revolutionary currents in the Social Democratic movement attended this conference—though it is true that they were not the only absentees. The leader of the Belgian Social Democrats, Vandervelde, announced, for instance, that he had no desire to meet his recent enemies, the Germans. Within the Berne International itself, there were sharp differences of opinion about the Treaty of Versailles, about Soviet Russia and about the war just ended. Soon afterwards, a number of the larger Social Democratic parties left the Berne International and formed their own international amalgamation of socialist parties, which became known as the Vienna International—or, as political commentators of the day termed it, 'Two-and-a-Half International'. This was a body led mainly by centrist parties accompanied by one or two left-wing Social Democrats of high standing, such as Bauer, Adler and Fort. It also included a number of Menshevik *émigrés*.

In May 1923, with capitalism beginning to stabilize itself throughout Europe, the Berne and Vienna Internationals joined forces. The unification congress held in Hamburg finally set up the Socialist Workers' International, bringing together virtually all the Socialist and Social Democratic parties that had survived or been reconstituted at the end of the eventful decade between 1914 and 1923. It was this new amalgamation of Socialist parties that was usually referred to as the Second International.

The First World War, caused by a crisis of world capitalism, actually made that crisis all the more acute. Almost every capitalist country experienced a political shift to the left in the moods and the thinking of the working class and the popular masses, a shift reflected in the creation of numerous Communist parties and, particularly, in the growing influence and numerical strength of the Socialist and Social Democratic parties. Although the Bolsheviks were highly critical of the resuscitated Second International, describing it as a stillborn organization, this was not the truth of the matter. Social Democracy proved a very influential force in post-war Europe. In 1928, the various Communist parties accounted for approximately 1,300,000 members (900,000 of whom were Bolsheviks), whereas the parties comprising the Socialist International had a total membership of 6,500,000.[28] The numbers of trade unions affiliated to socialist organizations had multiplied the pre-war total. In the pre-war period, it was exceptional for Social Democratic leaders to have any part in the governments of Western countries. Now it became the rule. In Germany, the Social Democrats participated in every coalition government between 1918 and 1930, and their party enjoyed a majority from 1928 to 1930, as they had done between 1918 and 1920. The Austrian Social Democratic party participated in the coalition government of 1918-20 polling no less than forty per cent of the votes and claiming a membership of almost 700,000. In Britain, the Labour Party was in power from January to November 1924 and then from May 1929 to August 1931. In Denmark, the Social Democrats formed a one-party government as early as 1924 and several years later headed a coalition government. In Sweden, the Social Democrats were by 1917 the largest single party in electoral terms, and in 1932 entered government to open a record period of rule.

In the 1920s and 1930s, the Second International retained Marxism as its official doctrine—or, at the very least, the main theorists of the organization considered themselves Marxists. Kautsky, Adler, Bauer and Hilferding, among others, attempted to analyse contemporary society from an orthodox Marxist standpoint, but at the same time they criticized the theory and political practice of

Bolshevism. However, the membership of the Second International continued to include parties with no allegiance of any kind to Marxism. The British Labour Party, for instance, formed in 1900, while 'arming itself' with some of Marx's ideas on political economy, turned elsewhere, to the Fabian Society, which stood for 'municipal socialism' and the peaceful, gradual evolution of capitalism into socialism, in order to equip itself with political and philosophical beliefs.[29] It is important to add that religion played a significant part in Fabian thinking and consequently in Labour-Party ideology.

The right-wing Social Democrats played a leading role in all the main parties of the Second International, and this tendency can be considered Marxist or socialist only in the formal sense. The political role of right-wing Social Democracy was more accurately defined by one of its German leaders as 'being the doctor at the bedside of sick capitalism'. In point of fact, the right-wing Social Democrats came more and more to fulfil the function of the traditional bourgeois liberal parties, a process mostly clearly noticeable in Britain where, under the two-party system, the Labour Party gradually took over from the Liberals, who survived but were reduced to insignificance as a political force.

The centrists had an important part to play in the Social Democratic movement, and especially through their most prominent leader, Kautsky. The left-wing Social Democrats, with their own particular function to fulfil, were highly critical of the Russian Bolsheviks in the 1920s, and especially their persecution of the Mensheviks and SRs, the overthrow of the Menshevik government in Georgia and the creation of a one-party system via the dictatorship of the proletariat. They approved of the Bolshevik decision to abandon War Communism in favour of NEP. All Social Democrats, however, united to condemn the trial of the right SRs in 1922 and the falsified trial of the Industrial Party and the Union Bureau of Mensheviks in 1930 and 1931. They were equally critical of enforced collectivization in 1930-32 and more so towards the campaign of terror in the late 1930s. It is significant that, on the formation of the new Second International, most of the leaders spoke out against the split between themselves and the extreme left-wing factions from which the Communist parties were soon to be formed. In the period between 1919 and 1922, European Social

Democracy was at one with Ramsay MacDonald, who said, in April 1919: 'In so far as the Socialist International at the present time is open to all shades of Socialist opinion and despite all the theoretical and practical disagreements resulting from Bolshevism I see no reason why the left wing has to cut itself off from the centre and form an independent group.'[30]

Social Democracy was still counting on the possibility of amalgamation with the Communists. In 1922, the Vienna International proposed that a special conference of the three Internationals—those of Berne and Vienna, and the Communist International—should be arranged, and this proposal was accepted by the Comintern leadership. The three executive committees met in Berlin in early April 1922. The Comintern delegation was headed by Clara Zetkin, and from Russia the Bolshevik Party sent Bukharin and Radek as delegates. There was some discussion of a proposal for an international workers' congress aimed at creating a united front of working people to resist the threat of war and the advance of capitalism. A working party was set up to deal with the preparatory details, but the differences proved too great and it was not long before the Comintern representatives walked out of the 'Commission of Nine' set up at the Berlin conference. The failure of this attempt to establish a united front rested not only with the leaders of European Social Democracy but also with the Comintern leaders, who, from the earliest days, took up extreme positions on many issues and may fairly be accused of sectarian dogmatism.

At the same time as the Social Democratic parties were preparing actively for the revival of the Socialist International, preparations were under way in Soviet Russia for the establishment of a new, third or Communist International. The idea had occurred to Lenin soon after the outbreak of the war and the collapse of the Second International, and gained strength with the emergence of small left-wing groups in the Social Democratic parties of Europe, all of them violently opposed to the war on grounds not far removed from those of the Bolsheviks. On his return to Russia after the February Revolution, Lenin called for a Bolshevik initiative. In his 'April Theses' he wrote: '10. A new International. We must take the initiative in creating a revolutionary International, an International directed against the social-chauvinists and against the "Centre".'[31]

Some days later, in a pamphlet entitled 'The Tasks of the Proletariat in Our Revolution', Lenin described the various groups that made up the movement of Social Democracy world-wide. His conclusion was that 'it is we who must found, and immediately, without delay, a new, revolutionary, proletarian International... This is the International of those "internationalists in deed" whom I specifically enumerated above. They alone represent the revolutionary, internationalist masses and not the corrupters of the masses. True, there are few socialists of that type, but let every Russian worker ask himself how many really conscious revolutionaries there were in Russia on the eve of the February-March Revolution of 1917. ...Our Party must not "wait", but must immediately found a Third International... To whom much has been given, of him much is demanded. There is no other land on earth as free as Russia is now. Let us make use of this freedom...to organize in a bold, honest, proletarian, Liebknecht way the foundation for a Third International, an International uncompromisingly hostile to the social-chauvinist traitors and to the vacillators of the "Centre".'[32]

However, the founding of the Third International proved to be beyond the Bolsheviks in 1917, and also in 1918, because of the complexity and seriousness of their own internal problems. But as soon as the situation in Russia settled down and began to improve a little, Lenin took the initiative and preparatory work began. The Party Central Committee met in late January 1919 and welcomed representatives from many foreign Communist parties—from Hungary, Poland, Austria, Germany, Finland and Latvia—as well as the Baltic Federation of Revolutionary Social Democrats and the Socialist Labour Party of America. The First Congress of the Communist International, or Comintern, was held in Moscow from March 2 to March 6, 1919. Other delegates in attendance included representatives of the Communist parties of the Ukraine, Estonia and Armenia, and also the Left Social Democratic Party of Sweden, individual leftist politicians from France, Chinese socialists and some others, though the overall numbers were kept small. In all, fifty-two delegates took part, representing thirty countries, and thirty-four of them had a vote.[33] The Congress ratified the Manifesto and Platform of the Communist International, Lenin's theses on bourgeois democracy and the dictatorship of the proletariat, his Appeal to Workers of All Countries and several other documents.

The Second Congress opened eighteen months later, in July 1920, in Petrograd, with an attendance reflecting the significant growth that the Communist movement had experienced in the meantime. There were 169 voting and forty-eight consultative delegates representing sixty-seven organizations from forty-one countries, including twenty-seven Communist parties and ten youth groups.[34] References were made to the growth of the movement in various countries and the Congress ratified numerous documents defining the organizational principles of the Communist International and its policy on problems of vital concern to the workers' movement. Conditions of entry and a rule-book were approved, the latter placing great emphasis on the principle of democratic centralism for the whole of the Communist movement. The leadership of Comintern possessed the same degree of authority *vis-a-vis* each individual party as did the Central Committee of the Bolshevik Party in relation to its own local party organizations. In essence, the Comintern—as was stated in the first paragraph of its Rule Book—set itself up as a single world-wide Communist party. National Communist parties comprised sections or branches of this united party and were obliged to implement the policy of the Comintern Executive Committee without question. The CEC had the power to annul any decision taken nationally, expel any leader from any Communist party, and even eject whole groups and organizations. All national programmes had to be presented to it for ratification.

The first man to be elected chairman of the Comintern Executive Committee was Zinoviev. He wound up the Second Congress with these words: 'We have approved the rule book of the Communist International. This is no empty formality. It is a strengthening of the formation of a single, united, international party of Communists which has only branches in various countries. (Applause)…Our adoption of the rule book indicates that we have closed ranks once and for all and we now have an international association of workers, an organization of blood brothers, centralized on an international scale.'[35] In formal terms, the Russian Communist Party had now become no more than one of the sections of the Comintern, but in fact the ruling hand of that Party, and the subsequent All-Russian Communist Party (Bolsheviks) was obvious to all and unchallenged on any side.

The Fourth Congress, which lasted for a month in Moscow, from

November 5 to December 5, 1922, was the last one attended by Lenin. This speech was dedicated to the fifth anniversary of Soviet power. Once again, a substantial expansion of the world Communist movement was reported. No less than 408 delegates (sixty-five of them consultative) attended the Congress, representing fifty-eight Communist parties in fifty-eight countries.[36] Such parties had sprung up by now on every continent, though almost all of them were very small in numbers and lacking in serious influence within their own countries. For this reason, the Comintern Executive Committee set each section the task of converting its Communist party into a mass party. Along with this went the task of winning over a majority of the workers to the Communist cause. Both the Third and Fourth Congresses passed resolutions requiring all parties 'to achieve the dissemination of Communist influence among the majority of the working class and the involvement of its decisive section in the struggle'.[37] In the capitalist countries, however, the majority of the workers were influenced not by the Communists but by the Social Democratic parties and the affiliated trade unions. Hence the logical demand for an intensification of the struggle against Social Democracy. The slogan of the 'united front', which was also being pushed at that time, really entailed struggling for a united front 'from below'. The Communist parties were to seek agreement with rank-and-file working-class Social Democrats and the grass-roots organizations of the Social Democratic parties and trade unions, while simultaneously stepping up the struggle against the reformist leadership of the Social Democratic movement and the Second International. One of the resolutions passed by the Third Congress of the Comintern stated: 'The Communist International must in future do battle not only against the Second International, against the Amsterdam International of Trade Unions, but also against the Two-and-a-Half International. Only through this *ruthless* struggle, proving day by day to the masses that the Social Democrats and centrists have no heart for fighting to overthrow capitalism or even for the most elementary and pressing needs of the working class, can the Communist International wrest from these agents of the bourgeoisie their influence over the working class. This struggle can be brought to a victorious conclusion only by the complete suppression of all centrist tendencies within our own ranks.'[38]

Once all the Social Democratic organizations had agreed to international unification at their Hamburg congress, an augmented plenary session of the Comintern Executive Committee was heard to pronounce the following confident prediction: 'That new arrival, the Second International, is a stillborn child. It will be buried either at the first sign of international conflict or the first clash of any significance between capital and labour. It is the last rival to the Communist International in the workers' movement, and one that guarantees success for the Communist International. The Hamburg International...will soon be recognized by the workers whom it is still deceiving for what it really is, a bastion of the bourgeoisie... The task of the Communist International and all its sections is to speed up the inevitable process of disillusionment... And the fiercer, the more urgent the struggle we wage, the sooner will the vast majority of the toiling and exploited masses realise that Communism alone is capable of ridding them of the horrors of capitalism and creating a better future for them.'[39]

These predictions never came true. The revolutionary crisis was ended by what was then called 'a temporary stabilization of capitalism'. The forces of reaction gathered strength in most countries. The fascist movement was getting stronger all the time. Only in one or two countries, France, Germany and Czechoslovakia in particular, did the Communist party manage to increase its membership and influence, and even there the majority of the work-force followed the Social Democrats as before, not the Communists. In the other capitalist countries, the Communist parties remained organizations of small political significance in the late 1920s. A few simple statistics illustrate this clearly. In 1928, the German Communist Party had a membership of 125,000 whereas the SPD could count on almost one million. In the election of that year, nine million people cast their votes in favour of the latter, while the Communists polled only 3,200,000. The French held an election the same year, and in it the Communists won approximately 1,100,000 votes—some 200,000 more than in 1924 but still far less than the total polled by the Socialists and Radical Socialists. In 1926, there were 65,000 declared Communists in France. In Czechoslovakia, the Social Democrats won about one million votes and thirty-nine seats in 1929, whereas the Communists managed 750,000 votes and thirty seats. In Austria, the few thousands of Communists compared badly with the hundreds of thousands of Social Democrats. The Communist Party of Great Britain had less than ten thousand members in 1928 and no members of parliament, whereas in 1929 the Labour Party won the election and formed the government. In Belgium, Communist Party strength stood at less than two thousand. In Sweden in the same year (1928), there were about fifteen thousand Communists but, following a split in the party, membership fell away drastically. There were no more than three thousand in Switzerland. The picture was worse still in the United States. This country had the largest working class in the world, yet in 1929 its Communist Party consisted of no more than ten thousand members. The conclusion that suggests itself is that the 'ruthless' and 'implacable' struggle against Social Democracy undertaken by the Communists and conducted throughout the 1920s did not achieve conspicuously successful results. This was no accidental failure. It must surely be admitted now that from the outset the whole question of Communist–Social Democrat relations was wrongly formulated and that, for their part, the Communists made far too many mistakes.

The first mistake was to take the experience gained in the Bolshevik struggle against the Mensheviks and SRs in Russia and apply it automatically to the activities of the Comintern, which were actually governed by quite different circumstances. We have already observed that in Western Europe, and even more in the USA and Japan, the bourgeoisie looked on Social Democracy as anything but its own buttress. The bourgeoisie had its own parties to rely on and in many countries these were permitting the advance of fascism. Thus the Communists' policy of directing the main thrust of their agitation and propaganda against the Social Democrats bore no relation to real socio-political conditions in the West. As in Russia, the Western Communist parties argued fiercely and bitterly against the Social Democrats and really did attempt to disseminate among the working masses the 'hatred, revolusion and scorn for those who think differently' that Lenin had called for, to wage 'a war of destruction' acknowledging no limitations other than those 'imposed by the criminal law'.[40] This tactic was wrong even in Russia; it was doubly wrong in the conditions of the outside world. In Russia, the Bolshevik and Menshevik factions had emerged simultaneously, and even as early as the revolutionary period 1905-

1907, the former had enjoyed greater influence over the working class. The situation changed during the First World War, when harsh repression curtailed their activities, but after 1917, with their return to legality and freedom of action, the Bolsheviks soon regained their decisive influence over the workers. An entirely different balance of forces existed in the capitalist countries, where young and inexperienced Communist parties, small in numbers and with no leaders who enjoyed mass popularity, were opposed by Social Democratic parties with, in most cases, four or five decades of experience behind them. These parties had a strong influence on the multi-million-strong trade unions and co-operatives as well as many other working-class political and educational organizations. It was, incidentally, by no means true that these parties took no interest in even the most elementary and pressing needs of the working class. They did not, of course, encourage the workers to think in terms of immediate violent revolution, but they did make a considerable contribution to the organization and education of the working class, to the creation of trade unions, the establishment of an eight-hour working day, pay increases and improved living and working conditions for a large section of the work-force of the Western world. This is why there was so little point in dismissing the Social Democratic leaders in blistering terms such as 'renegades', 'betrayers', 'traitors', 'enemies of the working class', 'agents of the bourgeoisie', and so on.

The working class in most Western countries had learned how to organize itself before any Communist parties were formed there. It was therefore a mistake for the Bolsheviks, when encouraging the slogan of a united front, to reject in advance all forms of coalition and alliance with Social Democratic workers' organizations. In doing so, they committed the 'united front from below' to certain failure. By the time of the Fifth Congress of the Comintern, it was necessary to admit publicly that the tactic of a united front had not brought tangible results for the Communist parties and, more specifically, that 'the parties of the Communist International at the present time often prove incapable of making use of the tactic of a united front as such' and that by the same token 'this tactic threatens to turn into a tactic of opportunism and a source of "revisionism".' The harsh message continued: 'The tactic of a united front is only a method of agitation and the revolutionary mobilization of the masses for the whole of a period. Any attempts to interpret this tactic as political coalition with counter-revolutionary Social Democracy amount to an opportunism which the Communist International repudiates.'[41] These directions may not have been 'opportunist', but they created a misguided sectarianism that led not to a united front but to the isolation of Communists in the working-class movements of the capitalist countries.

One of the most serious mistakes made by the Comintern was to declare war on the left-wing tendencies of Social Democracy, which were presented as an enemy no less dangerous than the right-wing Social Democrats. In point of fact, all the Western Communist parties, and even Russia's, arose from left-wing tendencies and groups within Social Democracy, which at the appropriate moment detached themselves to form independent parties. In the conditions of the class struggle, once the Communist parties had broken away the Social Democratic parties continued to generate left-wing groups and tendencies and these movements, as one might expect, began to criticize the right-wing of Social Democracy and the Communist movement alike. Thus, the left wing of Social Democracy found its own niche by a natural process. It ought to have been just as natural for the Communists to look on these left-wing Social Democrats as future allies and therefore to react with some restraint towards their critical comments, to concentrate on explaining to them their own policies and tactics, to seek agrreement with them wherever possible and always to consider and even try to implement the best of their ideas. The Comintern did not do this. It called for battle to be opened up on a new front—this time with left-wing Social Democracy. The programme adopted by the Sixth Congress in 1928 gave the following guidance: 'In the course of international revolution, particular significance as a major force of counter-revolution, actively combatting revolution and actively supporting the partial stabilization of capital, has been assumed by the ruling cadres of the Social Democratic parties and the reformist trade unions... Systematically conducting this counter-revolutionary policy, Social Democracy operates with its two separate wings: a right wing, overtly counter-revolutionary, essential for negotiating and establishing direct contacts with the bourgeoisie, and *a left-wing—for deceiving the workers with particular subtlety*. "Left-wing" Social Democracy, playing around with pacifist and sometimes even revolutionary phraseology, actually works against the proletariat, particularly at the most crucial moments...*and therefore amounts to the most dangerous of all the factions of Social Democracy*.[42]

The Communist International could not, or would not, see any positive significance in the way the Social Democrats, and particularly those of the left, resisted fascism. This indicated a serious underestimation of the fascist dangers and hindered the creation of a united front against it. Communism outside Russia was much too weak to offer any real resistance to the rise of fascism. Social Democracy, on the other hand, was a real obstacle to this power. The internecine left-wing struggle, waged so fiercely in the 'war of destruction' advocated by Lenin, brought nothing but delight to fascist groups and parties throughout Europe. The Comintern continued to withhold assistance from the Social Democrats and to underestimate the value of the democratic institutions and freedoms that were now being threatened by fascism. Worse than that, Communist propaganda and agitation introduced the new and false concept of 'social fascism', which was meant to define Social Democracy. The Comintern programme informed the world that 'by way of adaptation to the changing political situation the bourgeoisie is now employing the methods of both fascism and coalition with Social Democracy, the latter movement itself frequently playing a fascist role at moments of critical importance to capitalism. In the course of development it is revealing fascist tendencies.'[43] The literature of propaganda took hold of this thesis, embellished it and made of it a complete new theory. Here is an extract taken from the *Workbook for Institutions of Higher Education and Communist Institutions of Higher Education,* compiled by the Communist Academy's Institute of Economics: '"Social fascism" is one peculiar aspect of fascism, an agency of monopolistic capital within the working-class movement... Lenin established long ago that the bourgeoisie develops two main methods of domination: the method of violence and the method of "liberalism"... The method of violence is directly represented by fascism; the method of "liberalism" is represented by the Social Democratic aspect of fascism, or social fascism. ...For all the formal distinction existing between the more overt national fascism and the hypocritical social fascism, they both perform the same function, carrying out the requirements of the imperialistic bourgeoisie. The differences between the devices and phraseology of fascism and social fascism are explicable by the fact that each has its own specific tasks. Social fascism is summoned to recruit workers for the service of monopolistic capital, summoned to throw the revolutionary movement into confusion and to switch proletarian activity over to the service of capital in the guise of defending "the higher interests of the whole nation". The peculiar nature of the tasks confronting social fascism gives rise to numerous niceties of social demagogy—devil's advocacy in opposition (soon cut short when the social fascists are invited into government), adherence to Marxist phraseology, etc."[44] It goes without saying that this sort of propaganda was not destined to make a great impact on the working class or the progressive intelligentsia in the West, for whom Soviet textbooks written for Communist Institutions of Higher Education were not the only literature available.

By its insistence on automatically applying methods of revolutionary struggle that had once proved successful in Russian conditions to the substantially different circumstances in the capitalist countries, the Comintern was guilty of a dogmatism that was not to be shaken off completely even in the period 1935-37 when, after the triumph of fascism in Germany and the defeat of the Communists along with the Social Democrats, the Communist parties announced a change in strategy and tactics. A united front had helped prevent the victory of fascism in France in the 1930s, but it was not able to stave off the Second World War. The chance had gone. Responsibility for this failure rests not only with the Western bourgeois governments or Western Social Democracy but also with the leadership of the Comintern and the Bolshevik Party.

The Social Base of Social Democracy

These mistakes arose in no small degree from an overestimation of the revolutionary eagerness of the working class in the developed capitalist countries and their capacity and willingness to follow the example of the Russian working class. Similarly mistaken conclusions were reached in relation to the social base of Social Democracy. The Communists of the 1920s refused to accept the idea that Social Democracy might be able to reflect the interests and aspirations of the bulk of working-class Europe. Quite the reverse—it was commonly stated by representatives of the Communist movement that the Social Democratic parties, including not only right-wing Socialists but those of the centre and left as well, were, in terms of their social base, not working-class parties at all but 'bourgeois agencies' operating within the working class. The Comintern programme made it clear that 'Social Democracy is the mainstay of imperialism in the working class. International Social Democracy of all shades...has thus become a reserve of bourgeois society, its truest support. At certain times Social Democracy is obliged to move across and take up the position of an opposition party and even simulate the defence of the class interests of the proletariat in its economic struggle, in order to win the trust of the working class and then betray its interests all the more shamefully.'[45]

This dogmatic sociology was, of course, remote from the truth. At the beginning of the twentieth century, the working class in Western Europe and the USA was developing in conditions very different from those suffered by the working class of Russia, in both economic and political terms. In Russia, the Bolsheviks formed the nucleus of the working class. The larger the industrial enterprise and the more literate and effectively organized its work-force, the easier it was for the Bolsheviks to win a position of influence, because of the sharper awareness of the contradiction between the working class on the one hand and, on the other, the combined forces of autocratic, landowning Russia, world capital and the Russian bourgeoisie. The Mensheviks were also a working-class party, but they represented only a minority of the class; their influence extended to relatively few enterprises and professions—usually the better-paid ones—and to tradesmen. The SRs, of the left and the right, and the labour and populist Socialists were predominantly parties of the peasantry, though they appealed also to office-workers, students and the intelligentsia; they could rightly be described, in Marxist terms, as 'petty-bourgeois' parties.

In the Western capitalist countries in the 1920s, the social structure and the situation of the working class were different. The workers' political parties and their trade unions enjoyed full legal status, they were represented in the legislature and thus had some considerable opportunities to fight for their own rights within the limits of the law. The standard of living was higher. The situation of the peasantry was by no means the same; rural populations in the

West were smaller than in Russia and they suffered far less from latter-day feudalism. By and large they were not much inclined towards revolution. Even after the end of the First World War, the ruling classes in the West retained their dominion over vast colonial holdings in Asia, Africa and Latin America, and enjoyed a substantial return on capital investment in semi-developed and weak capitalist countries such as Russia, the Balkans, regions of South America and elsewhere. The Communist parties in these countries recorded some successes during the revolutionary crisis of 1918-1923. Even then, however, their influence was limited to a minority of the working class and even this was then restricted by the stabilization of capitalism and the resurgence of Social Democracy. Existence—as Marx put it—determines consciousness, and in Western Europe it happened that the great bulk of the industrial proletariat became more responsive to the idea of a gradual evolution to socialism than to calls for violent revolution. This was not altogether surprising. Even before the October Revolution, Lenin had foreseen that reformism or 'revisionism' would gradually get the upper hand in the European Socialist movement. In 1908, defining this extreme form of 'opportunism', he wrote: 'To redetermine one's behaviour from one event to another, to adjust to daily occurrences, to the twists and turns of political trivia, to lose sight of the basic interests of the proletariat and the fundamental characteristics of the whole capitalist order...to sacrifice these basic interests for the sake of momentary advantage, real or imaginary—such is the policy of revisionism.'[46] The developing reformist and revisionist tendencies in the Social Democratic movement were, however, given a particular explanation in Bolshevik literature: they were put down to degeneracy among the majority of the party workers, trade union leaders and workers' representatives in parliaments and municipalities. This became official Comintern doctrine, as may be seen from the following resolution, 'On Our Attitude towards "Socialist" Tendencies', passed by the First Congress: 'Petty-bourgeois "fellow travellers" of socialism have been pouring into the ranks of the official Social Democratic parties and have gradually changed the course of their policies in the direction of the bourgeoisie. From the leaders of the world-wide parliamentary labour movement, the trade union leaders and the editors and officials of Social Democracy a whole new caste has been formed, a bureaucracy that has its own self-seeking group interests at heart and has become hostile to socialism.'[47] This was only partly true, for the change occurring in the apparatus of the Social Democratic movement were a reflection of similar changes occurring deep within the working class itself.

Lenin wholly endorsed the thesis proposed by Marx and Engels concerning the revolutionary mission of the working class. It was his conviction that only a union between socialism and the working-class movement could open the way towards socialist revolution. He agreed completely with what Marx and Engels had written in *The Holy Family:* 'Not in vain does (the proletariat) go through the stern but steeling school of *labour*. It is not a question of what this or that proletarian, or even the whole proletariat, at the moment *regards* as its aim. It is a question of *what the proletariat is,* and what, in accordance with this *being,* it will historically be compelled to do. Its aim and historical action (are) visibly and irrevocably foreshadowed in its own life situation as well as in the whole organization of bourgeois society today.'[48] These principles, first enunciated in 1845, remained applicable even after the passage of seventy or eighty years, but there were numerous exceptions to the rule. The cases of England and the United States at the beginning of the twentieth century were such exceptions. These countries had the largest working classes and the highest degree of capitalist development, yet their left-wing parties and groups were the smallest and least influential. It was inappropriate to think in terms of the formation of a special bureaucratic caste within Social Democracy for that kind of bureaucracy had less influence in England and the USA than anywhere in continental Europe.

Another explanation of the slow development of revolutionary attitudes in working-class Europe rested upon the concept of 'the labour aristocracy'. This was a concept frequently used by Marx and Engels, mainly with reference to the upper strata of the working class in Great Britain, the controllers of the activities and political attitudes of some of the major British trade unions—various groups of skilled workers who had managed to win relatively high rates of pay for themselves. Marx and Engels did not claim that such workers were not exploited, but the degree of exploitation was clearly much lower than that suffered by the other categories of working men. In the second half of the nineteenth century, England made remarkable industrial advances, which allowed the English capitalists to cream off substantial profits without having to reduce rates of pay for their skilled workers. This was used by Marx and Engels as an explanation of the palpable decline in socialist attitudes among the British working class. Engels wrote in 1885: 'The truth is that while England's industrial monopoly has existed the English working class has enjoyed its advantages to a considerable extent. The advantages have been shared out very unevenly among the workers; a privileged minority has seized the largest part, though even the broad masses have been given a little something from time to time. This is why, ever since Owenism died out, there has been no socialism in England. With the collapse of the industrial monopoly, the English working class will lose its privileged position and all of it, including the privileged, leading minority, will find itself back on the same level as the workers in other countries. And this is why socialism will reappear in England.'[49]

The concept of a 'labour aristocracy' made its first appearance in Lenin's work in 1912 and its implications are those described by Engels. Attempting an explanation of the existence of 'liberal-bourgeois traditions hanging ominously over the *aristocracy* of America's working class', he wrote: 'The state of affairs in America shows us, as in England, a remarkably deep split...between bourgeois working-class policies and Socialist ones. For, however strange these words may sound, even the working class can lead the way towards bourgeois policies in a capitalist society if it loses sight of its goals of emancipation and comes to terms with hired slavery ...for the sake of imaginary "improvements" in its situation of slavery. The main historical reason for the particular prominence and (temporary) strength of bourgeois working-class policies in England and America is to be found in the latter's long-established political freedom and conditions—which have been extraordinarily propitious compared with those of other countries—favourable to the development of capitalism in depth and breadth. On the strength of these conditions an aristocracy has emerged within the working class and has tried to keep up with the bourgeoisie, thus betraying its own class.'[50]

The same concept recurs frequently in Lenin's preparatory notebooks for *Imperialism, the Highest Stage of Capitalism*, written between 1914 and 1916. Now the author linked the appearance of a 'labour aristocracy' with excess profits, drawn from the colonies and used in part to suborn sections of the working class. Lenin and the Bolsheviks generally were certain that neither the workers who happened to enjoy a comparatively privileged position nor the reformist Social Democracy that depended upon them could possibly inaugurate Socialism, or even desire it. The actual position and attitudes of this stratum of the working class were virtually never scrutinized in Bolshevik literature. The few pronouncements that were made created the impression that the 'labour aristocracy' was not subject to exploitation at all, that, in suborning these workers, the capitalists stopped exploiting them and gave them an equal share of their profits. In other words, the capitalists no longer appropriated all the surplus value created by the workers but, on the contrary, gave them back a part of the surplus value achieved through the exploitation of other, less skilled, workers and the toiling people of the colonial and semi-colonial countries.

The fact of the matter is that, in England, America and the countries of Western Europe, even the skilled workers were still subject to exploitation, albeit of a less harsh and brazen kind. Far from being given their improved material conditions by benevolent capitalists and factory-owners, they fought for, and won, these improvements in the course of a prolonged struggle, which was, indeed an economic rather than a political one. We must remember that the skilled workers were producing more goods per working day than the semi-skilled or unskilled work force, and that this was reflected in their higher rates of pay. This section of the working class was certainly not impervious to socialist propaganda, though it did consist of people who favoured the more moderate forms and methods of political struggle. Lenin, however, did not raise the question of a possible pact or union with the 'labour aristocracy' or indeed with any of reformists within the Social Democratic movement. Along with the other Bolsheviks, he placed all his hopes in the possibility that international capitalist rivalry, together with the spread of national liberation movements, would lead to a decline in the material prosperity of the upper strata of the working class. The 'labour aristocracy' would shrink and wither away and the working class as a whole would lean more and more towards revolution. It might have seemed that these hopes were being realized at the end of the First World War, when the countries of the West were plunged into a period of extreme difficulty that culminated in a profound economic crisis. This did, in fact, lead to a shift to the left among the working masses as well as exacerbating and extending all forms of the class struggle. Even after the storm of the immediate post-war years, no Bolshevik doubted that the days of capitalism were numbered and that it could not now count on a resurgence of any kind. At the Fifteenth Conference of the All-Russian Communist Party (Bolsheviks) in 1926, Trotsky was able to say: 'If we were to think that European capitalism could guarantee another resurgence for itself (and it is my opinion that capitalism has no chance of doing so), if theoretically we were to allow this possibility just for a moment, this would mean that, on a European and world-wide scale, capitalism has not yet quite exhausted its historical mission, that it is not yet imperialistic, decaying capitalism but capitalism still developing and leading the economy and culture onwards—but that would mean that we have arrived too soon.'[51]

At that time, of course, Trotsky was at the head of the party's Left Opposition, but his words were an expression not merely of left-wing thinking but also of majority Bolshevik and Western Communist opinion. Once the much more serious crisis of 1929-33 got under way, many Communists assumed that at long last the final crisis of capitalism had arrived. But history took a different path. In all the capitalist countries, the economic and financial crisis was weathered, albeit at the cost of sharpened class struggle and a shift to the left in the consciousness and political activity of a large section of the working class. Communist parties in many countries experienced a growth in membership. At the same time, however, other working-class or socialist parties took up more radical positions; this was reflected in the policies adopted by the Social Democratic movement, in which left-wing tendencies came to prominence and began to exercise their influence. On the other hand, many countries saw the economic crisis result in a movement to the right and a considerable growth of various nationalist and fascist parties, particularly in Germany. Under pressure from the working class and rank-and-file Communists, the leadership of the Comintern and its sections found themselves compelled to revise their sectarian attitude towards Social Democracy and other left-wing groups on the European scene. Communist literature began to admit adjustments to a number of previously firm theoretical principles. The mistaken expression 'social fascism' was cast aside. It was admitted that the Social Democratic parties and the trade unions were indeed working-class organizations, even though they inclined towards the right and were influenced by bourgeois thinking. Here is an extract from a resolution passed by the Comintern at its Seventh Congress in 1935: 'Without departing for a moment from our own independent work on Communist education, organization and mobilization of the masses, we Communists must ... contrive to arrange joint declarations with the Social Democratic parties, the reformist trade unions and *other organizations of working people* directed against the class enemies of the proletariat on the basis of short-term and long-term agreements... We Communists must reveal to the masses the sense of the demogogic arguments put forward by the right-wing Social Democratic leaders against a united front ... and establish the closest co-operation with the left-wing Social Democratic workers, functionaries and organizations that struggle against reformist policies and support a united front with the Communist parties.'[52] Similar changes were noticeable in the attitude now adopted by the Social Democrats towards the Communists. Georgi Dimitrov, who took over from Zinoviev, Bukharin and Manuilsky as leader of the Comintern Executive Committee, read a speech to the Seventh Congress of the Comintern in which he was obliged to observe that the Social Democracy had moved away from policies of class collaboration with the bourgeoisie, towards the policy of a united front with the Communist parties.[53] Many Social Democratic leaders were entering into agreements with the Communists. They did so with serious and understandable reservations, but in the uncomfortable and increasing awareness that, unless they co-operated with the Communists, and on a world scale with the USSR, victory over the ever-growing forces of fascism would be unattainable.

The Position and Role of the Communist Movement Today

A work such as this cannot even begin to consider the complex processes that occurred in the Communist and Socialist movements during the Second World War and the twenty-five years after it. Despite the forecasts and expectations of the 1920s and 1930s, capitalism survived the terrible shocks of the Second World War and the defeat of fascism. The Western capitalist countries, and Japan, have survived the break-up of their vast colonial empires and their replacement by independent Third World countries. During the war and immediately after it, capitalism suffered great losses, but the system as a whole has come through the crisis and in many respects has even increased its own might. The rates at which the economies of the capitalist countries developed in the 1950s and 1960s far outstripped the rates achieved in the 1920s and 1930s, and approximated to the rates of development in the socialist countries. Between 1950 and 1975 alone, industrial output in the advanced capitalist countries rose by 350%. It was capitalism that, in the post-war period, provided the impetus for the technological revolution and thus guaranteed prolonged and rapid material progress, unprecedented levels of economic development, a vast network of scientific and technological institutions and an awe-inspiring military machine.

This rapid development of capitalism, which was not allowed for by Marxist theory, has been accompanied by complex changes in the structure of capitalist society. In all capitalist countries, the working class has increased in numbers. There has been a great extension of that stratum of the work-force consisting of paid workers in trade and the service industries. Numbers of people engaged in scientific work, the intelligentsia and the student population have all grown considerably. At the same time, the numbers of people working on the land have diminished, and the conditions of agricultural labour have changed completely, so that the work is now akin to industrial labour with all its variations. The educational level of the working class, and all working people, has risen perceptibly. The structure of skilled labour has undergone a change. By 1975, skilled workers made up 39.2 per cent of the working population of the USA and semi-skilled workers accounted for a further 46.6 per cent; unskilled labour had fallen to 14.2 per cent. In 1974 in France, the proportions were: skilled workers, 40.3 per cent; semi-skilled, 39.6 per cent; unskilled, 20.1 per cent. In Germany the percentages were, respectively, 45, 36.2 and 18.8; in England 51.4, 26.4 and 17.7.[54]

By persisting in their struggle against the industrialists and the state, most workers in the West[55] managed to improve their material conditions in the post-war period. There was a significant broadening of the categories of goods and services considered essential to a minimum standard of living in the developed countries. The concept of a 'labour aristocracy' has lost all meaning; such people are virtually indistinguishable now among the great masses of skilled and semi-skilled workers. The only people who may be said to constitute a 'labour aristocracy' today—and then only with some reservations—are certain supervisors and engineers who are one or two rungs higher up the ladder of the modern production system. Their numbers have risen dramatically, and no one political party may count on their support.

None of this should be taken to indicate that Western capitalism has now overcome the bitter contradictions that characterized the system in its earlier stages of development. The contradictions still exist, and modern capitalism has long since prepared all the objective material prerequisites of a socialist reconstruction of society. Even so, socialism has yet to achieve victory. One reason for the long survival of capitalism is the discord between Communists and Socialists, which broke out with renewed acerbity at the end of the Second World War. The responsibility for this inability to find agreement rests equally with the Communist and Socialist movements.

During the Second World War, the Comintern was disbanded. It ceased to exist as a united Communist party. Once the war was over, one or two minor Third World Communist parties called for the reconstitution of some kind of international, but the majority of Communist parties were not interested. An attempt was made to set up a European organization for co-ordinating information of general use to the Communist movement—the Information Bureau known as the Cominform, with its centre in Belgrade, then in Prague. An international Communist newspaper began to be published, as they said, 'for lasting peace and popular democracy'. As things turned out, however, the Cominform met on only a few occasions and spent most of the time condemning the activities of the Communist Party of Yugoslavia. In 1956, the whole organization, including its publications, was wound up. No other international organization has arisen to take its place, since the various Communist parties were justifiably afraid of losing the independence and autonomy gained by the dissolution of the Comintern. The last remaining form of co-operative activity available to the Communist parties was a series of international congresses. But there have been only three such conferences, in 1957, 1960 and 1969, and there were noticeable absentees from the last of these, when a number of the major Communist parties felt unable to participate because of deep-seated differences. Berlin hosted a European Congress of Communist parties in 1976, and the only absentees were the Communist parties of Albania, Yugoslavia and one of the two Greek parties (in Greece, as in India and some other countries in Asia, Africa and South America, two or more 'parallel' Communist parties had by then emerged). The 1980 European Congress held in Paris scarcely counts as a success in view of the absence from it of representatives from Italy, Spain, Britain and some other European countries including Romania. An internationally circulated journal, *Problems of Peace and Socialism,* is still published from Prague; published in all the world's main languages, its purpose is the exchange of information between all Communist parties.

Differences of opinion have not prevented the significant growth of the Communist movement in the post-war period. Whereas in the 1930s only the USSR and Mongolia were ruled by Communist parties, Communists soon came to power in fourteen other countries of Europe and Asia, and then in Cuba. The 1960s and 1970s have seen groups and parties allied to the Communist movement take power in several countries of Africa and Asia. By the early 1970s, the socialist countries accounted for rather more than a quarter of the land surface of the planet and about a third of the world's population. The advanced capitalist countries occupied only about eight per cent of the land surface and accounted for some fifteen per cent of the world's people. Upwards of sixty per cent of the land and fifty per cent of the population of our planet belonged to Third World countries. At the same time (1971), industrial output was divided approximately as follows: capitalist countries—fifty-four per cent; socialist countries—thirty-nine per cent; Third World countries—seven per cent.[56]

The number of Communist parties has grown significantly, rising from about sixty parties with three million members in 1935 to seventy-five parties with thirty-three million members in 1957. By 1962, there were eighty-eight parties and forty-three million members, and, by the mid-1970s, nearly one hundred parties with around sixty million members.[57] It must be remembered, however, that by far the largest proportion of Communist party members are found in the socialist countries. In the advanced capitalist countries, Communist party membership rose in the post-war period, but not so steeply as that of the Social Democratic parties. Italy is the only country in which the Communist party has gained a predominant influence in the working class, ousting the Socialists from first place. The French party enjoyed a similar position for much of the post-war period, until the spectacular resurgence of French Socialism displaced it. In Spain, Portugal and Japan the Communist party has acquired, if not predominance, at least a significant influence on the working class. In virtually all other capitalist countries, the Communist party has failed to convert itself into a mass organization wielding significant influence.

In 1973, the Italian Communist Party had more than 1,600,000 members whereas the Social Democratic and Socialist parties together claimed only some 750,000. In the first post-war election in Italy, nineteen per cent of the population voted Communist. The French Communist Party had more than 400,000 members in 1973, as opposed to the Socialist Party's 110,000. In their first post-war election twenty-six per cent of the French people voted Communist, and by 1973 that proportion had fallen to twenty-one per cent. The Japanese Communist Party claimed about 300,000 members in 1972 and polled 5,500,000 votes—more than ten per cent of the electorate. The Socialist Party of Japan had only 50,000 members but it still attracted the votes of 11,500,000 citizens—twenty-two per cent of the electorate. In Spain, the Communist Party emerged from underground with more than 200,000 members, a similar number to those supporting the Socialist Party. In the election held in March 1979, however, the Socialists gained 121 seats compared with the Communists' twenty-three. In Finland, the Communist Party had about 50,000 members in 1973, and in 1975 received about twenty per cent of the votes. At the time, the Finnish Social Democratic Party, with a membership of about 100,000 attracted the votes of about a quarter of the electorate.

It is clear that in most European capitalist countries the Socialist parties exert a much stronger influence than the Communists. In Austria, for example, the Communist Party had about 25,000 members in the early 1970s and polled only just over one per cent of the votes cast in the election of 1971. At that time, the Austrian Socialist Party claimed a membership of 700,000 and won a majority in the same election with more than half the electorate behind it. In Belgium, the two Socialist parties (Flemish and Walloon) had 220,000 members in the mid-1970s, whereas the Communist Party could count on about 11,000. The Labour Party in Britain had at that time some 6,300,000 members (including trade union affiliations); this large figure compares with a mere 30,000 in the Communist Party, which could not muster a single Member of Parliament. There are no Communist deputies in the West German Bundestag—in the 1974 election the 40,000 members of the Communist Party of West Germany was able to win only 0.3 per cent of the electorate. In the same country, the Social Democratic Party has more than a million members. Turning to Sweden, we note that, whereas in that same period the Communist Party had about 16,000 members and polled less than six per cent of the votes, the Social Democratic Party had 900,000 members and polled between forty and fifty per cent. The Social Democratic Party in Switzerland had a membership of some 70,000 and was able to attract a quarter of the votes in the most recent general election; the Communist Party in the same country had three thousand members and less than three per cent of the votes. The same story emerges in most of the other countries of Western Europe. In Holland and Denmark, the Communist Parties, with, respectively, 12,000 and 8,000 members, polled 4.4 and 3.6 per cent of the votes. In Norway 5,000 Communists achieved eleven per cent of the votes, a fairly high proportion but still well behind the ruling Labour Party with its membership of about 180,000.

The picture is somewhat different in the USA where the Communists have failed to make any impression at all, before or after the war. Membership of the US Communist Party never exceeded 12,000 throughout the 1970s. The difference here is that in the USA the Socialists too have been unable to establish any kind of solid or strong political organization. In Canada, the Communist Party has made little headway and lags well behind the socialist (New Democratic) party.[58]

Thus it emerges that since the war the various Social Democratic parties have not only re-established, but have actually advanced their positions in the capitalist world. Steps have been taken to re-establish the international organizations, which had to suspend operations during the war. As early as 1947, a committee was set up in London to co-ordinate international Socialist conferences. Comisco, as it was called, made the necessary preparations for the Socialist International of 1951. This was a newly constituted international alliance of Social Democratic parties. Its first meeting, held in Frankfurt, approved the declaration of 'The Aims and Tasks of Democratic Socialism', later known as the 'Frankfurt Declaration'. It was decided to reconvene the Socialist International at congresses held every two or three years. Between congresses, the leadership was to rest with a Council of the International composed of two members from each party. A secretariat was set up to take care of day-to-day business and the headquarters were located in London. The first elected chairman of the association was the eminent Austrian socialist, Pitterman, who was succeeded in the mid-1970s by the head of the West German Social Democratic Party, Willy Brandt.

In the early 1950s, the Socialist International embraced thirty-nine Socialist parties. Left-wing moods and tendencies had been very strong in the late 1940s, when governments in several capitalist countries included not only Socialist but even Communist members, but now, in the bleak conditions of the Cold War, the countries of Western Europe witnessed a transfer of allegiance by the electorate to the clerical, Conservative, and traditional Liberal parties of the middle class. Then, in the period between 1961 and 1964, a reverse occurred; local, parliamentary and presidential elections all over Western Europe returned results indicating a sharp swing to the left. The overall Socialist vote rose substantially. By 1970 the Socialist International had grown even larger, with fifty-four member parties speaking for more than fifteen million people. Disregarding block membership, like that of the trade unions, the Socialist International represented approximately ten million individuals. Some seventy-eight million Europeans had cast a Socialist vote and it was clear that the Socialist parties were well ahead of the Communists in influence. In the ten West European countires, Socialist parties were either in power or participated in coalition governments. At the same time, two-thirds of all Socialist parties belonged to Western Europe. In 1970, Latin America had eight representatives in the Socialist International and the whole of Asia had only nine. The Labour Parties of Australia and

New Zealand were members. There were no representatives at all from Africa unless we include the offshore island states.[59] In the early 1960s, the Socialist International included nine émigré parties from Central and Eastern Europe, bringing the overall formal total of member parties to more than sixty.

The late 1970s saw a gradual decline in the influence of Social Democracy throughout Europe. This process has had some connection with the simple fact that the Social Democratic parties in power have proved incapable of making any real impact on the inexorable crisis in the capitalist economy over this period. In Britain, the Labour Party has been voted out. In Sweden the Social Democratic Party has suffered defeat after more than forty years of government. The Portuguese Socialists have lost power too, and the Socialist vote has declined in other countries. In country after country, the Social Democrats have split. The elections to the European parliament resulted in limited success for the left-wing parties, including the Social Democrats, compared with the conservative and centre parties. At the same time, however, the Social Democrats have tightened their grip in West Germany and Austria. The conservative parties, as experience in Britain and Sweden shows clearly, have proved equally incapable of overcoming the growing problems of the economy. It seems likely that the 1980s will see a renewal of Social Democratic influence and, more specifically, of the left-wing tendencies within the Socialist International.

In the last decade, the Socialist International has taken steps to extend its influence beyond Western Europe. The returns have not been impressive. The ruling Socialist Party of Senegal has been recruited, as well as Social Democratic parties from India, Costa Rica, El Salvador, the People's Republican Party of Turkey and one or two others. Most of the newly acquired member parties are small in numbers and influence. the most obvious reason for this is that the reformist ideology of the International evokes a response primarily among the better-off strata of the working class. It is thus quite difficult for the Social Democratic movement to find a social base in the backward, impoverished countries of the Third World.

In contemporary Soviet journalism, and in our handbooks, we often read that it is the working class that provides the social base for Social Democracy. For instance, the Social Democratic Party of Denmark is described as 'uniting considerable numbers of workers, officials and also the petty bourgeoisie and the intelligentsia'. The more radical Left Socialists are presented as 'expressing the interests of a section of the workers'. The Socialist Party of France is said to unite 'the workers in several industries (in textiles and mining), considerable numbers of officials, teachers and the intellectual engineers and technicians'.[60]

Nevertheless, Communist literature still harks back all too frequently to the days when not only Social Democratic parties but even trade unions outside Communist-controlled alliances were debarred from classification as working-class organizations. For instance, a Bulgarian scholar first of all describes the movement as 'the bearer of bourgeois ideology and the conductor of bourgeois policies in the workers' movement' and goes on to state that it is primarily 'a petty-bourgeois tendency and movement, in some particulars not far removed from the other movements of the bourgeoisie.'[61] Time after time, a party like the West German SDP is described as unambiguously 'bourgeois' or 'of the pro-monopolist type'.[62] Evaluations such as these are so tendentious and unreliable as to be without worth. It may be true that many of the leaders of Social Democracy are practically indistinguishable from bourgeois liberal politicians and seem to belong more to the bourgeoisie than to the working class, but the same cannot be said of the Social Democratic movement as a whole, and it is even less true of the majority of Social Democratic parties and their organizations. In today's capitalist societies reformism has every right to exist, not merely as a bourgeois institution but as part of the working-class movement. This is something all Communists should accept and take into account.

There are today a number of parties describing themselves as 'Socialist' or 'Social Democratic' that are definitely not working-class institutions. The Social Democratic Party of Portugal, for instance, is a typical party of the right, worlds apart from the Socialist Party of the same country, which belongs to the Socialist International. The Social Democratic Party of Italy has also disqualified itself from any place in the working class. It rests exclusively on the petty bourgeoisie and the world of officialdom, which cannot be said of the Italian Socialist Party, with its continuing significant influence among the workers, the trade unions and the co-operative movement. The Pacifist Socialist Party of the Netherlands consists almost entirely of the middle bourgeoisie, intellectuals and the clergy. In France, the republican 'Radical Socialists' are, in fact, one of the most ancient parties of the French bourgeoisie, whereas it is the country's Socialist Party, another member of the Socialist International, that may be described as one of the historic parties of the French working class. Political parties are not to be judged by what they call themselves. A true socialist party may well include in its ranks certain welcome 'outsiders'—intellectuals, office-workers, petty bourgeoisie and students—but it must attract a majority of its members voters from among working people. On the other hand, the commitment of such a party to reformist policies will distinguish it from a Communist party.

The Ideology of Social Democracy Today

It is difficult to be brief about the theoretical principles and ideology of Social Democracy, which have a hundred years of exceedingly complex evolution behind them. However, one or two outstanding features of that evolution are worth brief examination in the present context.

The first consideration is that the theories and programmes underlying Social Democracy have undergone substantial alteration according to changing economic, social and political circumstances in the capitalist world. The arrival and development of imperialism, two cruel, imperialist-inspired world wars, the collapse of the colonial systems accompanied by the swift growth in the economy and the military might of capitalism, the emergence of national and even supra-national monopolies, changes in the structure of capitalist society—all of this, naturally enough, found expression in the policy documents and theoretical attitudes of the Social Democrats. Second, the ideology of the movement has been much affected by the constant in-fighting between various groups and tendencies within it and equally by the ongoing arguments conducted directly with the apologists of capitalism and other anti-socialist ideologies. Even today there are substantial differences between the right-wing, centrist and left-wing organizations making up the Socialist International, in terms of both ideological conviction and political behaviour.

Third, Social Democratic thinking has been conditioned by the development of the Communist movement, and the creation and progress of Communist countries and other countries of 'real socialism'. Social Democracy and Communism have tended to regard each other as bitter enemies, and so, anti-Communism has become the hallmark of most Social Democratic attitudes and policies.

A fourth source of influence on the movement has been provided by the local conditions in which it has developed. German Social Democracy has been greatly affected by Marxism but this is scarcely true of the British Labour Party, which has been shaped primarily by religious and ethical thinking. As one Labour leader put it, 'I believe that first and foremost the creation of the socialist movement has been conditioned by religion',[63] whereas Willy Brandt, the German SDP leader, is on record as claiming that 'we all stand on the shoulders of Marx'.[64]

Marxism is no longer part of the official teaching of the Socialist International. The Frankfurt Declaration laid great stress on philosophical neutrality as a basic principle: 'Socialism is an international movement not requiring strict unanimity of opinion. It does not matter whether a Marxist or any other method of analysis lies at the basis of socialist convictions, it does not matter whether they are inspired by religious or humanitarian principles—they are all striving towards a single goal, a system of social justice, a better life, freedom and peace throughout the world.'[65] A German theoretician gives a further explanation of this principle of Social Democracy: 'The Christian teaching about the nature of man and his ethical requirements, human rights as proclaimed by the French Revolution, the ethics and philosophical ideas of Kant, Hegel's dialectical philosophy of history, Marx's critique of capitalism, Bernstein's critique of Marxism, Rosa Luxemburg's theory of spontaneity, the critique of Bolshevism, the free socialism of Schumacher, the latest pronouncements by Ernst Bloch, Horkheimer and Adorno, Habermas, Kolakowski, Djilas, etc.,—these are, in a manner of speaking, the accumulated and co-ordinated credentials of democratic socialism, which together amount to a single ethical creed.'[66]

On the continent at least, Marxism continues to exercise a strong influence on the Social Democratic movement, and its terminology retains its long-standing popularity. For instance, Willy Brandt has written: 'Karl Marx is not merely one of the great Germans. He belongs to the eminent company at the head of the European movement of liberation. Marx's greatest qualities have always been a striving towards freedom, towards the emancipation of man from slavery and dependence. This was the main theme of the thinking and practice of Marx.'[67] Brandt places great emphasis on Marx's continued struggle for the triumph of democracy, for the self-determination and equality of nations, his readiness to co-operate with other socialist and democratic movements and his protest against social and economic injustice. A connection is suggested between the rising interest in Marx and Marxism and the emergence on the world political scene of dozens of new countries and nations wishing to build up a new life for themselves without using the old capitalist models. This 'renaissance' of Marxism is something that Social Democracy is obliged to reckon with. At the same time, however, there are some Marxist concepts that Brandt utterly repudiates; the analyses of the class character of bourgeois society, of the necessity for the destruction of the bourgeois state and its replacement by a dictatorship of the proletariat, and of the inevitability of proletarian immiseration are prominent among them. It is necessary today to abandon the Leninist reading of Marx, which still links Marxism with the conspiratorial traditions of the Russian revolutionary underground, Brandt considers, and to re-examine the excellent 'updating' of Marxism carried out by Eduard Bernstein.

Another European politician who has much to say in favour of Marx is the leader of the Austrian Social Democrats, Bruno Kreisky. He acknowledges Marx as the greatest contributor to the unification of socialism and the workers' movement. In his words, 'Marx's greatest single historical achievement was to have given the workers' movement one main political aim—the building of socialism'.[68] But, Kreisky goes on to say, this is no reason to demand that anyone who joins the movement must swear an oath of allegiance to Marxism and unquestioningly accept its whole philosophy and theoretical base. In contrast, a German theoretician, W. Eichler, claims in *An Introduction to Democratic Socialism* that it is wrong to demand that Social Democrats dissociate themselves once and for all from Marxism. 'If we are imprudent enough to meet that demand,' he tells us, 'that would mean a denial of our traditions and our very sense of truth, the essence of the scientific principles on which socialism is based'.[69]

Of course, Social Democratic thinking today is anything but free from disparaging comment on Marx and his teachings. Another Austrian expresses the opinion that 'Marxism is an obsolete theory relating only to one specific period of history',[70] while a Swiss Social Democrat states his unequivocal belief that 'Marx's theory as a general theory of socialism for today is a reactionary one'.[71] Harold Wilson once said, characteristically, that in the whole of his life he had never managed to get through more than a few pages of *Das Kapital*.

Let us accept that there are many shades of opinion in the Social Democratic movement, just as there are many differences between socialists internationally. There are nevertheless a number of ideological criteria that serve both to define the character of Social Democracy in general and to distinguish it from orthodox Communism on the one hand and from allied bourgeois or religious convictions on the other. Foremost among them is the principle of 'democratic socialism'. At first sight it appears that this principle should be entirely acceptable to Communists who, after all, stand for both socialism and democracy. But many articles and books have been written in the USSR with the express purpose of criticizing it. Let us take, for example, the following statement by G. Shakhnazarov: 'From the theoretical standpoint, the concept of "democratic socialism" itself does not stand up to criticism, for socialism in its truest sense can be nothing other than democratic. We may speak of the assertion of socialist principles in various forms and conditions but we have no right to attempt to take these variations to absurd extremes and divide the tree of socialism artificially (in theory and in practice) into two opposite branches.'[72] It would not be difficult to demonstrate the falseness of this kind of reasoning; reference to the *Communist Manifesto* alone would suffice. What is curious is that in some respects Shakhnazarov aligns himself with such commentators as Solzhenitsyn, Maximov, Shafarevich and the like. These people also object to the principle of 'democratic socialism' but on entirely opposite grounds—it is their belief that 'socialism in its truest sense' can never under any circumstances be democratic.

What, then, do the Social Democrats themselves understand by the term 'democratic socialism'? There are a number of different interpretations. Let us turn again to Willy Brandt. 'Democratic socialism is not a philosophy of life. It does not set itself up as a theory or an ideology intended to annul or replace all previous concepts by rendering them worthless or almost worthless. On the contrary it is a doctrine that borrows the best from other people not in order to create a single conception out of this conglomeration but only to enrich its own content.'[73] This sort of definition is open to considerable doubt. The concept of 'democratic socialism' is, of course, part of Social Democratic ideology, and in this respect the opinion expressed by Palme has more justification than that of Willy Brandt.[74] It is also true that most ideologies, including Marxism-Leninism, claim that, far from arising in a vacuum, they are assimilating 'the best' parts of all preceding ideological systems. Such claims are more easily made than substantiated. Here is another definition: 'It is a scientifically orientated concept of practical action. It is open to all sorts of philosophical and religious persuasions as far as its moral stance is concerned and equally to various scientific and theoretical conceptions which allow a constant critical reappraisal of its aims and methods.'[75] But this is not the only form of socialism that claims a scientific basis; Marxism-Leninism does so as well.

At its simplest, the formula 'democratic socialism' asserts that Social Democrats are on the side of socialism, and not capitalism. This does not mean they will support any form of socialism—it must be a socialist society in which the social injustices of contemporary capitalism have been put right and, what is just as important, one in which all the democratic values of modern Western civilization have been preserved: freedom of speech and freedom of the press, freedom of political organization and association, political and ideological pluralism, freedom of movement and personal initiative. The British Labour Party's 1970 manifesto for 'A Socialist Britain' promised solemnly to 'improve the quality of our democracy' and 'give more power to the people'.[76] Two years later, the leadership of the Austrian Socialist Party made the following declaration: 'Everywhere today the Social Democratic parties are flushed with a renewed, manly sense of responsibility. They do not want only to exercise political power, they want to carry out their governmental functions in the full awareness that the realization of the ideas of Social Democracy at the present stage in the development of our society is an assignment of historical importance... and that a categorical imperative of the socialist movement is a classless society.'[77] Such a society must be democratic as well as socialist. As Kreisky has put it, 'today's business includes solving the problem of democratizing all spheres of life in society'.[78] Brandt has made the same point: 'The present phase in the development of German and European Social Democracy—the determining of the tasks before us in the seventies—includes the realization of the aims of Social Democracy. We are convinced that without democracy in a state or society, without shared participation and responsibility in every major sphere, there will be no stable democracy... Our aim must be the implementation of Social Democracy, i.e. the democratization of our society.'[79]

The claims advanced by the right-wing leaders of Western Social Democracy should not be taken at face value; they are not all necessarily sincere. What they do indicate unmistakably, however, is the high degree of popularity enjoyed by such ideas among the workers in Western countries. Even if Social Democracy has not had much success in actually 'building a socialist society', the movement has done a great deal to democratize social life. This fact alone explains why the working class entrusts governmental power to Social Democratic parties sooner than to the parties of the bourgeoisie.

When pressed to refine and elucidate their concepts of socialism, the leaders and theoreticians of the Social Democratic movement usually proceed with great caution. Kreisky once said that since there were already seventy-two different definitions of socialism, it would not make a great deal of difference if he added a seventy-third. In fact there are many more than that, but this does not free those concerned with the building of socialism from the obligation to explain in some detail what they actually envisage. On another occasion, Kreisky gave the following definition. 'Democratic socialism is a political principle rather than a form of society. Social Democracy is the awareness of a political goal that we are approaching, fully aware that the approach cannot be more than asymptotic.'[80] Since an asymptote is a straight line that continually approaches a curve but never meets it, Kreisky's definition can scarcely be considered satisfactory.

By declaring themselves on the side of socialism, the Social Democrats are obliged to a greater or lesser extent to criticize capitalist society. In June 1962, a Socialist conference in Oslo approved a policy declaration entitled *The World Today: a Socialist Perspective*. This document expressed the view that capitalism was incapable of solving the main problems facing humanity. In particular, it could not avoid recurrent crises, unemployment and poverty. The capitalist world continued to concentrate economic power in monopolies directed primarily by the profit motive rather than by any desire to satisfy the social and cultural requirements of the population. 'Society is still divided into different classes, each enjoying a different status and standard of living, based on accidents of birth and inheritance.[81] In 1976, François Mitterand used the occasion of the Thirteenth Congress of the Socialist International to denounce monopolistic capitalism as the main enemy of Social Democracy.[82] Leaders like Palme, Brandt and Kreisky, who either are or have recently been in power, have been more cautious in their criticism of capitalism. But even these people are not afraid to refer to the 'crisis of capitalism' and the 'murderous competition that strengthens concentration and throws millions of unemployed workers on the rubbish heap of society'.[83]

When drawing comparisons between capitalism and socialism, even the leading theoreticians of Social Democracy differ considerably in their interpretations of such concepts as 'socialism', 'equality' and 'social justice.' Modern Socialists are genuinely indifferent to the motivation impelling people towards socialism. They are happy to welcome into their ranks atheists and believers, Christians and Muslims, agnostics and supporters of Marxist theory. The only thing that matters is one's attitude towards democracy and socialism. This cannot hold much appeal for Communists, who are much more exacting about the philosophical views of their followers, yet it is this wide tolerance that guarantees the flexibility of the Social Democratic movement, which is seen by many as a great advantage over the rigid stance of the Communists.

Those who claim adherence not just to socialism but to *democratic* socialism dissociate themselves in every way from Communists and from Communist-ruled states. The latter are not considered democratic, and many Social Democrats would go so far as to claim that they are not socialist either. At the Thirteenth Congress of the International, Willy Brandt declared: 'We oppose the tendencies in capitalism towards the limitation of freedom and the alienation of man from society, and equally we oppose Communist dictatorship... Neither America nor Russia has fulfilled the great hopes of mankind. I do not claim that we Social Democrats shall be able to realize those hopes but at least we are responsible for their continuing vitality.'[84] A superficial glance at Social Democratic policy statements concerning democratic socialism might give the impression that they do not differ greatly from the statements so frequently made by orthodox Communists. The former chairman of the Socialist International, B. Pitterman, has often claimed that the first aim of democratic socialism is to rid the world of the disasters brought about by the capitalist hunger for profit. 'We want a world in which individual people and nations can live together in peace, where the principles of social justice will obtain both within the individual states and in the international community at large.'[85] Here is an extract from the programme of the Belgian Socialist Party in the early 1970s: 'Socialism alone is in a position to defend humanity from its besetting dangers. A Socialist party refuses to become integrated into the surrounding society. Its aim is to achieve for every person the economic, social, political and cultural conditions needed to guarantee his full development.'[86] The programme of the Socialist International makes the same claim. The aim is to create a society guaranteeing political, economic and social democracy; 'whereas the ruling principle of capitalism is the extraction of personal profit, the main principle of socialism is the satisfaction of people's need.'[87] Socialists differ from bourgeois democrats in their insistence not only on civil and political rights but also on economic and social rights for each individual, including the right to work, access to medical care, old age pensions and sickness benefits, the right to leisure, the right to child care, equal educational opportunities, and so on. The programme goes on to commit Socialists to fight for the removal of all forms of discrimination on grounds of sex, race, social origins or domicile. It rejects anarchy in production and insists upon a planned economy subordinated to the interests of society as a whole.[88]

The distinction between Communism and Social Democracy—about which we shall have more to say shortly—is to be seen clearly in their differing attitudes to the private ownership of the means of production. Orthodox Marxism stipulates that all such private ownership must be abolished. Social Democracy, on the other hand, in every one of its post-war programmes, has expressed the view that the private ownership of means of production is defensible *provided that it does not hamper the creation of a just social order*. Freedom of personal initiative that does not conflict with the interests of society at large is considered by the Social Democrats to be one of the fundamental democratic freedoms. One of their favourite mottoes is, 'private enterprise where possible, state control where necessary'. The possibility, even the necessity of nationalizing a large portion of the means of production, is taken for granted, but the necessity has to be demonstrated in every instance and, in any case, the nationalization of any corporation or enterprise must be carried out without violence of any kind to the previous owner.

It is a deeply held Social Democratic conviction that, even under socialism, various forms of property-owning are permissible—state, municipal, collective and private. A mixed economy is considered the best guarantee against the concentration of economic power in the hands of a few people, even where these represent the state, and also the best guarantee of democracy. No one in the Soviet Union suggests reintroduction of private ownership in the means of production—the only discussion is of ways to encourage personal initiative in production and services. Yet in the developed capitalist countries, practically every Communist party asserts its belief in a mixed economy and declares that, in the event of a transfer of power to the Communists or a left-wing bloc, the new state would expropriate only the huge monopolies, the banks and businesses operating on a national scale. In this respect, the distinctions between Communists and Social Democrats are matters of quantity rather than quality.

In many Western countries, another fast disappearing distinction between Communists and Socialists concerns plans for the political and cultural reconstruction of society. Many Western Communists today are convinced of the need for both tolerance and pluralism. They defend the rights of political minorities to put forward their views and to st up their own organizations. They assert the need for complete freedom of conscience. Communists and Social Democrats alike envisage the broadest possible liberalism in the cultural life of socialism.

In international relations, Social Democrats invariably stand for peace, peaceful coexistence, an extension of detente and international cooperation. Here is another extract from the programme of the Socialist International: 'Democratic socialism rejects all forms of imperialism. It fights against the exploitation and oppression of any people ... it fights for peace and freedom throughout the world, for the creation of a world without any exploitation or enslavement of man by man and people by people, for a world in which the development of personality is the basis of the fruitful development of humanity.'[89] Social Democrats believe that peace on earth must be pursued not only by the amelioration of inter-state relations, arms limitation, and so on, but ultimately by the creation of some form of world government that will put into practice the principles of Social Democracy and make use of 'extensive executive power' in order to guarantee 'freedom for all peoples', to remove the threat of war and establish international cooperation. A world government of this kind is envisaged in the official programmes of the Socialist International as a vital institution in the society of the future.[90]

Another important and recurrent consideration in Social Democratic policy documents is 'the quality of life'. This notion envisages going beyond the various economic demands, and other such *quantitative* material considerations, to create new demands involving a *qualitative* improvement in the position of the working class. It is sometimes referred to as 'the central idea of democratic socialism',[91] and has been explained as follows: 'The quality of life means nothing more than a high standard of living. Quality of life presupposes freedom, including freedom from fear. It includes security on the basis of human solidarity, the chance of participation and self-assertion, the full employment of one's strength in work, practical activity and communal life, the enjoyment of nature and culture and the opportunity to remain or to become healthy...'[92]

The second fundamental principle of Social Democracy is *reformism*. What divides Communists from Social Democrats is not so much a difference of ultimate aims; it is their quite distinct attitudes to the methods of attaining these aims. It was this very issue that led first to the division of the Russian Social Democratic Party into Bolsheviks and Mensheviks and subsequently to the broader division of the whole socialist movement into Communists and Social Democrats.

The latter take the view that socialism can be constructed only in a society with a highly advanced capitalist economy and that even then the process must be a gradual one, enjoying the support of a majority of the population and relying on existing democratic institutions, general elections, referenda, the parliamentary system and municipal organs. The essential point is that the transition to socialism can be effected, indeed must be effected, by means of a series of reforms and not by violent revolution and dictatorship, temporary or permanent. Under fascism, of course, the Socialist parties did not appeal for reforms, they supported armed conflict. They still support armed conflict on occasion, in the case of colonial peoples for whom there exists no possibility of achieving independence by peaceful methods. (It is also true, of course, that right-wing Social Democratic leaders have been supporters of colonialism and of colonial wars). However, given the conditions now obtaining in Western capitalism, with its well developed democratic institutions, Social Democrats are content to work for a peaceful and gradual transition to their objectives. Social Democrats are not, and have no wish to be, revolutionaries. They are reformists and they consider this to be their greatest virtue. Here is Kriesky again: 'Wherever a modern industrial society exists, social development is not to be determined by revolutions. These do not constitute a political category of real significance. We must acknowledge forthrightly that society can only be changed through a continual process of reform.'[93] A German Social Democratic leader, G. Werner, affirms that 'Capitalism is not something that can be overthrown. We must concern ourselves only with the idea of changing it.'[94] The leaders of the British Labour Party share the same view. In 1952, Richard Crossman published a collection of *New Fabian Essays* in which the aims of the British Labour movement were defined as follows: 'The true aim of the Labour movement has always been not the dramatic capture of power by the working class, but the conversion of the nation to the Socialist pattern of rights and values; not the violent destruction of one economic system and the substitution of another, but the voluntary acceptance of the need for socialism...'[95] Such attitudes explain why Social Democratic ideologists turn to philosophers like Popper, whose belief is that only charlatans claim to be able to see very far into the future, from which it follows that the only realistic policy is one which aims at altering existing institutions one by one and solving private problems step by step.[96] The only constructive method of reforming present-day reality was by a gradual process of 'social engineering'.[97]

But do Communists not also accept the importance, the inevitability, of reforms? Do they not also support the struggle of the working class to improve its living conditions within the existing framework of capitalist society? This is true, but there is an essential difference. Communists usually reject any possibility of achieving the necessary transition from one socio-economic system to another *through reform alone*. Social Democrats do admit this possibility and, in their policy documents at least, strive towards it. Some of them attempt to distinguish between 'system-stabilizing' and 'system-changing' reforms, it being understood that only the latter type will further the cause of socialism. But many right-wing Social Democrats actually reject any such formulation. Helmut Schmidt is on record as claiming that 'the only rational possibility is a systematic and gradual changing of society through specific reforms... The distinction between "system-stabilizing" and "system-changing" reforms observed at present in the German Social Democratic Party must be abandoned. Any social reform changes society and, therefore, "the system".'[98]

Acceptance of reformism naturally involves rejection of the fundamental Marxist idea of the state as the political power of a *class*. This does not deter the Social Democrats, who believe that the state has long since ceased to be what Marx and Engels described as 'the executive committee of the bourgeoisie'. According to them, the modern state is an organ of power transcending class considerations, and its main function is to maintain domestic peace and to defend all classes in society against possible abuse at the hands of other groups. By way of proof, the Social Democrats point to their own increasingly wide access to the highest positions of the state. The Italian Socialist Pietro Nenni has said: 'As a result of a whole century of workers' struggle, the state, while retaining the character of a superstructure overtopping the economic and communal organization of society, no longer represents the dictatorship or monopoly of a single class, in other words the strongest class in economic terms, but now reflects the social balance... which is gradually maturing in our social life.'[99] Willy Brandt is of the same opinion: 'We must look on the civilized democratic state as an organized and legalized association of the people entrusted with the task of guaranteeing security, freedom and justice.'[100] Only such a state is to be trusted with a monopoly of legitimate violence, by which Brandt means not revolutionary violence but the various activities associated with police work and warfare. In their much-publicized correspondence, Brandt, Palme and Kreisky roundly condemn revolutionary violence as an anti-democratic method dreamed up by the 'elitist way of thinking' of Communists and Anarchists and irrelevant to Western Europe.

The question of reform, its nature and its extent, divides not only Social Democrats from Communists but the Social Democratic movement itself. As once before, in the period between the wars, Social Democracy is dominated at present by its right wing, though the centrists and the left-wingers are now speaking out more and more. There is no difference of opinion about improvements in health and welfare, social security measures and consumer protection; in any case, reforms like these are often effected without pressure from Social Democrats. But left-wing Social Democrats frequently express dissatisfaction at the over-cautious attitude of their movement, and its governments, towards capitalist property. In Western Europe today, a large portion of the economy is state-controlled. In the USA, after the Second World War, many state-run industries were transferred to private control, but in Europe the reverse process occurred. There was extensive nationalization, carried out with the consent and cooperation of the owners. The Labour administration in Britain nationalized the coal and steel industries and the railways. In France and Italy, the giant Renault and Fiat companies have passed into state control, as have radio and television in a number of European countries. Banking is largely independent but many countries offer a state-controlled banking service as well. There can be no doubt that Social Democracy has had a large hand in the creation of these state holdings, but it is equally true that nationalization, which swept ahead in the immediate post-war period, has not grown much in the last twenty-five years. The vast capitalist monopolies, on the other hand, have expanded considerably and some of them now operate umbrella organizations covering dozens of countries. These multinational corporations are based for the most part not in Europe but in the USA. They represent a serious and active threat to public ownership, and so far Social Democracy has a poor record of opposition to them. This is all the more disappointing when we look back to statements such as the following, taken from a Socialist International policy declaration approved in 1962: 'Democratic socialism has achieved a great deal, but there are even larger problems ahead that need to be solved. There is no single method of overcoming the shortcomings of today's society. In order to arrive at a fair distribution of wealth we insist on the extension of public ownership and control, the passing of laws directed at curbing the power of private monopolies, a radical reform of the tax system and consumer protection. State intervention, with the support of democratically taken decisions, is vitally necessary to guarantee rapid economic development, adequate investment and the speedy introduction of the latest achievements in technology. This makes economic and social planning the main function of government.'[101] Of all the capitalist countries, the one with the best record of state control over the economy in the post-war period was Austria. Yet the Socialist Party could say in 1966: 'The economic power of the huge monopolies is on the increase, as is their influence on politics and the state, which is inconsistent with principles of democracy. The economic dependence of working people on capitalist control over the means of production still remains, though in an age of political equality it is felt more cruelly than ever. The free development of the human personality demands a system of socialized economy purged of the interests of private and state capitalism.'[102]

The German Social Democratic Party expresses itself in these terms: 'In large-scale economies the right to exert control belongs to a handful of people... As a result of this, private ownership of means of production has lost much of its controlling significance ... In the event that a healthy system of relations in regard to economic power cannot be guaranteed by other means, socialized property-owning is both expedient and essential.'[103] The Belgian Socialist Party for its part demands '... the socialization of those branches and businesses that exert a decisive impact on the development of the economy or which extend to their owners the power of influencing the activity of enterprises responsible for the smooth development of the economy, and particularly those in energy and credit facilities.'[104]

However, when a Social Democratic party comes to power in

Western Europe most of this talk of confronting the great monopolies is set aside. Various excuses are made. The usual explanation is that the capitalist economies are so interdependent that the nationalization of monopolies is possible only on a continental scale. It is also said that state-run enterprises are less efficient than private ones and therefore less profitable. There is some truth in both assertions, but there are also many contrary arguments, and examples of selfish capitalist practice conflicting with national and social interests. Even these seem insufficient to galvanize Social Democratic governments into meaningful activity. It is as if modern capitalism is seen still to play a progressive role. Here is a statement by Willy Brandt that amounts to a direct contradiction of his own party's policy: 'Must we in our part of the globe renounce the advantages of the market economy? Must we undertake the risk of setting up an economy directed from a single centre? I believe that all our mature experience speaks against our taking that path and for our developing market strengths and competitiveness still further and in the most comprehensive manner.'[105] The Young Socialists in the German SDP are clearly out of sympathy with this kind of argument. They continue to insist on the nationalization of all key sectors of the West German economy and the introduction of a system by which private investment can be controlled and regulated. This proposal was, however, rejected by the 1975 Party Conference at Mannheim. Still, the discussion goes on, kept alive by the Social Democratic left, one of whom has insisted on the introduction of reforms 'aimed at the self-determination of man and his participation in all spheres of life in society, at the ending of alienation and social and mental impoverishment, at the setting up of a social system that no longer allows domination over other people, power uncontrolled by democratic means, and in which government is reduced to a functionally essential minimum. We repudiate the sort of reformism that is directed only at social adaptation, integration and increasing the technical efficiency of the existing system.'[106]

This kind of attitude appears to be becoming more widespread and active, but it has yet to determine the general profile and policy of Social Democracy in the West.

The Communist—Social Democratic Controversy

One conclusion that emerges clearly from all this is that in many respects Communists and Social Democrats are 'relatives'. Nevertheless each subjects the other to severe criticism. Right-wing Social Democrats stand accused by the Communists of hypocrisy and deception. The Swedish Social Democrats, for example, have had forty years to achieve their goals—and has a socialist society been constructed? Improvements have certainly come about in the material and social conditions of the workers, but within the framework of capitalism. No attempt has even been made to begin the socialization of monopolistic capital. By the early 1970s, only nine of the fifty largest industrial undertakings in the country were run by the state, its municipalities or the cooperatives; fifteen old-style financial dynasties controlled the rest. Olof Palme has had to admit that 'all the reforms we have brought about have led on to great success but, to tell the truth, they have not touched daily life in the work process'.[107] It may be for this and similar reasons that the Social Democratic Party has declined in influence over the last decade and finally been replaced in government by a bourgeois coalition.

The experience of Sweden has much to teach us if we wish to analyse the real possibilities open to Social Democracy. It is being studied elsewhere in Europe. The French Socialist Robert Pontillon, considering the electoral debacle of the Swedish Social Democrats, has said: 'The contemporary socialist movement has yet to discover its own path in the pressurized conditions of capitalism, which hamper the movement towards socialism, and in a society of coercion that overwhelms man and stifles democracy. The Swedish experiment was an attempt to discover that path. Thus the defeat suffered by the Swedish Social Democrats gives pause for thought— and not only in Stockholm ... In order to maintain consistency, sooner or later reformism is going to have to depart from the framework of reforms as such.'[108] The same criticisms apply also to the Social Democrats in Norway who have been in power, except for a few short intervals, for almost half a century, and also to those of Denmark and Britain, who have enjoyed power for more than twenty years in all, without undertaking the kind of reforms needed to transform capitalist society. The same is true in West Germany: ten years and more of Social Democratic rule without any real progress in the direction of socialism.

It is understandable that Communists should have become used to claiming that Social Democrats, far from reforming capitalism, move to rescue it when difficulties arise. This is not to say, of course, that Communists oppose any reform likely to benefit the working class; obviously, when it comes to choosing between a bourgeois and a Social Democratic government, Communists vote for the latter, as they did over a period of years in Sweden. But it remains true that the Social Democrats have not yet been able to come up with effective measures to solve the growing crisis of capitalism and to facilitate the transition to socialism. Mollet, leader of the French Socialists in the late 1960s, admitted as much: 'In no country where the Social Democrats have been in power (in some cases for many years) have they managed to reform the economic order'.[109] François Mitterand does not retract this admission, but he goes on to say: 'Opportunism and betrayal have seriously compromised reformism, which, however, I do not condemn. It seems to me, moreover, that this is the only course of action today, now that revolution is impossible and undesirable.'[110]

Communists cannot forgive Social Democrats for abandoning the concept of the class struggle and promulgating instead the unthinkable idea of class collaboration, or for their anti-Communist and anti-Soviet posture. It should not be forgotten, however, that Social Democrats do condemn many of the shortcomings of capitalism. Their condemnation is for the most part sincere, and has its part to play in the struggle for socialism. It is difficult to understand the irritation that comes over many Communist writers and thinkers at the mere mention of the phrase 'democratic socialism'. A German Communist leader, Max Schefer, to take one example, summarized his criticism of the Social Democrats in this way: 'So-called democratic socialism is not a variation of socialist ideology; its place is not between capitalism and socialism. No, it is a constituent part of imperialist policy and ideology. It struggles against socialism and its ideology from the standpoint of state monopoly capitalism.'[111] If Social Democracy really is a constituent part of imperialism and state monopoly capitalism, how are we to explain the urgent appeals for unity of action between Communists and Socialists that resound today from the platform of every international gathering of Communist parties?

The experience of history has shown that the weakest aspect of the Social Democratic movement is its reliance on reformism—its tendency to exaggerate the possibilities of reformist activity and its sworn resistance to revolutionary methods. Back in the 1930s, Otto Bauer arrived at this sober assessment of the possibilities, the significance and the historical role of reformism: 'reformist socialism is nothing more or less than the inevitable ideology of the working class at a particular stage in its development, when the working class is still not strong enough to overthrow the capitalist social order but is strong enough to make successful use of democratic institutions in struggling to improve its own living standards within the framework of capitalist society.'[112]

His successor Bruno Kreisky gives an entirely different definition of reformist socialism when he claims that Social Democracy works on an understanding that 'sooner or later the quantity of reforms will turn into a new quality'.[113] This political use of dialectics is one which Communists, naturally enough, cannot bring themselves to accept.

Just as Communists criticize the ideology and practice of Social Democracy, so the Social Democrats criticize the ideology and practice of Communism. Their criticism extends to all aspects of the movement and to the internal and foreign policies of the socialist countries. It must be remembered that, at the beginning of the century, European Social Democrats supported the Mensheviks rather than the Bolsheviks; they considered the revolution in Russia to be premature and repudiated Lenin's interpretation of 'the dictatorship of the proletariat'. After the October Revolution, most of the leaders of Social Democracy utterly condemned the widespread application of revolutionary terror and many other aspects of War Communism. Worst of all, from their point of view, was the suppression of the Menshevik and Socialist Revolutionary parties, who belonged to the international community of socialism. (This criticism has come down to the present day and is still directed at the countries of Eastern Europe, which ban many Socialist parties with leaderships formed in emigration and now affiliated to the Socialist International.) Social Democratic attitudes to the Revolution varied widely. Many German Social Democrats welcomed Russia's withdrawal from the war, whereas those of France and England condemned the Peace of Brest-Litovsk. Most left-wing Social Democrats hailed the Revolution, and many Social Democratic organizations and trade unions raised the anti-interventionist slogan 'Hands off Russia!'. On the other hand, the powerful impact of the event clearly frightened the leaders of the right. Scheidemann said bluntly in 1918: 'Today Bolshevism is more of a danger than the Entente'.[114]

Some leading Social Democratic theorists assured their readers that the Revolution in Russia was not really socialist but bourgeois-democratic in character. Soon after October Karl Kautsky wrote: 'Thanks to democracy a world-wide and peaceful form of the proletarian revolution without bloodshed or violence has now become possible. Under democratic conditions revolution itself will not arise so abruptly and will not engender new fighting men and new programmes as it does in bourgeois revolutions. Thus proletarian revolution is no doubt less dramatic, less interesting and less satisfying for the literary man with a taste for new sensations. It is a more arid and less eventful affair than a bourgeois revolution. If the contemporary Russian Revolution is rich in dramatic incident and unprecedented sensation this shows yet again that, according to its actual content and despite all the intentions of its leading elements, it is a bourgeois revolution.'[115] This interpretation of events was to be given widespread currency in many theoretical surveys produced by Western Socialists and expatriate Russians. P. Garvi, a member of the Menshevik Central Committee in 1917, wrote as follows ten years later: 'The history of the Provisional Government is the history of the withdrawal of the propertied classes one by one from revolution. What soon came to be established was in fact dual power, which led to inevitable crises in authority... The Russian bourgeoisie, wing-clipped and spineless, self-interested and short-sighted, proved incapable, even in the person of its intelligentsia, of directing its own bourgeois revolution. Fear of the proletariat weakened it in advance and pushed it steadily into the arms of land-owning counter-revolution. This weakness on the part of the Russian bourgeoisie was mistaken by the working class for its own strength. By the will of history it was called to take up the pioneering, leading role in a bourgeois-democratic revolution. It is hardly surprising that it surrendered so readily to Bolshevik promptings about the seizure of power; it is hardly surprising that it mistook the *bourgeois* revolution for its own *proletarian* revolution; it is hardly surprising that under Bolshevik leadership it began to "deepen" the revolution, thus forming an abyss down which were lost not only the socialist illusions of October but also the democratic victories of February.'[116] Such ideas gave rise to the still widespread theory—subscribed to by members and non-members of the Social Democratic movement alike—that *state capitalism* was the basis of the Soviet social system. This, in turn, leads to the idea that a kind of 'new class' has been formed in the USSR, and now subordinates and exploits the other classes in our country. In recent years, this theory has been associated with the Yugoslav theorist Milovan Djilas, who wrote a book actually entitled *The New Class*, but this work was merely echoing the long-standing opinion of a whole current in inter-war Social Democracy. This approach is not shared by all Soviet specialists and bourgeois ideologists. Many Western writers and journalists have attempted to show that, on the contrary, what has occurred in the Soviet Union is indeed an 'authentic' socialist revolution and that an 'authentic' form of Socialism has been installed there—socialism being unable to survive without 'Red terror', enforced collectivization, recurrent 'purges' and a one-party dictatorship. Even among the Social Democrats the idea of state capitalism as the basis of the Soviet system has lost a great deal of ground. Instead there is more and more talk of 'bureaucratic' or 'authoritarian' socialism.

Social Democrats have always been critical of the organizational principles of the Communist parties, and especially of democratic centralism, on the grounds that it is bound to give rise to bureaucratic centralism, which itself leads to a situation in which the party apparatus dominates the movement and stifles the normal processes of discussion and development. Similarly, much criticism is directed against the dependence of the USSR and other socialist countries on centralized leadership and planning in economic affairs. The system is seen in the West as unnecessarily cumbersome and bureaucratic, suicidally inflexible, conservative, resistant to technological change and hostile to all forms of personal or (worse still) private initiative. A further object of critical assault in the Social Democratic press is the absence of real democracy in the USSR and the socialist countries, and particularly the infringement of civil and political freedoms. The lack of an independent press, the curtailment of free speech, freedom of assembly and demonstration, the overdependence of trade unions on the Party bureaucracy, the ban imposed in practice on political minorities, who may not formulate and defend new positions or set up new organizations, the absence —even the prohibition—of political and intellectual opposition, the electoral system, which recognizes only one party and only one candidate to represent it, the virtual conversion of the Party apparatus into the machinery of state itself, the too rigid imposition of Party control on all social organizations—all of this provides the soil for a rich harvest of Social Democratic criticism. When Social Democrats take it upon themselves to review the history of the USSR and the CPSU, they attempt to show that the obvious economic and cultural achievements of the Soviet Union have been purchased at too high a price. They point to the crimes committed by Stalin and condemn the universal terror that dominated our country and others during his rule, causing the deaths of many millions of innocents. Stalin's policy of enforced collectivization is criticized both *per se* and because it created an unwieldly and largely inefficient system of agriculture. The foreign policy of the Soviet Union is often roundly condemned by Social Democratic parties in the West, particularly the entry of Warsaw Pact troops into Hungary in 1956. More recently, Soviet involvement in Afghanistan has attracted similarly hostile criticism. The persecution of Soviet dissidents and their various groups and organizations also arouses the indignation of the Social Democratic movement.

Much of this criticism is all too justified, though on many occasions the Social Democrats are guilty of needless exaggeration. A good example is to be found in Bruno Kreisky's *The World in Which We Live*. At one point he says: 'The idea of a planned economy is entirely discredited as a result of its total collapse in the Communist states... Communist society deprives men of everything whereas a Social Democratic society, on the contrary, enriches men by creating more space for decision-making in their personal lives and the opportunity of participation in the affairs of society as a whole.'[117] It is almost superfluous to counter this argument by reminding Kreisky that centralized planning in the socialist countries, whatever its many shortcomings, has proved its relative effectiveness beyond reasonable doubt, and that Communist society has provided something for modern man whereas Social Democracy has yet to establish a 'Social Democratic society' anywhere in the world. One of the commonest critical devices of Social Democracy is the association of Communist societies with extreme manifestations of bourgeois totalitarianism. The Austrian right-wing Socialist R. Hartl writes as follows: 'At the centre of the entire Social Democratic effort stands man as a concrete entity, and not an abstract design as under Communism, or an unfettered private economic unit harming the quality of life as under a bourgeois democracy with a Conservative majority... Social Democrats are neither the gravediggers nor the saviours of capitalism, they are the pioneers of a new, better, fairer and more humane order of existence in the conditions of the only alternative to capitalism and Communism—Social Democracy itself.'[118] The leader of the Socialist International expresses a similar view: 'Democratic socialism stands ranged against both monopoly capitalism and any form of totalitarian economy'.[119] And in a basic policy document of the Socialist International, *The Aims and Tasks of Democratic Socialism*, we read this comment: 'Communism is the instrument of a new imperialism... By producing enormous contrasts in the distribution of wealth and privilege it has created a new class-conscious society.'[120]

This two-way criticism provides material enough for us to go on for many pages. There is practically no aspect of Socialist or Communist activity that has escaped hostile criticism from the ideological adversary. At the same time, however, the Social Democrats themselves, while rejecting every word of criticism from Communist quarters, often find it necessary to acknowledge many shortcomings within their own movement. The same is true, *mutatis mutandis*, of the Communist side. Even more curiously, the two parties often resort to the same forms of self-justification. Social Democrats tend to extol the virtues of their own experience and activities with a backward glance at the old maxim of Bernstein— the movement is all, the goal is nothing. In other words, Social Democrats enumerate the specific achievements of their movement but they claim nevertheless that, far from being the end of their democratic process, these are in fact just a beginning.[121] In 1958, the German Social Democrat Willy Eichler said that 'socialism always remains an unrealized ideal with its tasks unfulfilled.'[122] Essentially the same words were repeated fifteen years later by Willy Brandt: 'Democratic socialism has no ultimate aim; it should be understood as a permanent series of tasks,'[123] The Communists are no different. For all the many books and articles written about 'developed socialism', when they encounter fair criticism from the Social Democrats, they often refer the critics to these words written years ago by Lenin: 'Socialism is not a ready-made system doing a great favour for mankind. Socialism is the class-struggle of the contemporary proletariat proceeding from one aim today to another tomorrow, in the name of its principal goal to which it draws nearer every day.'[124]

The Prospects for Cooperation

We have already seen that the Socialist-Communist united front of the war years soon fell apart and was replaced during the Cold War by embittered ideological and political rivalry. This rivalry, albeit conducted with a little less acrimony, continues to the present day. It is clear enough that complete unity of opinion and political behaviour between Communists and Social Democrats is neither possible nor even necessary. In a number of respects, the mutual criticism existing between the two groups is essential and healthy for both. However, vicious enmity benefits neither group. History has shown that it does untold harm to both Social Democrats and Communists, not only by alienating the two parties that constitute the left in capitalist societies but also by creating a split within the working class, their common social support. The working class has a great desire for unity in the defence of its own interests. Any strike or demonstration requires united action on the part of all involved. A host of other struggles involving working people—protection of the environment, the removal of racial discrimination, the winning of equal rights for women, and so on—also require, not uncoordinated measures, but mutually agreed procedures accepted and pursued by all working-class parties and organizations. Even when extreme right-wing Socialist leaders and extreme left-wing Communists insist on prolonging furious controversy, both Communist and Social Democratic workers must attempt to maintain class solidarity in their workplaces and make sure that the leaders on both sides are aware of this and take it into account.

The coordination of interests and activities between Socialists and Communists frequently requires the two groups to sink their differences in an election pact designed to defeat the bourgeois parties. Even in the absence of formal agreements between the two parties, Communists have often stood down in favour of the Socialist candidate. The Socialists have sometimes reciprocated, though this is rare. In some Western countries this kind of cooperation exists at both local and parliamentary level—Sweden experienced it for many years. It remains true, however, that these occasional examples of cooperation, or at least coordinated activity, have been few and far between. The unfortunate fact is that the differences that now separate Communists from Social Democrats are so wide and so deep that one begins to wonder whether even cooperation, let alone any kind of solid alliance or united front, is still within the bounds of practical possibility.

In countries with a Communist government, not only is there no cooperation with Social Democratic parties; the latter have no legal right to exist. After 1922, the Russian Mensheviks continued as a group only in emigration. Today's Socialist International includes nine *émigré* Social Democratic groups originating in Eastern Europe. In capitalist countries, however, Communists consider the coordination of their own activities with those of the Social Democrats a possible and even desirable aim. At the 1969 International Conference of Communist and Workers' Parties it was announced that 'Communists, because they place decisive significance on the unity of the working class, declare themselves in favour of cooperation with Socialists and Social Democrats in order to set up an advanced democratic order today and build a socialist society tomorrow.'[125] This message was spelt out more specifically at the Brussels Conference in 1974: 'The working class and democratic forces, which are faced with the same problems, must also step up their own common struggle. It is quite possible today to define certain aims for democratic renewal, in the struggle for which all the forces at present representing the working class, the toiling people, the middle strata of Europe's capitalist countries, can come together and act cooperatively. This policy of a broad union of all the democratic, progressive and peace-loving forces of the people is based on mutual respect and the acceptance of the equality, variety and autonomy of each contributory force. For Communists this is a permanent policy, a matter of principle, effected today in accordance with the specific conditions in each country—in the name of democracy and social reform today and tomorrow in the name of the building of socialism ... The Communist parties in the capitalist countries of Europe emphasize their desire to establish contact and engage in consultations with Socialist and Social Democratic parties, and to undertake concerted action in order to achieve aims related to the essential needs of working people.'[126] Mindful of the modest progress that had been recorded in joint activities, the Berlin Conference of 1976 announced that the Conference welcomes the successes in the development of cooperation between Communist and Socialist parties which have been achieved in a number of countries ... (It) considers that the radical interests of the working class and all toiling people require the overcoming of all obstacles standing in the way of cooperation and complicating the struggle of the toiling masses against monopoly capital, against the forces of reaction and conservatism.'[127]

What has been the Social Democratic response to appeals such as these? In countries where the Social Democrats are in power or enjoy a predominant influence over the working class, they have tended to reject proposals for cooperation, though without denying the Communists their right to exist as a party under the law. Willy Brandt has been prominent among those Social Democrats who oppose joint ventures with the Communists: 'The Social Democratic Party of Germany cannot get jumbled up with Communist parties or groups, or undertake popular front policies or so-called unity of action.'[128]

The Social Democratic weekly *Vorwärts* responded as follows to the Berlin proposals: 'The meeting in East Germany, with its concluding document and its twenty-two speeches, has once again shown us some old facts: on their way towards future power in Europe, the Communists see an insuperable obstacle in Social Democracy. Their proposal for cooperation is an attempt to get round this obstacle. The declaration on rapprochement and equal rights conceals the unchanging claim to the sole possession of progressive political principles and an attempt to disrupt the powerful movement of Social Democracy.'[129] This view might usefully be compared with the opinion of Kautsky, who claimed that 'both these parties are proletarian ones; they both draw their strength from the proletariat'. Hence, the mere fact that Communists and Socialists espouse different interpretations of Marxism 'should not prevent the formation of a coalition when it comes to defending so great a common aim as democracy'.[130] Today, however, in West Germany and Austria of all places, proposals for cooperation are rejected out of hand. 'These two currents,' as Bruno Kreisky put it, 'have moved so far apart that they have turned into out-and-out antagonists.'[131]

The problem of unity cannot be solved without reference to the internal circumstances of the two camps. It is hard for Communists to think in terms of cooperation with the right-wing groups that dominate the major Social Democratic parties at present, but they can at least consider the possibility of joint work with Social Democrats of the left or even of the centre. Germany's left-wing Young Socialists recently called for joint campaigns with the Communists. The reaction of the Party leadership was to demand that the young left-wingers revoke this decision, taken in conference at Hamburg, or else risk expulsion from the Party. The Young Socialists came into line, but insisted in doing so that the SPD's embargo on all contacts with Communists was 'formally valid but essentially wrong'.[132] There is much less hope of cooperation in the case of small Communist parties that have proved incapable of reconciling themselves to the enormous changes occurring in the developed capitalist countries and have therefore stuck to dogmatic principles on all the major issues—it happens, unfortunately, that the Austrian and West German parties come into this category. The Social Democrats, for their part, do not respond with any enthusiasm even to Communist parties that have greatly changed their approach to political problems in the modern world. Referring to the Italian party, Willy Brandt said recently: 'Here we see an interesting anti-dogmatic process, but unfortunately no one can say how far it will go. At the very outset, the Communists ought to outline their position more clearly. But even if it is nothing more than a tactical ploy, it must result eventually in a number of changes.' Even then, he went on to emphasize, all these processes and adaptations applied for the time being only to Italy—in other countries the situation remained unchanged.[133] On another occasion, asked about Eurocommunism, Brandt expressed interest in what was happening in the Italian and Spanish Communist parties but added that in their present policies he could see no basis for an alliance.[134]

The misgivings of the Social Democratic leadership are based on a suspicion that agreements between Social Democracy and Communism will benefit only the latter. As a German commentator remarked in the early 1970s: 'Open contacts with Social Democracy can only heighten the prestige of the German Communist Party and counteract the dangers of its isolation... Thus cooperation and unity in action must be seen as wrong and dangerously short-sighted. They would reinforce the Communist Party, weaken the Social Democratic Party and assist the forces of conservatism in West Germany in their battle against democracy.'[135]

The West German situation is not typical of the Western countries; it corresponds roughly to the state of relations between the two movements in the 1950s when the Socialist International officially debarred its members from all cooperation with the Communists. But the impulse towards cooperation remained strong in many countries, and in 1972 the International removed the formal embargo, leaving the decision to the party in each individual country. The right-wing leadership, while accepting the need for the lifting of this ban, continued to look with extreme disfavour on any agreements made with the Communists. This attitude was reflected in a resolution passed at the Eleventh Congress of the Socialist International held at Eastbourne: 'In the process of seeking united activities with Social Democratic parties, Communist parties usually have as their ultimate aim one-party government and hegemony, in the struggle for which they strive to make use of the participation of democratic forces only to eliminate them subsequently as independent organizations.'[136] Communists have every right to consider this an unfair representation of their actions and motives. There is plenty of evidence to support the sincerity of the many statements made by Western Communist parties acknowledging the principle of pluralism and renouncing any prospect of a one-party system. This is a genuine political development and not a tactical ploy. On the other hand, one can see that the history of the Communist movement gives Social Democracy reason for concern over its ultimate destiny in the event of the Communists coming to power. Even in Western Europe, not many decades ago, a 'united front' invariably meant a Communist-controlled front. But in reality the leadership of a political alliance cannot be dictated, it must be earned. Nowadays Communist proposals for cooperation do not, as a rule, presuppose Communist hegemony. At the Twenty-Second Congress of the French Communist Party, Georges

Marchais stated that there should be both cooperation *and* competition between Socialists and Communists in France. This competition, however, could not take the form of 'an attempt by one partner to strengthen his ranks at the expense of the other and then impose his own will; the relationship ... must be based on equality of rights and obligations in the honest fulfilment of duties jointly undertaken'.[137]

The clearest sign of a change in Social Democratic attitudes to cooperation with the Communists was the governmental programme signed by Marchais and Mitterand in June 1972 and accepted also by the Left Radicals. The resulting Union of the Left had mixed fortunes in the years that followed. Nearly victorious in the presidential election of 1974, it was cheated of a majority in the legislative elections four years later. The reasons for the latter were both external—the ideological and political mobilization of the right—and also internal: the rapid growth of the Socialists caused understandable unease in the PCF and provoked the Marchais leadership into damaging sectarianism.[138] But despite these setbacks, the policy of unity has now given the Fifth Republic its first president of the left, backed by an absolute majority in the legislature. The 'competition' mentioned by Marchais has to date run heavily against his own party, yet the pact was maintained to the point of victory, and the new Socialist government includes four Communist ministers. The governmental and wider political experience of France in the coming years may be decisive for the future of Socialist-Communist relations in Western Europe.

It must be emphasized that Communists have not been the only ones to issue unrealistic demands in relation to united fronts. Social Democrats have often been guilty of the same thing. Attempts by the leaders of Social Democracy in Belgium and Finland to limit the independence of their counterpart Communist parties in order to strengthen their own positions brought no benefit to either side. Some Social Democratic leaders require the Communists to accept virtually every last detail of Social Democratic policy and tactical thinking, and also to renounce all former international contacts—in other words, to cease being revolutionaries, in the exclusive interests of Social Democratic reformism. Bruno Kreisky makes no attempt to conceal this. If the Communists wish to become truly democratic and worthy of an alliance they must give up their main political creed; 'then,' says Kreisky, 'there will be nothing left of the Communists, they will have turned into Social Democrats with a somewhat more revolutionary turn of phrase'.[139]

Olof Palme, for his part, has attempted to prove that the historic controversy between Communists and Social Democrats has been settled—in favour of the latter. All that remains is for the Communist parties to become reincarnated as reformist organizations perhaps 'somewhat more radical than the Social Democratic and Socialist formations.'[140] He is quite clearly wrong. The controversy is not yet settled, though it has been very instructive. Experience has shown the value of reformism as a means of improving society in particular circumstances of time and place. But it has also shown the value of the revolutionary method—again according to the circumstances. Moreover, history has revealed innumerable miscalculations, errors and crimes on the part of Social Democrats and Communists alike. It is true that the history of the Social Democratic movement contains no grisly figures like Stalin. This is explicable not only in terms of the restraint and respect for democracy shown by Social Democrats but also by the relatively limited scale on which they have operated and their frequent withdrawal from political responsibility at certain critical moments in world history. Historical and contemporary experience shows that the ideological baggage of Social Democracy contains a number of old, unserviceable doctrines that should be got rid of at the earliest opportunity. The baggage of the Communist movement is equally in need of spring-cleaning.

Cooperation between the two movements remains vitally necessary. Throughout the 1970s ,contacts and agreements were established, with the full approval of both party leaderships, in a number of countries—France, Italy, Japan, Finland, Sweden, Portugal, Luxemburg and Greece. In some cases, these came about in the face of disapproving Social Democratic leaderships—notably those of West Germany and Austria. France has now gone furthest of all in this direction, and quite new and testing forms of cooperation—and competition—are now on the agenda. At certain critical moments of the Portuguese revolution, working agreement was reached by the country's Socialist and Communist parties, and it is a matter for great regret that the alliance proved insecure. Particular importance attaches to the united Communist–Social Democratic front established in Chile, its electoral victory, its governmental record, and its downfall. As the official journal of the Socialist International wrote: 'What occurred in Chile cannot be forgotten by any socialist government in the world. The government of President Allende was elected by the people and for three years, when in power, it checked every step taken against the constitution and the law. President Allende put together a political grouping that united Communists, Socialists and Christians for victory over the reactionaries, for the achievement of autonomy and independence, for Chile's own road to socialism.'[141] In this document, for the first time in its history, the Socialist International was obliged to concede that at least one Communist party had shown a willingness to respect the constitutional norms of a democratic state. (The Social Democrats, however, have their own good reasons for not accepting too broad an interpretation of this idea.) The Chilean experience remains a crucial reference for the future.

The 1970s also saw the first significant contacts between delegations from various Socialist parties and the ruling circles of the CPSU. Talks were held with the Social Democratic parties of West Germany, France and Finland, with the Socialist Party of Belgium and with the British Labour Party. In 1974, the November Conference of the Belgian Socialist Party welcomed for the first time, among other Communist guests, representatives of the CPSU. And, at long last, Moscow has played host to a delegation from the leadership of the Socialist International, holding talks on many vital issues related to disarmament and peace. Such overtures, which would have been inconceivable in the 1950s and even later must be built upon in the years ahead.

The evolution of Social Democracy has been much more than an aberration. It has corresponded to the social and economic situation of a significant section of the European working class. In this movement no less than in that of Communism, the formula 'existence determines consciousness' has found confirmation. There is no doubt that Communists must wage war on opportunism and reformism; they cannot and must not abstain from criticism of many of the doctrines promulgated by Social Democracy today. But they must not anticipate that such criticism will do away with every last vestige of Social Democratic influence and every last reformist principle. The Social Democrats continue to enjoy a wide social base among the working class, and this situation will not be altered by any amount of propaganda and agitation. Criticism must go hand in hand with cooperation. It is obvious that capital will not voluntarily relinquish its economic and political power. It will do so only by *yielding to force,* the force of a united movement of working people. Such socio-economic upheaval can be brought about without recourse to the open and direct violence that has traditionally marked social revolution. In spite of the great and growing might of the capitalist governmental machine and military apparatus, it remains possible that a relatively peaceful and gradual transition to socialism could be achieved in Western countries, through the existing democratic institutions and with the support of a majority of the working class and allied wage-earners, the young and the intelligentsia.

If agreement—and, beyond that, unity—is to be achieved between the two movements, it will be essential for strong criticism to be directed against the dogmatic anti-Communist rantings of right-wing Social Democratic leaders and likewise against the equally dogmatic, anti-democratic modes of thinking and behaviour that distinguish many of today's Communist leaders. It must be clearly recognised that the sections of the working class on which Communist parties depend have become for the most part moderate in their choice of methods of struggle. What they want is democratic socialism, and they prefer to achieve it without civil war or direct violence, without bloodshed and armed uprisings. Conversely, the section of the working class on which present-day Social Democracy is dependent has become noticeably more radical. These working people, blue-collar and white-collar alike, are protesting against the decay of their material situation, against unemployment, inflation and the threat of war. They are demanding more from their leaders than fine talk about democratic socialism, and insist on far-reaching social reforms capable of transforming capitalist society. Thus we see in the process of creation the objective basis for a united front of left-wing parties which, according to specific circumstances in individual countries, may well prove attractive to moderate left-wing elements in other parties. A united front of this kind could maintain its existence both before and after coming to power.

The split between Socialists and Communists helps capitalism to extend its lease of life in the Western world, but it does nothing to cure its chronic and incurable diseases, which have been getting steadily more serious in recent years. However sickly capitalist society becomes, it will not collapse automatically. In order to triumph over capitalism, it will be necessary to fight hard. This fight, if it is to have a successful outcome, must be carried on by Communists and Socialists working together. But unity is out of the question unless both movements are prepared to introduce changes in their political strategy and tactics. To put it bluntly, they must take one or two steps towards each other. Communists must recognize that Social Democracy is not a sham but a legitimate force representing the political aspirations of a significant section of the working class that longs for socialism but not at the cost of social gains already achieved—it *does* now have more to lose than its chains. They must also recognize that even the Communist-voting section of the working class is more moderate in its political intentions than it was sixty years ago. Communists must find a way of maintaining their organization and revolutionary spirit while crediting the long-scorned democratic institutions of Western society with far greater value than they have ever done before. Meanwhile, Socialists must, for their part, become more radical in their demands for the reform of capitalism. A union of Communists with a new political face and Socialists with more radical, more decisive policies—this is what is wanted, this is the greatest hope for socialism in Europe.

References

Note:- Citations from the works of Lenin and Stalin have here been retranslated from the Russian and are referred to the standard Russian editions. For the reader's convenience, parallel references to English editions have been added, in almost all cases. In the case of Lenin, references are to the *Collected Works*, London 1960-70; the English title or description is given, followed by the abbreviation CW and the number of the volume in which the text appears. Passages from Stalin's writings are referred to various corresponding English editions.

INTRODUCTION

1. *Russkaya Mysl'*, Paris, July 22, 1976.
2. V.I. Lenin, *Polnoye Sobraniye Sochineniy*, vol. 34, p.116 ('From a Publicist's Diary', CW, 26).
3. *Problemy Mira i Sotsializma*, 1978, 2, p.19.
4. *Novoye Vremya*, 26, 1977, p.11.
5. Wolfgang Leonhard, *Eurokommunismus*, Berlin-Darmstadt-Vienna 1979, pp. 26-27.
6. R. Titzck, 'Eurokommunism—ein troianisches Pferd', *Die Welt*, May 3, 1977.
7. *Osteuropa*, no. 10, Stuttgart, 1978.

CHAPTER 1

1. Lenin, vol. 18, p.345 (*Materialism and Empirio-Criticism*, CW, 14).
2. N. Bukharin, *Put' k sotsializmu v Rossii*, New York 1967, p.214.
3. Lenin, vol. 44, p.225 ('The Importance of Gold Now and After the Complete Victory of Socialism', CW, 33).
4. J.V. Stalin, *Sochineniya*, vol, 6, p.70-71 (*Leninism*, vol. 1, Moscow-Leningrad 1934, p.14).
5. *Bolshevik*, no. 2, 1925.
6. *Komintern v dokumentakh*, 1919: 32, Moscow 1933, p.9.
7. *VKP (B) v rezolyutsiyakh*, Moscow 1936, p.596.

8. *Obshchestvennyye nauki*, no. 2, 1979, p.9.
9. *Die Zeit*, 28 April, 1978.
10. *Republika*, 2 August, 1978.
11. *Pravda*, 11 May, 1979.
12. Lenin, vol. 4, p.184 ('Our Programme', CW, 4).
13. *Pravda*, 'Tezisy k 100-letiyu so dnya rozhdeniya V.I. Lenina', 23 December, 1969.

CHAPTER 2

1. Marx and Engels, *Sochineniya*, 2nd edn., vol. 7, p.31 (Marx, *Surveys From Exile*, London 1973, p.61).
2. Ibid., p.91 (p.123).
3. *Bol'shaya Sovetskaya Entsiklopediya*, 1st edn,. vol. 6, p.483.
4. Marx and Engels, vol. 28, p.427 (*Selected Correspondence*, London 1934, p.57).
5. Ibid., vol. 22, p.61.
6. Ibid., vol. 19, p.27 (*Selected Works*, London 1968, p.331).
7. Lenin, vol. 4, p.219 ('A Draft Programme of Our Party', CW, 4).
8. *Istoriya Vtorogo Internatsionala*, Moscow 1965, vol. 1, p.161.
9. Marx and Engels, vol. 22, p.201 (*Selected Works*, p.262).
10. E. Bernstein, *Istoricheskiy Materializm*, St. Petersburg 1901, p.228.
11. *Das neue Programm der Sozialistischen Partei Osterreiches. in Protokoll. Ausserordentlicher Parteitag der Sozialistischen Partei Osterreiches*, Vienna 1958, p.116.
12. *Vtoroy s'yezd RSDRP: protokoly*, Moscow 1959, p.420. See also Lenin, vol. 6, p.229 ('Notes on Plekhanov's Second Draft Programme', CW, 6).
13. Lenin, vol. 11, pp.75-6 ('Two Tactics of Social Democracy in the Democratic Revolution', CW, 9).
14. Stalin, *Voprosy Leninizma*, Moscow 1946, p.108 (*Leninism*, vol. 1, pp.261-62).
15. Lenin, vol. 38, pp.385-88 ('Greetings to the Hungarian Workers', CW, 29).
16. Ibid., vol. 39, p.14 ('A Great Beginning', CW, 29).
17. Ibid., vol. 38, p.377 ('Foreword to "Deception of the People..."', CW, 29).
18. Ibid., vol. 33, p.26 ('The State and Revolution', CW, 25).
19. L.S. Gaionenko, *Rabochiy klass Rossii* v 1917g., Moscow 1970, p.72.
20. Lenin, vol. 41, p.77—Lenin's italics ('"Left-wing" Communism—an Infantile Disorder', CW, 31).
21. Ibid., p.35 ('The State and Revolution', CW, 25).
22. Ibid., p.90-91.
23. Ibid., p.49.
24. Ibid., p.44.
25. Ibid., p.100-101.
26. Marx and Engels, vol. 28, p.602.

27. M. Robespierre, *Izbrannyye Proizvedeniya*, Moscow 1965, vol. 3, p.91.
28. Lenin, vol. 38, p.301 (my italics, RM) ('The Third International and Its Place in History', CW, 29).
29. Ibid., vol. 12, p.288 (my italics, RM) ('The Victory of the Kadets and the Tasks of the Workers' Party', CW, 10).
30. Marx and Engels, vol. 5, p.431 (my italics, RM).
31. Lenin, vol. 33, p.100.
32. Ibid., p.35.
33. Marx and Engels, vol. 22, pp.200-201.
34. Lenin, vol. 37, p.246 (Lenin's italics) ('The Proletarian Revolution and the Renegade Kautsky', CW, 28).
35. Ibid., vol. 38, p.308 ('The Third International and Its Place in History', CW, 29).
36. Ibid., vol. 37, p.496 ('Theses and Report on Bourgeois Democracy and the Dictatorship of the Proletariat', CW, 28).
37. Lenin, vol. 37, p.462 ('Letter to the Workers of Europe and America', CW.
38. *Leninskaya teorlya sotsialisticheskoy revolyutsii i sovremennost'*, P.N. Fedoseyev, S.V. Aleksandrov, V.V. Zagladin, V. Ya. Zevin, N.V. Tropkin, ed., Moscow 1975, p.420.
39. V.E. Guliyev, *Demokratiya i sovremennyy imperializm*, Moscow 1970, p.120.
40. *Voprosy Istorii KPSS*, no. 6, 1980, p.16.
41. *Bol'shaya Sovetskaya Entsiklopediya*, vol. 7, 1972, p.177.
42. G. Kh. Shakhnazarov, *Fiasko Futurologii*, Moscow 1978, p.228.
43. Yu. A. Krasin, *Revolyutsiyey Ustrashennyye*, Moscow 1975, p.285.
44. Lenin, vol. 37, p.245 ('The Proletarian Revolution...', CW, 28).
45. Ibid., vol. 36, pp.503-504 (CW, 27).
46. Ibid., vol. 44, p.465.
47. Ibid., vol. 12, p.321 ('The Victory of the Kadets...', CW, 10).
48. Ibid., p.320.
49. Ibid., vol. 41, pp.383-91 ('A Contribution to the History of the Question of Dictatorship', CW, 31).
50. *Voprosy Leninizma*, p.116 (*Leninism*, vol. 1, p.266).
51. Lenin, vol. 50, p.26 CW, 44; see also *Pravda*, January 22/23 1918.
52. Lenin, vol. 43, p.42.
53. Ibid., vol. 45, p.190 (CW, 33).
54. Ibid., vol. 5, p.8 ('Where to Begin', CW, 5).
55. *Istoriya KPSS*, B.N. Ponomaryov, ed., Moscow 1969, p.26.
56. Lenin, vol. 19, p.369.
57. Ibid., vol. 32, p.307 ('The Enemies of the People', CW, 25).
58. Ibid., vol. 34, p.222 ('The Russian Revolution and Civil War', CW, 26).
59. Ibid., pp.290-91 ('Can the Bolsheviks Retain State Power?', CW, 26).
60. Ibid., pp.320-21.

61. Ibid., vol. 37, p.264 ('The Proletarian Revolution...', CW, 28).
62. Ibid., p.213 (Moscow Party Workers' Meeting, November 27, 1918, CW, 28).
63. *Sovetskoye narodnoye khozyaystvo b 1921-25g.* Moscow 1960, p.29.
64. Lenin, vol. 44, p.427 (CW, 45).
65. *Istoriya KPSS,* vol. 4, book 1, Moscow 1970, p.8.
66. Lenin, vol. 42, p.208 ('On the Trade Unions, the Present Situation and Trotsky's Mistakes', CW, 32).
67. Ibid., vol. 45, p.357.
68. *Voprosy Leninizma,* Moscow 1946, pp.118-36 (*Leninism,* vol. 1, pp.274-96).
69. Lenin, vol. 39, p.134 All-Russian Congress of Workers in Education and Socialist Culture, July 31, 1919, CW, 29).
70. Ibid., vol. 41, p.236 (CW, 31).
71. *II Kongress Kominterna: stenograficheskiy otchet,* Petrograd 1921, pp.64-5.
72. Lenin, vol. 43, p.42 (Tenth Congress of the RCP(B), March 9, 1921, CW, 42).
73. Ibid., vol. 36, p.199 ('The Immediate Tasks of the Soviet Government', CW, 27).
74. Ibid., vol. 45, p.20 ('The Conditions for Admitting New Members to the Party', CW, 33).
75. Ibid., vol. 54, p.291.
76. M. Gorky, *Sobraniye Sochineniy,* vol. 29, pp.484-85.
77. N. Ustryalov *Pod znakom revolyutsii: sbornik stat'ey,* Harbin 1925, p.7.
78. Ibid., p.60-61.
79. Lenin, vol. 45, pp.93-94 (CW, 42).
80. *VKP (B) v rezolyutsiyakh,* vol. 1, Moscow 1936, pp.474-75.
81. Jaroslav Mateka, *Gottwald,* Prague 1971, p.240.
82. D. Nemes, 'Iz urokov klassovoy bor'by za vlast' v Vengrii', *Problemy Mira i Sotsializma,* no. 9, 1976, p.23.
83. M. Thorez, *Oeuvres choisies,* vol. 11, Paris, p.489.
84. *Informatsionnoye soveshchaniye predstaviteley nekotorykh kommunisticheskikh partiy: sbornik,* Moscow 1948, p.15-16.
85. I. Goushka and K. Kara, *Kharakter narodno-demokraticheskoy revolyutsii,* Moscow 1958, pp.484-488.
86. M.B. Kitin, ed., *Sotsializm i ideologicheskaya bor'ba,* Moscow, p.338.
87. Yu. Krasin and B. Leybzon, *Revolyutsionnaya teoriya i revolyutsionnaya politika,* Moscow 1979, p.110.
88. Lenin, vol. 37, p.304 ('The Proletarian Revolution...', CW, 28).
89. *Problemy Mira i Sotsializma,* no. 11, 1978, p.21.
90. *Avante,* October 21, 1974.
91. *Cahiers du communisme,* no. 23, 1976, p.63.
92. S. Carrillo, *Eurocommunism and the State,* London 1977, p.141-49 (Carrillo's italics).

93. *Die Zeit*, February 10, 1978, p.9.
94. *L'unità*, February 1976.
95. Lenin, vol. 38, pp.385, 388 ('Greetings to the Hungarian Workers', CW, 29).
96. Ibid., vol. 33, p.34 ('The State and Revolution', CW, 25).
97. Étienne Balibar, *On the Dictatorship of the Proletariat*, NLB, London 1977.
98. *Pravda*, April 18, 1980.
99. Lenin, vol. 6, p.229 (my italics, RM) (CW, 6).
100. Ibid., vol. 38, p.308 ('The Third International...', CW, w9).
101. Ibid., vol. 34, pp.192-93 ('The Impending Catastrophe and How to Combat It', CW, 25).
102. Ibid., vol. 43, p.228 ('The Tax in Kind', CW, 32).
103. Krasin and Leybzon, p.78.
104. K.I. Zarodov, *Tri Revolyutsii v Rossii i Nashe Vremya*, Moscow 1977.
105. Ibid., pp.522-23.

CHAPTER 3

1. Cf. Marx and Engels, vol. 4, pp.498, 500-501.
2. Ibid., vol. 8, pp.205-206 (*Surveys From Exile*, p.237).
3. See ibid., vol. 25, part 1, p.422.
4. Ibid., vol. 18, p.154.
5. Ibid., vol. 17, pp.342, 346 (*Selected Works*, pp.291, 294).
6. Ibid., vol. 22, p.237.
7. V.V. Shulgin, *Dni*, Leningrad 1926, p.159.
8. *Proletariy*, August 23, 1917.
9. Lenin, vol. 12, p.231 ('A Tactical Platform for the Unity Congress of the RSDWP', CW, 10).
10. Ibid., p.130 ('Socialism and Anarchism', CW, 10).
11. Ibid., pp.317-318 ('The Victory of the Kadets...', CW, 10).
12. Ibid., vol. 30, p.322 ('Lecture on the 1905 Revolution', CW, 23).
13. Ibid., vol. 31, p.18 (Letters From Afar', CW, 23).
14. *VKP (B) v rezolyutsiyakh i resheniyakh*, vol. 1, Moscow 1936, p.22.
15. Lenin, vol. 31, p.115 (CW, 24).
16. Ibid., vol. 34, pp.304-305 (CW, 26).
17. Ibid., vol. 36, p.6 (Extraordinary Seventh Congress of the RCP(B), March 6-8, 1918, CW, 27).
18. Ibid., vol. 35, pp.238-39 (CW, 26).
19. Ibid., vol. 37, p.105 ('The Proletarian Revolution...', CW, 28).
20. Ibid., vol. 36, pp.50-51 (Extraordinary Seventh Congress, CW,27).
21. Ibid., pp.212-13.
22. CW, 28.
23. Ibid., vol. 38, p.2 (March 1919, CW, 29).
24. Ibid., p.89 ('Draft Programme of the RCP(B)', CW, 29).
25. Ibid., p.220 ('Reply to an Open Letter by a Bourgeois Specialist',

CW, 29).
26. Krasin and Leybzon, p.138-39.
27. Lenin, vol. 54, p.502.
28. Ibid., vol. 41, p.77 ('"Left-wing" Communism...', CW, 31).
29. Stalin, *Voprosy Leninizma*, Moscow 1946, pp.32-35.
30. *Komintern v dokumentakh*, Moscow 1933, pp.63, 58.
31. Lenin, vol. 37, p.493 ('Theses and Report...', CW, 28).
32. *Komintern v dokumentakh*, p.112.
33. Ibid., p.115.
34. *Velikaya Oktyabr'skaya Sotsialisticheskaya Revolyutsiya*, Moscow 1977, p.606.
35. Ibid., p.668.
36. *Protokoly zasedaniya VTsIK, IV sozyva*, Moscow 1920, pp.36-37.
37. *Velikaya Oktyabr'skaya Sotsialisticheskaya Revolyutsiya*, p.246.
38. *Voprosy Istorii KPSS*, no. 11, 1976, p.11.
39. N. Bugay, 'Revkomy kak chrezvychaynyye organy diktatury proletariata', *Voprosy Istorii*, no. 11, pp.5-6.
40. *Sobraniye uzakoneniy RSFSR*, nos. 1-2, 1920, p.5.
41. Lenin, vol. 51, p.231 (CW, 44).
42. Bertrand Russell, *The Practice and Theory of Bolshevism*, London 1949, pp.40-43.
43. *Sotsialisticheskiy Vestnik*, no. 1, 1922, p.17.
44. F. Dan, *Dva goda skitaniy*, Berlin 1922, pp.113-14.
45. K.V. Gusev, *Partiya Eserov*, Moscow 1975, p.346.
46. *Yezhenedel'nik VMS*, February 25, 1923.
47. *Zvezda* (newspaper), Yekaterinoslav, March 17, 1920.
48. *Byuleten' No. 1 IV Vseukrainskogo S'yezda Sovetov*, Khar'kov 1920, p.42.
49. *Voprosy Leninizma*, Moscow 1946, pp.118-19 (cf. *Leninism*, vol. 2, pp.275-76).
50. *Kommunisticheskiy Internatsional v Dokumentakh*, Moscow 1933, p.409.
51. Ibid., p.18.
52. *Bol'shevik*, no. 3, 1951, p.57.
53. *Materialy VIII S'yezda Italy'yanskoy Kommunisticheskoy Partii*, Moscow 1957, pp.180, 181.
54. *Problemy Mira i Sotsializma*, no. 4, 1974, p.69.
55. *Kommunisticheskoye Dvizheniye: problemy teorii i praktiki*, Prague 1978, pp.257-58.

CHAPTER 4

1. Barbara Ward, *Five Ideas that Change the World,* New York 1961.
2. *Problemy Mira i Sotsializma*, no. 10, 1978, p.67 (my italics, RM).
3. A. Meyer, *Leninism*, Harvard 1957, p.176.
4. J. Dunn, *Modern Revolutions*, Cambridge 1972, p.46.
5. T.H. von Laue, *Why Lenin? Why Stalin? A Reappraisal of the*

Russian Revolution 1900-1930, Philadelphia, New York 1964, pp.109, 120.
6. See Marx and Engels, vol. 18, p.305.
7. See Engels, ibid., vol. 18, pp.511-12.
8. Ibid., vol. 22, pp.533-35 (*Selected Works*, pp.655-56).
9. Ibid., p.544 (*Selected Works*, p.664).
10. Ibid., vol. 36, pp.217-18 (*Selected Correspondence*, p.434).
11. N. Ya. Eydel'man, *Sergey Murav'yov-Apostol*, Moscow 1976.
12. P.N. Tkachov, *Izbrannyye proizvedeniya*, vol. 6, Moscow 1932, p.90.
13. Ibid., vol. 2, p.266.
14. Ibid.
15. *Nabat*, nos. 1-2, 1877, p.17.
16. *Vtoroy s'yezd RSDPR: protokoly*, Moscow 1959, p.181.
17. Ibid., pp.181-82.
18. Lenin, vol. 11, p.39 ('Two Tactics...', CW, 9).
19. Ibid., vol. 49, p.347.
20. Ibid, vol. 31, p.458.
21. L. Trotsky, *Fevral'skaya Revolyutsiya*, Berlin 1931, pp.167-68 (*The History of the Russian Revolution*, London 1934, vol. 1, pp.158, 159).
22. Lenin, vol. 32, p.50 ('Report on the Results of the Seventh (April) All-Russian Conference of the RSDWP(B)', CW, 41).
23. D. Shub, *Politicheskiye deyateli Rossii 1850-1920gg.*, New York 1969, p.71.
24. P.N. Tkachev, *Izbrannyye proizvedeniya*, vol. 3, Moscow 1932, p.71.
25. Lenin, voi. 31, p.147 ('The Dual Power', CW, 24).
26. Ibid., vol. 40, pp.4-7, 10. ('The Constituent Assembly Elections and the Dictatorship of the Proletariat', CW, 30).
27. Ibid., vol. 34, p.241 ('The Bolsheviks Must Assume Power', CW, 26).
28. Ibid., vol. 40, p.11-12 ('The Constituent Assembly Elections...', CW, 30).
29. Ibid., p.13.
30. Cit. G. Safarov, *Osnovy Leninizma*, Leningrad 1924, p.332.
31. Lenin, vol. 40, pp.16-17 ('The Constituent Assembly Elections...', CW, 30).
32. K. Kautsky, *Die Diktatur des Proletariats*, Vienna 1918, p.15.
33. Lenin, vol. 37, p.254 ('The Proletarian Revolution...', CW, 28).
34. See Bukharin, *Izbrannyye Proizvedeniya*, p.69.
35. *Komintern v rezolyutsiyakh i dokumentakh* (1919-32), Moscow, 1933, p.40.
36. Lenin, vol. 12, pp.179-80 ('The Present Situation in Russia and the Tactics of the Workers' Party', CW, 10).
37. Quoted from *Drapeau Rouge*, organ of the Belgian Communist Party, February 5, 1976.
38. *L'Humanité*, November 18, 1975.

CHAPTER 5

1. K. Zarodov, *Tri revolyutsii v Rossii v nashe vremya*, 1975, pp.44-45.
2. Marx and Engels, vol. 4, p.334 (*Collected Works*, Vol. 6, pp.351,52).
3. Ibid., vol. 7, p.32 (*Surveys From Exile*, p.62).
4. Ibid., vol. 39, p.76.
5. L. Trotsky, *Nasha Revolyutsiya*, 1906, pp.277-78 (*The Permanent Revolution and Results and Prospects*, New York 1969, pp.104-105).
6. Ibid., pp.285-86 (p.115).
7. Lenin, vol. 26, pp.354-55('On the Slogan for a United States of Europe', CW, 21).
8. Trotsky reprinted his article in a collection entitled *A Programme for Peace (Programma mira)*, published in August 1917. He also included it in his Collected Works, the publication of which began in the USSR in the early 1920s. See Trotsky, *Sochineniya*, vol. 6, part 1, pp.89-90.
9. Lenin, vol. 30, p.133 (CW, 23).
10. Ibid., pp.218, 219-20 ('Principles Involved in the War Issue', CW, 23).
11. Ibid., vol. 27, p.81 ('On the Two Lines in the Revolution', CW, 21).
12. *Sed'moy S'yezd RKP, stenograficheskiy otchet, 6-8 marta 1918g.* Moscow-Leningrad 1923, p.20.
13. *Severnaya Kommuna*, March 14, 1919.
14. *Stenograficheskiy otchet Mossoveta*, no. 20, 1920. The present quotations are taken from their original sources. In the fourth and fifth (Russian) editions of Lenin's collected works his statements have been distorted. Phrases are omitted and the first text includes the arbitrary addition of the phrase 'the eventual victory of revolution', which Lenin did not write. The second and third editions contain no distortions. Even the fifth edition, incidentally, includes a number of analogous statements, as, for instance, in vol. 36, p.382, where Lenin says: 'We do not close our eyes to the fact ... that we alone by our own strengths cannot completely achieve socialist revolution in a single country'.
15. *Sochineniya*, vol. 17, part 1, p.195.
16. Lenin, vol. 44, p.36 ('Theses for a Report on the Tactics of the RCP', CW, 32).
17. Ibid., vol. 45, p.370 (CW, 33).
18. Ibid., p.377.
19. Ibid., pp.308, 309 ('Speech at a Plenary Session of the Moscow Soviet', November 20, 1922, CW, 33).
20. *1905 god*, predisloviye, Petrograd 1922, pp.4-5 (*1905*, London 1972, pp.vi-vii).
21. *Sochineniya*, vol. 3, part 1, pp.92-93.
22. *5 let Kominterna*, 1924, pp.250, 487-88.
23. Stalin, vol. 8, p.61 (*Leninism*, vol. 1, p.40).
24. Ibid., (*Leninism*, vol. 1, p.297).

25. M. Mekler, *O pobede sotsializma v odnoy strane,* Leningrad 1926, pp.30-31.
26. *VKP (B) v rezolyutsiyakh,* vol. 2, Moscow 1936, pp.29-30.
27. Cit. Stalin, *Voprosy Leninizma,* Moscow 1946, p.141 (cf. *Leninism,* vol. 1, p.302).
28. F. Vaganov, *Pravyy uklon v VKP(B) i yego razgrom,* Moscow 1970, pp.51-2.
29. Bukharin, *Put' k sotsializmu v Rossii,* New York 1967, p.340.
30. *Sochineniya,* vol. 13 p.348 (*Works,* vol. 13, p.288f.).
31. Trotsky, *Permanentnaya Revolyutsiya,* Berlin 1930, pp.168-69 (*The Permanent Revolution and Results and Prospects,* p.280).
32. *Chetvyortyy Internatsional i voyna,* Geneva, 1934, p.18.
33. *Russkaya Revolyutsiya i mirovaya revolyutsiya,* unpublished manuscript, p.12.
34. *Sochineniya,* vol. 5, pp.82-83—my italics, RM (*Works,* vol. 5, p.84).
35. Lenin, vol. 45, p.361 and *passim.*
36. *Sochineniya,* vol. 13, p.325 (*Works,* vol. 13, p.288f.).
37. Bukharin, *Put' k sotsializmu,* p.97.
38. *Nauchnyy Kommunizm,* no. 2, 1979, p.86.
39. *Problemy Mira i Sotsializma,* no. 4, 1979, pp.68-69.

CHAPTER 6

1. G. Noske, *Von Kiel bis Kapp,* p. 69.
2. *Delo naroda,* July 16, 1917.
3. Marx and Engels, vol. 4, p.453 (*Selected Works,* p.59).
4. Ibid., p.454 (p.59).
5. Ibid., pp.455-56 (pp.59-61).
6. Ibid., pp.458-59 (pp.62-63).
7. Ibid., vol. 16, p.669.
8. Ibid., vol. 33, pp.537-39 (*Selected Correspondence,* pp.162, 163).
9. Ibid., vol. 33, pp.537-38 (pp.329-30).
10. Ibid., vol. 38, p.132.
11. Ibid., vol. 22, p.425.
12. S. Sobornsky, *Mezhdunarodnoye rabocheye dvizheniye v tsifrakh i faktakh,* Leningrad 1926, p.18.
13. *Istoriya 2-ogo Internationala,* vol. 2, Moscow 1966, pp.342, 285
14. Marx and Engels, vol. 4, p.459 (*Selected Works,* p.63).
15. Ibid., vol. 36, pp.215, 217 (*Selected Correspondence,* pp.431, 433).
16. Ibid., p.217 (p.433).
17. Lenin, vol. 15, pp.297-301 (CW, 12). In such disagreements Stalin, of course, was to dispense with even the general civil limitation imposed by law.
18. Stalin, *Oktyabr'skaya Revolyutsiya i taktika russkikh kommunistov, Voprosy Leninizma,* Moscow 1946, pp.94-95 (*Leninism,* vol. 1, pp.124-25).

19. *Istoriya VKP (B): Kratkiy Kurs,* Moscow 1938, p.343.
20. Lenin, vol. 37, pp.191, 193 ('The Valuable Admissions of Pitirim Sorokin', CW, 28).
21. Ibid., p.218.
22. Ibid., pp.380-81 ('Speech at a Presnaya District Workers' Conference', CW, 28).
23. Ibid., vol. 38, p.266 (Extraordinary Plenary Meeting of the Moscow Soviet of Workers' and Red Army Deputies, April 3, 1919, Resolution, CW, 29).
24. V.A. Antonov-Ovseenko, *Zapiski o grazhdanskoy voyne,* Moscow 1933, vol. 4, p.113.
25. *Proletarskaya Revolyutsiya,* 1925, No. 6, p.139-141.
26. Lenin, vol. 50, p.307 (May 7, 1919, CW, 36).
27. Ibid., vol. 39, pp.415-16 ('Closing Speech on Report of CEC', CW, 30).
28. *Kommunist,* no. 2, 1968, p.90; also 1980, No. 5, p.34.
29. Sidney Webb, *Socialism in England,* London 1889.
30. *L'Humanité,* April 15, 1919.
31. Lenin, vol. 31, p.116 ('The Tasks of the Proletariat in the Present Revolution', CW, 24).
32. Ibid., pp.177-78 (CW, 24).
33. I.S. Yuzefovich, *Osnovaniye Kommunisticheskogo Internatsionala,* Moscow-Leningrad 1940, p.164.
34. *Kommunistichekiy Internatsional v dokumentakh,* Moscow 1933, p.89.
35. *Doklady Vtoromu Kongressu Kominterna,* Petrograd 1921, pp.12-13.
36. *Kommunisticheskiy Internatsional v dokumentakh,* p.293.
37. Ibid., p.299.
38. Ibid., p.201.
39. Ibid., pp.375-76.
40. Ibid., vol. 15, pp.297-301.
41. *Kommunisticheskiy Internatsional v dokumentakh,* p.407.
42. Ibid., pp.10-11.
43. Ibid., p.12.
44. *Imperializm i vseobshchiy krizis kapitalizma,* Moscow-Leningrad 1931, pp.507-508.
45. *Kommunisticheskiy Internatsional v dokumentakh,* pp.10-11.
46. Lenin, vol. 17, p.24 ('Marxism and Revisionism', CW, 15).
47. *Kommunisticheskiy Internatsional v dokumentakh,* p.74.
48. Marx and Engels, vol. 2, p.40 (*Collected Works,* vol. 4, p.37).
49. Ibid., vol. 21, pp.204-205.
50. Lenin, vol. 22, pp.231-32.
51. *XV-aya Vsesoyuznaya Konferentsiya VKP(B),* Moscow 1926, p.532.
52. *Rezolyutsii VII Vsemirnogo Kongressa Kommunisticheskogo Internatsionala,* Moscow 1935, pp.10-11.
53. G. Dimitrov, *Nastupleniye Fashizma i Zadachi Kommunisticheskogo*

Internatsionala v bor'be za yedinstvo rabochego klassa, Moscow 1935, p.28.
54. N.P. Pavlov, *Nauchno-tekhnicheskaya revolyutsiya i problemy struktury rabochey sily,* Moscow 1978, pp.68-69.
55. References like this, to 'the West' in general, are meant to include Japan.
56. *Narodnoye Khozyaystvo SSSR 1922-72,* Moscow 1972, p.62.
57. *Kommunist,* no. 5, 1980, p.34.
58. Statistical data on party membership have been obtained from the following works: *Politicheskiye Partii,* Spravochnik, Moscow 1974; the Yearbook of the *Bol'shaya Sovetskaya Entsiklopediya,* Moscow 1979; *Kommunisten der Welt über ihre Partien,* Prague 1976; W. Leonhard, *Eurokommunismus,* Berlin-Darmstadt-Vienna, p.52.
59. Statistical data on the Social Democratic parties have been obtained from the following sources: *Problemy Mira i Sotsializma,* no. 1, 1971, p.81; *Noveyshaya Istoriya Zarubezhnykh Stran: Yevropa i Amerika, 1939-75,* Moscow 1978, pp.536-37; *Socialist Affairs,* no. 6, 1975, p.106.
60. *Politicheskiye Partii,* Moscow 1974.
61. N. Ananiyeva, *Sotsializm po tu storony gorizonta,* Sofia 1977, p.22.
62. *Rabochiy klass i sovremennyy mir,* no. 3, 1976, p.64.
63. J.N. Evans, *Great Figures in the Labour Movement,* London 1966, p.118.
64. W. Brandt, *Friedrich Engels und Sozialdemokratie,* Bonn-Bad Godesberg, 1970, p.11.
65. *Declarations of the Socialist International,* London 1964, pp.3-4.
66. *Problemy Mira i Sotsializma,* 1973, No. 8, p.22.
67. W. Brandt, *Karl Marx und Sozialdemokratie,* Frankfurt-Köln, 1977, p.143.
68. B. Kreisky, *Die Zeit in der wir leben,* Vienna-Zurich-Innsbruck, 1979.
69. W. Eichler, *Zur Einführung in den demokratischen Sozialismus,* Bonn-Bad Godesberg, 1972, p.41.
70. *Die Zukunft,* no. 5, 1972, p.5.
71. *Die neue Gesellschaft,* no. 5, 1969, p.510.
72. G. Shakhnazarov, *Fiasko Futurologii,* p.145.
73. *Die neue Gesellschaft,* no. 19, Bonn 1972, p.864.
74. W. Brandt, B. Kreisky, O. Palme, *Briefe und Gespreche 1972-75,* Frankfurt-Cologne 1975, p.20.
75. G. Wuthe, H. Junker, 'Demokratischer Sozialismus' in W. Eicher, *Konsensus und Konflikt,* vol. 1, München-Wein 1975, p.143.
76. *Socialist International Information,* 1970, No. 9-10, p.138.
77. *Vorwärts,* April 27, 1972; *Die Zukunft,* 1972, No. 9, p.1.
78. *Die neue Gesellschaft,* no. 3, 1970, p.290.
79. *Vorwärts,* May 21, 1970.
80. *Borsenkultur,* August 8, 1979.
81. *Socialist International Information,* nos. 24-25, 1962, pp.355-56.

82. *Voprosy Istorii KPSS*, no. 12, 1977, p.69.
83. Brandt, Kreisky, Palme, p.30.
84. Brandt, December 26, 1976.
85. *Socialist International Information*, nos. 16-17, 1969, p.191.
86. *Socialist Affairs*, no. 5, 1974, p.84.
87. *Yearbook of the International Socialist Labour Movement*, 1956-57, London 1956, p.43.
88. Ibid., pp.42-43.
89. Ibid., p.45.
90. *Vorwärts*, June 20, 1962, p.8; *Arbeiter-Zeitung*, 1978, 20-21.
91. *Frankfurter Rundschau*, September 24, 1973.
92. *Vorwärts-Dokumentation*, July 19, 1973.
93. *Der Spiegel*, February 28, 1973, p.102.
94. *Die neue Gesellschaft*, no. 1, 1971, p.4.
95. R. Crossman, *New Fabian Essays*, London 1970, p.26.
96. *The Poverty of Historicism*, London 1957.
97. In much the same way, an earlier Social Democratic generation had turned to Kant, who insisted on 'the sovereign method of reform'.
98. *Kritischer Rationalismum und Sozialdemokratie*, Berlin-Bonn-Bad Godesberg 1975, p.viii.
99. *Avanti*, September 5, 1965.
100. Brandt, Kreisky, Palme, p.22.
101. *The World Socialist: the Socialist Perspective*, Socialist International, p.7.
102. *Die Osterreichische Sozialdemokratie im Spiegel ihrer Programme*, Vienna 1966.
103. *Grundsatzprogramm der Sozialdemokratischen Partei Deutschland*, p.15.
104. 'La Charta Doctrinale '74', *Le Peuple*, November 18, 1974.
105. Brandt, Kreisky, Palme, p.66.
106. *Die neue Gesellschaft*, no. 7, 1975, p.585.
107. *Le Monde*, July 19, 1972.
108. *Quotidien de Paris*, September 23, 1976.
109. *Le Nouvel observateur* October 28, 1968, p.24.
110. F. Mitterand, *Un socialisme du possible*, Paris 1970, pp.13-17.
111. *Problemy Mira i Sotsializma*, 1973, No. 8, p.26.
112. O. Bauer, *Zwischen zwei Weltkriegen?* Bratislava 1936, p.318.
113. *Arbeiter-Zeitung*, November 10, 1973.
114. Prinz Max von Baden, *Erinnerungen und Dokumente*, Stuttgart-Berlin-Leipzig 1927, p.580.
115. K. Kautsky, *Proletarskaya revolyutsiya i yeyo programma*, p.106, quoted from the anthology, *Diktatura proletariata i sovremennyy revizionizm*, Moscow-Leningrad 1931, p.130.
116. P. Garvi, *Zakat Bol'shevizma: 10 let diktatury*, Riga 1928, pp.5-7.
117. B. Kreisky, *Die Zeit in der wir Leben*, Vienna-Munich-Zurich-Innsbruck.
118. *Die Zukunft*, no. 2, 1972, p.18.

119. Ibid., no. 3, 1970, p.289.
120. *Declarations of the Socialist International*, 1, 1964, p.3.
121. K. Schacht, *Bilanz Sozialdemokratischer Reformpolitik*, 1976, p.39.
122. *Socialist International Information*, no. 39, 1958, p.586.
123. *Voprosy Istorii KPSS*, no. 4, 1977, p.90.
124. Lenin, vol. 23, p. 54 ('Conversation', CW, 19).
125. *Mezhdunarodnoye Soveshchaniye Kommunisticheskoy i Rabochikh Partiy: Dokumenty i materialy*, Moscow 1969, p.306.
126. *Rabochiy Klass i sovremennyy mir*, no. 3, 1974, p.155.
127. *Konferentsiya Kommunisticheskikh i Rabochikh Partii Yevropy* (Berlin, June 29-30 1976), Moscow 1977, p.21.
128. *Vorwärts*, August 24, 1972.
129. Ibid., July 29, 1976.
130. H. Weber, *Das Prinzip Links: Eine Dokumentation*, Ulm 1973, p.210-11.
131. B. Kreisky, *Aspekte des demokratischen Sozialismus*, Munich 1974, p.102.
132. *Pravda*, April 9, 1977.
133. *Der Spiegel*, January 26, 1976.
134. *L-76*, no. 5, 1977, p.147.
135. *Die neue Gesellschaft*, no. 2, 1972, p.142.
136. *Socialist International Information*, no. 14, 1969, pp.147-8.
137. *L'Humanité*, October 25, 1974.
138. See, for example, Marchais's remarks in *L'Humanité*, March 19, 1975.
139. *Der Spiegel*, April 1977.
140. O. Palme, *Le rendezvous suédois*, Stockholm 1976, p.97.
141. *Socialist Affairs*, vol. XXIII, no. 8, 1973, p.85.

Index

Adler, Max, 234, 235
Adorno, Theodor, 263
Allende, Salvador, 290
Antonov-Ovseenko, Vladimir, 230-1
Antonov, A.S., 57

Bakunin, Mikhail, 208, 209, 211, 212
Balibar, Etienne, 78
Barnai, Ferenc, 7
Bauer, Otto, 6, 234, 235, 278
Bebel, August, 13, 144, 212, 214, 216
Berdyaev, Nikolay, 152
Berlinguer, Enrico, 24
Bernstein, Eduard, 13, 32, 214, 263, 264
Blanqui, Auguste, 12, 29, 142, 207, 211
Bloch, Ernest, 263
Brandt, Willy, 259, 263-6, 268, 273, 276, 283, 287
Bukharin, Nikolai, 6, 13, 64, 65, 159-60, 179, 181, 186, 192, 237, 253
Bugay, N.F., 124

Caesar, Julius, 40
Carrillo, Santiago, 75-6
Cavaignac, General Louis, 41
Chernov, Victor, 204
Chernyshevsky, Nikholai, 18, 218
Chiang Kai-shek, 135
Connolly, James, 6
Cromwell, Oliver, 40
Crossman, Richard, 272
Cunhal, Alvaro, 73

Dan, Fyodor, 127, 218
Darwin, Charles, 25
Denikin, General Anton I., 157-8, 204, 228, 231-3

Dimitrov, Georgi, 6, 253
Djilas, Milovan, 281
Dühring, Eugen, 209, 214
Dunn, J., 141
Duvalier, Francois, 41

Ebert, Friedrich, 204, 205
Eichler, Willy, 264, 283
Engels, Friedrich, 11, 14, 29-31, 41, 76, 80, 85, 94-7, 141-4, 167-9, 194, 207-17, 219, 249-50, 273
Eydelman, N. Ya, 145

Farakos, G., 72
Farouk, king of Egypt, 145
Fischer, Ernst, 71
Franco, Francisco, 41, 69, 75
Ford, Gerald, 7

Garaudy, Roger, 71
Garbai, Alexander, 205
Garvi, P., 280
Gorky, Maxim, 65
Gottwald, Klement, 69, 136
Goushka, I., 71
Gruppi, Luciano, 77
Guesde, Jules, 212
Guliyev, V.E., 46

Habermas, Jürgen, 263
Hartl, R., 282
Hegel, G.W.F., 263
Herzen, Alexander, 18
Hilferding, Rudolf, 235
Hitler, Adolf, 41, 69, 205
Hyndman, Henry, 214

Jaures, Jean, 214

Kamenev, L.B., 58, 64, 180, 182-3, 230-1
Kant, Immanuel, 263
Kara, K., 71
Kautsky, Karl, 32, 44, 48, 50, 61, 81, 110, 156, 158-9, 171, 235, 237, 279-80, 286
Kerensky, Alexander, 104
Kissinger, Henry, 7
Kokoshkin, F.F., 52
Kolchak, Admiral Aleksandr, 121, 157-8
Kornilov, General Lavr, 54, 82, 104, 204, 224, 228
Krasin, Yu. A., 48, 111
Krasnov, General Petr, 121
Kreisky, Bruno, 264, 266-7, 268, 272, 273, 279, 282, 286, 289
Krupskaya, Nadezhda, 16
Ksenofont, F., 16
Kun, Bela, 205
Kursky, D.I., 52, 124

Lafargue, Paul, 169, 212, 214
Lasalle, Ferdinand, 30, 207, 209, 211, 212
von Laue, T.H., 141
Lavrov, Pyotr, 146-7
Lenin, Vladimir, 3, 5, 6, 12-26, 33-40, 44-52, 54, 58-68, 72, 76, 78, 80, 82-8, 105-16, 119, 129, 150-163, 170-80, 190, 192, 215, 217-27, 229-33, 237, 242, 245-6, 248, 250-2, 279, 283
Leybzon, B.M., 111, 113
Liebknecht, Karl, 204, 205
Luxemburg, Rosa, 6, 204, 205, 263

Makhno, Nestor, 57, 204, 230-2
Mao-Tse Tung, 21, 134
Marchais, Georges, 24, 73-5, 165-6, 288, 289
Marcuse, Herbert, 89
Martov, Y., 156, 218
Martynov, A.S., 36
Marx, Karl, 5, 11-26, 29-31, 42-3, 55, 56, 76, 80, 85, 94-98, 141-4, 167-9, 192, 194, 207-17, 219, 248, 249-50, 263, 264, 273
Maskalov, V., 58
Mazurenko, G.P., 204

Mazzini, Giuseppe, 211
Menert, Klaus, 7
Millerand, Alexander, 13, 214
Miliukov, P., 102
Mitterand, Francois, 268, 278, 289
Molotov, Viacheslav, 62
Mussolini, Benito, 41

Nasser, Gamal Abdel, 145
Nenni, Pietro, 273
Newton, Isaac, 26
Nicholas, tsar of Russia, 98, 226
Noske, Gustav, 204, 205

Owen, Robert, 211

Palme, Olof, 268, 273, 277, 289
Papaioannu, G., 6-7
Pasadovsky, K., 147-8

P'eng P'ai, 134
Pestel, P.I., 145
Petrovsky, G., 128
Pilsudski, Joseph, 56
Pitterman, B., 259, 268
Plekhanov, Georgi, 6, 13, 32, 53, 81, 148, 212, 214, 218
Pletnyov, V.F., 65
Pompey, 39
Ponomaryov, Boris, 19, 23
Pontillon, Robert, 277
Popper, Karl, 272
Proudhon, Pierre Joseph, 30, 207
Pyatakov, Y., 64

Radek, Karl, 237
Robespierre, Maximilian, 40
Russell, Bertrand, 125-6

Salazar, Antonio, 41, 69, 75
Shafarevich, I., 197, 265
Schefer, Max, 278
Scheidemann, Philipp, 204, 279
Schmidt, Helmut, 273
Shakhnazarov, G.N., 48, 265
Shaumyan, S., 92
Shingarev, A.I., 52
Shulgin, V.V., 102
Skobelev, Mikhail, 102, 204
Solzhenitsyn, Alexander, 4, 8, 265
Somoza, Anastasio, 41, 87
Sorge, F.A., 212-3

Stalin, Joseph, 6, 16, 20-1, 23, 51, 63, 68-9, 130, 136, 149, 180-93, 224-8, 282
Sulla, Lucius Cornelius, 40
Sverdlov, Iakov, 115
Svyatitsky, N.V., 153

Tchakev, Pyotr, 18, 146-7, 152
Thorez, Maurice, 69
Tito, Joseph Broz, 3
Trotsky, Leon, 17, 63, 64, 150, 169, 172, 175-6, 179-89, 190, 196-7, 252

Ustryalov, N., 65-7

Volkov, Yuri, 47
Vyshinsky, Andrei, 192

Ward, Barbara, 139
Wedemeyer, Joseph, 30
Werner, G., 272
Wilson, Harold, 264
Wrangel, General P., 56-7

Yudemich, General Nikolai, 232

Zarodov, K.I., 90-1, 93, 140, 167
Zetkin, Clara, 237
Zhdanov, A.A., 70
Zinoviev, A.A., 197
Zinoviev, Gregori, 17, 18, 60-1, 63, 64, 180, 182-5, 239, 240, 253
Zotov, V., 78